About the

Mary has written numerous technical and academic articles and is an experienced lecturer and presenter, but this is her first book. She practices as an osteopath in Wiltshire, treating people, horses and dogs. She is a trustee of the Sutherland Cranial College of Osteopathy (SCCO) and is a member of the Royal Society of Medicine and the Association of Animal Osteopaths. She was formerly a marketing consultant, with five years' experience at what is now PricewaterhouseCoopers, and three years with strategy consultancy P-Four (now part of WPP). She began her marketing career with Cadbury's confectionery and retains a lifelong love of chocolate.

Mary was born and raised on a farm on the edge of the south Shropshire Hills, the youngest of four children. She attended Shrewsbury High School from age four to eighteen. She spent much of her childhood on horseback, which left her with permanent damage to her right eye, a broken nose, a broken kneecap and a broken coccyx. She has been bitten, kicked, rolled on, dragged, and has fallen off too many times to recall, but she still rides racehorses for fun.

STRANGER IN MY HEART

STRANGER IN MY HEART

MARY MONRO

Unbound

This edition first published in 2018

Unbound

6th Floor Mutual House, 70 Conduit Street, London W1S 2GF

www.unbound.com

All rights reserved

© Mary Monro, 2018

The right of Mary Monro to be identified as the author of this work has been asserted in accordance with Section 77 of the Copyright, Designs and Patents Act 1988. No part of this publication may be copied, reproduced, stored in a retrieval system, or transmitted, in any form or by any means without the prior permission of the publisher, nor be otherwise circulated in any form of binding or cover other than that in which it is published and without a similar condition being imposed on the subsequent purchaser.

ISBN (eBook): 9781911586685

ISBN (Paperback): 9781911586692

Design by Mecob

Cover image:
© Shutterstock.com

Printed and bound in Great Britain by Clays Ltd, Elcograf S.p.A.

Permissions

Max Hastings *Nemesis*
Reproduced by permission of Harper Collins Publishers Ltd © 2007 Max Hastings

E Jones & S Wessely *British POWs; From Resilience to Psychological Vulnerability: Reality or Perception?*
King's Centre for Military Health Research, 20th Century British History, 2010, vol 21, 2, p163-183.
Reproduced by permission of Oxford University Press.

Frank McLynn *The Burma Campaign: disaster into triumph 1942-45*
Yale Representation Limited, 47 Bedford Square London WC1B 3DP
Reproduced with permission of the Licensor through PLSclear.

Laurens van der Post *Yet Being Someone Other*
From *Yet Being Someone Other* by Laurens Van der Post, published by Chatto & Windus.
Reproduced by permission of The Random House Group Ltd. © 1982

Edwin Ride *BAAG: Hong Kong Resistance 1942-45*
From *BAAG: Hong Kong Resistance* by Edwin Ride © Oxford University Press 1982. All rights reserved.
Reproduced by permission of Oxford University Press (China) Ltd

Dear Reader,

The book you are holding came about in a rather different way to most others. It was funded directly by readers through a new website: Unbound.

Unbound is the creation of three writers. We started the company because we believed there had to be a better deal for both writers and readers. On the Unbound website, authors share the ideas for the books they want to write directly with readers. If enough of you support the book by pledging for it in advance, we produce a beautifully bound special subscribers' edition and distribute a regular edition and e-book wherever books are sold, in shops and online.

This new way of publishing is actually a very old idea (Samuel Johnson funded his dictionary this way). We're just using the internet to build each writer a network of patrons. Here, at the back of this book, you'll find the names of all the people who made it happen.

Publishing in this way means readers are no longer just passive consumers of the books they buy, and authors are free to write the books they really want. They get a much fairer return too – half the profits their books generate, rather than a tiny percentage of the cover price.

If you're not yet a subscriber, we hope that you'll want to join our publishing revolution and have your name listed in one of our books in the future. To get you started, here is a £5 discount on your first pledge. Just visit unbound.com, make your pledge and type MONRO18 in the promo code box when you check out.

Thank you for your support,

Dan, Justin and John
Founders, Unbound

With gratitude to James Monro, who has always been my biggest supporter.

Super Patrons

Beatrix Alberga
Chas Alexander
Mickael Teixeira Alves
Joanna Aspin
Tony Banham
Richard Best
Sue Bishop
Jeanette Bolingbroke
Jeannine Bolingbroke
Amanda Boxer
James Bradshaw
Jennie Bradshaw
Richard Brighten
Joel Brightman
Ben Caldecott
Julian Caldecott
Karen Carroll
Teresa Caldecott Cialini
Tessa Clarke
Penelope Cowdy
Kat Crooks
Virginia Darragh-Williams
Stephen Delaney
David Douglas-Mort
Tony Dumbreck
David Duncombe-Anderson
June Evans
Gillian Ford
Another Friend
Charles Garrard
Richard Goldsbrough
Dawn Gorman

Nick Gosset
Donna Greaves
Mary Green
Andy Greene
Thelma Grimes
Sarah Grogan
Caroline Harmsworth
Caroline & David Hobbs
Jenny Holloway
Caspar Hull
Martin Humphrey
Leroy James
Janet Johnston
Emma Jones
Dan Kieran
Russ King
Jane Kinsey
Tim Kirkpatrick
Mary Law
Martin Lilley
Sophie Lippiatt
The Macaulay-Brooks
Angus Mackintosh
Jane Manning
Roger Mant
Meg McDonald
Alison McEwan
Joan Millington
John Mitchinson
Alexander Monro
Duncan Monro
Georgie Monro
James Monro
Robert Monro
Stefan Monro
Barbara Moulang

Nicholas Ostler
Jane Dunn Ostler
Sue Phillips
Garry Phillipson
Justin Pollard
Daryl Rush
Erica Russell
Michael Shea
Fred Sieders
Lesley Smith
Andrew Stevenson
Christian Sullivan
Mrs Gloria Taylor
Nick Trevor
Charles Vallee
Lisa White

越挫越勇

'The more one is defeated, the more courageous one is.'[1]

Chinese proverb

Alis et animo

'Wings and courage'

Monro family motto

---

1. The Chinese People at War: Human Suffering and Social Transformation, 1937–1945 Diana Lary (CUP, 2010).

Author's Note

Twenty per cent of net proceeds will be donated to the Riding for the Disabled Association.

List of Illustrations

Figure 1: Battle of Hong Kong 8–25 December 1941

Figure 2: Hong Kong Island as at 18 Dec 1941

Figure 3: Sham Shui Po Camp

Figure 4: Major John Monro's route across China, 1942

Figure 5: Map of Burma 1944–45

Figure 6: John Monro, Tenzing Norgay and another Sherpa, 1946

Preface

This story is centred around a biography of my father, Lieutenant Colonel John Monro, who died in 1981 before I had a chance to get to know him properly. His mystery was enhanced by his refusal to say much about his life, but fortunately he was a great communicator in writing. I have been able to learn much about him from his letters, reports and diaries and by retracing his journeys across China. He was as stoic in his endurance of the trials he faced in the Far East in the Second World War as he was in coping with the tribulations of everyday life in Shropshire in the 1960s and '70s. Understanding him has led to a deeper relationship with him and to a greater understanding of myself. Ancestor worship is a rather Chinese trait, but can we ever really know ourselves without knowing those who moulded us and whose wisdom lies within us, waiting to be discovered?

Dad was very much the 'stiff upper lip' Englishman, his fortitude developed at boarding school and at the Royal Military Academy, Sandhurst. He learned at a young age to handle challenges and to manage risk and complexity. His learning not only enabled him to cope with adversity but to positively relish it. Dad was born in 1914, a year of the Tiger in the Chinese calendar, symbolising leadership and courage. That particular year was associated with the element Wood, representing strong moral sense and selflessness. This resonates with my understanding of the characteristics that defined how he approached the world. (He married a Rabbit and had two Rabbit daughters – fine if his leadership went unquestioned, otherwise less harmonious! My brothers were more compatible signs – a charming, intelligent Snake and a good, dependable Ox.)

My father had a great affinity with the Chinese, whose stoicism is a deeply ingrained national trait. The 'War of Resistance against Japanese Aggression 1937–45', as the Chinese usually call the Second World War, was a prolonged test of resilience. The Chinese people were killed in their millions, the government was weak and corrupt, the economy was in tatters, famine was widespread, neighbour turned against neighbour, families were scattered and lost and yet the nation survived. No war heroes were acknowledged. There were no war memorials or public cemeteries commemorating the dead. People had no idea what had become of their families. The old social structures had been destroyed. China was almost immediately thrown into civil war, during which there was further upheaval and suffering. The people were tested again in the Great Leap Forward of the late 1950s and the Cultural Revolution of the 1960s and '70s. Again they just kept going, supported by the Confucian ideals of self-discipline, humility and sense of obligation, under the impersonal and inevitable Mandate of Heaven (the idea that there could be only one legitimate ruler of China at a time, and that this ruler had the blessing of the gods). I am lost in admiration for the Chinese people's apparently infinite capacity to endure suffering, to put the past behind them and to face the uncertain future unflinchingly.

Writing this book has been an exercise in resilience in its own right. The journey began several years ago when I was prompted to pay some attention to my long-deceased father. The process of reading and transcribing his documents was only the beginning. The words needed the breath of life – I had to walk the talk if I hoped to understand this man. But I didn't want to go to China unless I could speak the language a bit, introducing more complexity and dimension to what was fast becoming a major project in my life. Learning Mandarin opened my mind to Chinese culture and history. When I finally arrived in China, treasures fell on me like rain.

My father's handwriting wasn't the tricky part of transcribing the documents. They were full of army abbreviations, cultural references that went straight over my head and Chinese place names in a version of romanisation that is no longer in use (the Chinese government introduced a new system in 1958). The blessed internet is a fantastic research tool. Who was Hore-Belisha, for example, that Dad grumbles about making the troops soft? Apparently he was Secretary of State for War 1937–40, after having been transport minister, when he introduced the well-known and still used Belisha beacon for pedestrian road crossings. He was a bright and capable man who foresaw the importance of airpower, but he upset a lot of military top brass with his progressive notions and was removed from office in 1940.

The place names were more difficult to decipher. Undaunted, I bought a map of southern China and tried saying place names out loud. Waichow in my father's documents is now spelled Huizhou. Kweilin is now Guilin. Easy! Except that Chinese towns and cities often have two or more utterly unrelated names. Shaoguan was also known as Kukong, for instance. But the more difficult it was, the more intriguing it became. Some places simply no longer exist. The metropolis of Shenzhen was built by bulldozing out of existence many villages that Dad passed through after he crossed the border into China. Search though I might for Pokut, it is no longer there.

It has been a long, hard road but all the more rewarding for it. Along the way my relationship with my father has expanded enormously and I have immensely enjoyed learning about China. I have also been surprised to develop an interest in military history. I chanced upon a lesser-known story of the Pacific War, connected to my father, which, had things gone according to plan, might have shortened the war and saved millions of lives. I was amazed to find that I could research this story from the comfort of my sofa – President Franklin D. Roosevelt's library, containing all his correspondence for his whole term of office, is available online, for free. I am an osteopath, and one of the sayings passed down to us over the generations is: 'To the digger who will dream and the dreamer who will dig, I say dig on.' Well, here are my excavations.

Contents

	Dedication	xxix
	Foreword	xxxi
1.	The Call to Adventure	1
2.	Hong Kong 1941	19
3.	Escape	35
4.	China's War	55
5.	Road Closed and Open	69
6.	Crossing the Threshold	77
7.	Entering the Middle Kingdom	87
8.	Rosy Cloud Mountain	101
9.	Expanse West	109
10.	Mountain Minorities	119
11.	Wartime Capital	129
12.	The Devil in the Detail	149
13.	Onward Journey	175
14.	The Path into the Light	197
	Structure of the Royal Artillery in the Second World War	209
	Bibliography	211
	Acknowledgements	215
	Patrons	217

For Julian Caldecott, without whose love, support and belief this would not have been possible.

Foreword

BUCKINGHAM PALACE

An inspiring story of a Royal Artillery Officer, his capture and escape from the Japanese invasion of Hong Kong, concern for Prisoners of War left in Hong Kong and his subsequent understanding and support at the very beginnings of the Riding for the Disabled Association (RDA) are remarkable in themselves. That his story has been told by his daughter after her own challenging travels is just as remarkable. As President of the RDA I am delighted to remember and celebrate Lieutenant Colonel John Monro's role in the creation of the movement and to thank his daughter Mary for the extraordinary level of research and continued support for RDA.

1

The Call to Adventure

Who am I? Is my individuality a sum of my own life's experiences plus some DNA that dictates eye colour, hair waviness and the like, or am I a node in the web of lives that connects ancestors to descendants? Am I a storage vessel for all the lives that came before me, whose characteristics, experiences, dreams, passions and neuroses permeate me, the palette that makes up the painting of me? Some examples: 'I can be stubborn,' I confess; 'You wouldn't be your mother's daughter if you weren't,' says Aunt June; there's been a doctor in every generation of the family for hundreds of years, and the tradition continues into the generation below me; when I visited the Monro clan castle (acquired by the clan chief in the 14th century) for the first time, north of the Black Isle near Inverness, why did the view across the water feel so utterly familiar to me? To understand who I am, the place to start seems to be with my parents, those strangers called Mum and Dad – reduced to title and role – whose individuality is lost to the inevitably selfish child.

'Your father was one of the 20th-century Greats, you know,' said an old friend of the family at my mother's 80th birthday party in 2007. Jane Cordingley had been my older sister Kathy's best friend and lived with us during her last two years of school, when her father, a vicar, had been appointed to a far distant parish. She remained in contact with our family even after my sister died in 1987. Jane's well-meant comment shocked me – I realised that I did not know my father at all. What could she mean? Dad was a farmer, formerly an army officer, loved his food, loved his country sports and classical music. Absolutely reliable at falling asleep in front of the TV news. Not really what you could call 'great'. I was aware that he had escaped from a Japanese prisoner of war camp in Hong Kong during the Second World War and made his way across China to Chongqing. I also knew that he had been awarded the Military Cross for this act of courage. Was that it? I was too stunned to ask, but Jane's casual remark stayed with me and slowly germinated into a question that had to be answered. At the time I thought I was searching for Dad's identity, but eventually it dawned on me that this was a voyage of self-discovery.

My father, Lieutenant Colonel John Monro, died in 1981 when he was 67 and I, the youngest of his four children, was just 18. His death opened a void in my heart that I found unintelligible. Dad was old compared to my contemporaries' dads and young to pass away, with the combined effect that I knew no one in a similar situation. In our family we didn't discuss feelings, and so I was left with a startled and silent sense of loss. Still in the parent–child relationship with him, I never really knew him as an individual. Who had he been before he became a farmer? Why did he become a farmer and not remain an army officer? What was it about him that made him a 'Great'? And how did he influence my life through his choices?

I had a gorgeously innocent childhood on the farm, not appreciating Dad's role in setting up for us such a life of stability and fun, ease and hard work, freedom and responsibility. The farm was the traditional small, mixed type of a kind that has now almost disappeared, along with the social and natural capital embedded in that gentle approach to land management and food production. On 200 acres there were dairy cows, pigs, sheep, grain crops and sugar beet, with enough left over for grassy paddocks for the horses. Dad's working day began early with milking the cows and feeding the other animals. Mondays and Thursdays were pig-mucking-out days and he would come into breakfast stinking of pig manure, even after removing his overalls. Days could be very long, with crop harvesting in the summer and a final feed of hay for the cattle at 10pm on winter nights. The farm kept three men busy, along with my father, and the family were also expected to muck in at the busiest times and over the Christmas holidays. Bale stacking, grain shovelling, hand-weeding the fields for wild oats and ragwort, and helping cows to calve were all in a day's work. I witnessed my first operation when a heifer was delivered of her calf by caesarean section, still standing but sedated – I must have been ten or eleven.

Silky bantams scratched around the yard and periodically produced tiny clouds of fluffy chicks. They and the hens were regularly stalked by the local foxes, who used to kill them all from time to time. The hens and bantams were not only prey but also predators – their dinosaur heritage poking through – of Mum's magnificent vegetable garden. They pretended to be after grubs and worms, but they used to steal what they could. Mum worked hard to feed us on home produce – she grew everything from seed, tended the garden diligently and then froze vegetables, and jammed or bottled fruit. Her damson cheesecake is legend. She always had a few hens for eggs and occasionally requested a pig or sheep for the freezer. We drank milk fresh from the cow, the flavour varying according to the season and the diet that the cows were eating, a joy extinguished by pasteurisation. Mum resisted an entirely domestic life by volunteering for administrative roles in the Women's Institute, the Pony Club and the Meals on Wheels service, despite my father's preference for her to stay home. Both parents had long dreamed of the farming life and they loved it, even on days when we were snowed in or the cattle had escaped from their field to create muddy havoc in the neighbourhood.

It wasn't all a bucolic, new-mown-hay-scented scene. My father suffered an appalling series of crises in the 1960s, which must have tested him almost as much as the worst days of his experiences in the Second World War. There is a kind of courage that allows you to run into a burning building to rescue someone. There is another kind that sustains you through year after year of suffering.

When our family first moved to the farm in 1960, my parents owned some land on the far side of a main road, and the horses in that field escaped onto the road. Two of them collided with vehicles and were killed, including a home-bred filly and Dad's hunter. He later sold that land so that the horses were never put in that position again. In the early years of his farming career there were severe winters (especially 1962/3, the coldest winter of the 20th century) with deep snow that sometimes isolated the farm, so that the milk from the dairy herd had occasionally to be poured away, uncollected and uncompensated. The cows had to be taken to a stream to drink as all the water pipes had frozen, prolonging an already exhausting day's work. It must have been a bitter blow when Dad's farming career was still in its infancy.

The following summer, after I was born, Mum suffered a postnatal depression, which must have been hard for both of them as she was normally so unflappable. My 12-year-old sister was being very challenging, with temper tantrums well outside the norm, even for someone in the grip of puberty, and this may have aggravated the situation. My mother's mood was so low that my father took her to the doctor, highly unusual for the times, let alone in my 'stiff upper lip' family. I don't know whether she was given any treatment, but at that time postnatal depression was not widely recognised. She recovered, somehow, and suffered no lasting ill effects.

Having weathered that storm, in 1967 there was an outbreak of foot-and-mouth disease in Shropshire, when many cattle in the county were slaughtered and the movement and sale of unaffected animals was prohibited. This was another serious financial setback that must have left Dad wondering if he could really support his newly expanded family through agriculture. Then in 1969, when I was six, I had a near-fatal accident when a pony kicked me in the head, breaking my nose and permanently damaging my right eye. Dad drove to hospital, with me sitting on Mum's lap. The only moment that I remember of the accident is looking at my blood soaking into her pale-blue dress as we drove to town and wondering if the stain would come out. Apparently I asked, 'Am I going to die?' It must have been a heartbreaking moment for them both, and a question that they couldn't bear to contemplate. For some reason this incident didn't put me off horses, and I suppose my parents can't have forced me back onto a pony, or I would have remembered it, and I may well have demanded it. In any case, I carried on riding, often exploring the local lanes and bridle paths alone.

A couple of years later another calamity occurred when Mum had a catastrophic fall out hunting. She was riding Dad's hunter when he tripped going down a steep and narrow track, pitching her over his head. It was immediately clear that the injury was serious, but no ambulance could reach her there, and instead several other riders went to her aid and she was bundled into a Land Rover and driven to hospital. My brother James and I had been with her, riding our ponies, and I was kept out of the way by being told to lead her horse home. She had fractured several vertebrae in her neck and upper back and was incapacitated for weeks, before making a slow recovery. She was very lucky that she wasn't paralysed. Dad had to add all her domestic duties to his already full workload. Friends and neighbours were very kind, bringing numerous meals for us – Dad was no cook – but he had to do everything else. I remember him coming home from the supermarket with all sorts of exotic foods that we never normally ate. Mum ran a thrifty household, serving a regular menu of meals each week, and Dad was astonished to discover that the supermarket sold other things. His penchant for Chinese and Indian food was unleashed upon us, when all we wanted was macaroni cheese for supper on Tuesday as usual. I don't recall him being overwhelmed by the situation. I still went to school, the laundry got done, life carried on as normal.

As well as involving us in the responsibilities of the farm and the joy of the outdoor life, Dad wanted us well educated. He borrowed money from his family to put the four of us through private schools, which he believed would be best for us. Dad's father had been a solicitor and his mother's family were also solicitors, and all in all there was a certain expectation of academic success.

Dad himself had been sent to Chillon College in Switzerland from age 13 to 18. The school had taken over the old Hotel Byron, on the shore of Lake Geneva, in the 1920s when the formerly grand hotel fell on hard times. In its prime it had hosted many luminaries of the 19th century, including Wagner, Liszt and Victor Hugo. Sometimes called the 'Swiss Eton', the college was described by the *Lausanne Gazette* as having 'a battalion of little Anglo-Saxons animating the corridors of the hotel'.

Chillon certainly inspired Dad's passion for mountaineering, but I don't know if his experience there was entirely positive. I suspect that he was first sent to boarding school at a young age; likewise, he sent my brother James to boarding school at seven and my brother Robert at eight. I believe that James was often miserable at preparatory school, but there was no question of him being sent somewhere else, despite my mother pleading on his behalf. Boarding schools could be traumatic. Alex Renton, who wrote a review in the *Guardian* of *Boarding School Syndrome* by Joy Schaverien (2015), says about his own researches with former pupils: 'The schools of the elite suffered the same cover-ups and the same astonishing failings in regulation and in policing as did the hospitals, care homes and young offenders' prisons. The difference? As several correspondents put it, in anger or amusement, "Posh people's parents paid to have them abused."' Even in Victorian times, it was well recognised that boarding schools were home to alarming numbers of deaths, from starvation, abuse or suicide. Children's complaints were not tolerated or taken seriously – indeed, the brutality was thought to make men of them. I have to assume that my father's experience was sufficiently positive (either directly or with the benefit of hindsight) to lead him to send his sons down the same path, but he did seem deaf to their opinions on the subject, sticking obstinately to his decision.

The Monro stubborn streak is not to be underestimated. Our ancestor Dr Alexander Monro *secundus* (1733–1817) was a renowned anatomist and there is a part of the brain named after him. It is a connecting opening between the lateral ventricles and the third ventricle – Dr Monro was the first to fully describe (in a paper published in 1764) how all four ventricles (the fluid-filled cushions deep in the brain) communicate with each other. A colleague suggested that the ventricles were also continuous with the central spinal canal inside the spinal cord. Dr Monro's response was essentially: 'No. I have spoken. It is not so.' Authoritative, stubborn and wrong.

Boarding school has its merits and suits some children very well. Dad told of how they flooded the tennis courts in winter to make a skating rink, which he loved, and he retained a lifelong fondness for mountaineering and French, skills that he learned at school. The discipline of boarding school life certainly rubbed off on him. He had registered my older brother, Robert, for Shrewsbury School but changed his mind when he found that the headmaster allowed 'long' hair and encouraged girls to come and join in school activities. He was also unimpressed when the head said he sent the bright boys to university and the dim ones to the army! Perhaps this hit a raw nerve – Dad's younger brothers, Robert and Michael, both studied medicine at Caius College, Cambridge University, with Robert later becoming a successful surgeon and Michael a GP, while my father chose a military career.

We were not asked our opinion about our schooling or given a choice, as children usually are nowadays. I think Dad regarded the purpose of education to be a source of inspiration and a broad springboard to life's possibilities. He expected us to do our best and to become independent, responsible adults. He must have resisted his own parents' (spoken or unspoken) expectations that he should become a solicitor, and he passed this down to us by not putting pressure on us to follow a particular career path. It was like being steered by subtle and unseen forces of which you were barely aware, but with a huge amount of freedom between these invisible traces.

It seems that the discipline and fortitude learned at school stood Dad in good stead when it came to battle and enduring hardship on his escape journey. Yet it might also have formed his emotional reserve – at worst a lack of capacity for intimacy, even with immediate family. This is not a rare feature of someone of his generation and background. Perhaps the armouring formed at school was reinforced during the war years and then was difficult to shake off, even when it was no longer useful.

I never saw my parents argue, never saw them cry or show any strong feelings at all. Even when Dad was furious he was generally very restrained and philosophical about it. I still feel embarrassed about some of the annoying and stupid things that I did, for which I was not admonished. I caused a minor car accident once and Dad just said that it was his duty as a parent to pay for his children's mistakes. I probably benefitted from being the last of four children – and the most conforming and easy to manage. My sister, Kathy, the firstborn, was contrary in the extreme, actively seeking to zag to everyone else's zig, and she especially seemed to enjoy goading my father.

I suppose she was trying to escape the rigid carapace of Victorian mores to become a liberated woman of the 1970s. I remember her Afghan coat, her ancient Morris Minor post van and its interior painted with a vivid rainbow, her bralessness and the exotic recipes that she would gather on her travels, a sort of hippy Elizabeth David. She would pick fights with Dad at every opportunity. He would silently tolerate most things, but direct attacks on the values he held most dear would spark a blazing row. It was attention-seeking behaviour in Kathy, which showed little regard for anyone else's feelings. According to my mother, this antagonistic behaviour began when Robert was born, sibling rivalry in the extreme. Sadly, she never grew out of it, as I found when I tried to reconcile with her during her last illness (liver and pancreatic cancer) and she stubbornly refused. She was then 35 and I was 23. Her chief communication style was argument and, in the end, it may have been her anger that killed her – in traditional Chinese medicine, anger hurts the liver. In many ways she was very similar to our father, and her determination to succeed in her own way, against all odds, was an example of the apple falling close to the tree. Perhaps she was unconsciously trying to live up to the standard of courage that he had set. She was much more relaxed and at ease with her friends, with whom she formed deep, lifelong bonds.

Like so many of his generation, Dad never spoke of his wartime experiences – or, if he did, he saved it for British Legion meetings. For that matter, he never spoke to me of anything much. He was always busy with the farm and only really engaged with me when it concerned the horses. When I came home with my school report he filed it neatly and made no comment. If I was ill, Mum looked after me. When Mum went out for the evening, I cooked supper while Dad worked in his study or watched TV. If they had friends round for supper I got out of the way. If my parents went on holiday by themselves, I was sent to stay with a school friend. Family holidays were rare for a busy farmer and usually involved visits to relatives. It all seemed perfectly normal at the time, but looking back it seems a rather limited relationship. A generational thing? Or something more related to his life experiences? Perhaps my teenage infatuation with Clint Eastwood, in his spaghetti western phase, was art imitating life, with my rugged, silent hero riding into town and righting wrongs for everyone.

Aside from a fondness for Chinese food, Christmas letters from his old Chinese interpreter, Cheung Yan-lun, plus the occasional unexpected appearance of Mr Cheung's sons for visits, there were no clues as to Dad's wartime history in China. In Dad's study there was a copy of *The Royal Artillery Commemoration Book 1939–1945*, which included his account of the battle of Hong Kong and of his escape. I had read this as a child, but its significance escaped me at the time. I've asked my mother about whether he ever talked to her about his escape and she says not. This silence is eloquent. If I had done what I eventually realised that he had done, it would have coloured my conversation for the rest of my life. Such reticence is far from unique, and may have created other cultures in response, to fill the gaps, as it were. It seems to have led, for example, to the current vogue for researching family history. Many people are only able to find out what their ancestors did in the world wars through official documents such as military records, or letters and diaries that have been rediscovered. Rarely has the former combatant said more than a few words himself.

But the gravid silence is highly ambiguous. Does it imply respect for those who didn't come home? Respect for those killed by the survivor? A modest desire not to seem self-congratulatory about surviving? A reluctance to relive the experience? A wish to let the past remain in its place and to live in the present? A feeling of being unwilling or unable to describe the experience to anyone who didn't share it? Conflicted feelings about an experience that was both the most exciting and most horrific of your life? Keeping a lid on wartime experiences to combat the onset of psychological symptoms that might attract stigma (veterans of the First World War had been shot for shell shock)? Knowing that your entire generation shared the experience, so that there is the constant but unspoken understanding and support of all of your contemporaries? Sparing one's relatives from horror? Maintaining the habit of secrecy that had been necessary in war? Equating bravery with brevity?

The annual commemoration of the Great War (later known as the First World War) with two minutes' silence is a ritualised version of the night vigil, when the dead were watched over by their surviving comrades. The purpose was to protect them against mutilation, looting or being dragged away by scavengers; to guard their honour rather than as an act of remembrance. Perhaps war survivors, particularly from the First and Second World Wars, spent the rest of their lives guarding the honour of their dead and of their own scorched youth. Much has been written about post-combat stress, but there is little on the subject of this silence, the men who didn't show frank signs of psychological disorder, despite what they had been through. It seems that the silence is so common as to be taken for granted. Yet, in the present day, it also seems strange to us, in our assumption that talking is necessary to process difficult life events and complex emotions. For these men, perhaps silence was the simplest source of peace, the ultimate shock absorber and safety net.

Dad was always keen to share his interests with us. He had had horses during his army career in the Royal Artillery. He rode in many point-to-point races, the pinnacle of his achievement being to come third in the Military Gold Cup at Sandown in 1951, riding his horse Sidewalk, who he trained himself. From 1969 to 1979 he was secretary of the South Shropshire Hunt, often leading the field over huge hedges or unopenable gates on his heavyweight hunter, Henry. Mum had also been brought up on horseback, so between them it was inevitable that their children would ride. My parents were busy, so encouraging my passion for riding was a stroke of genius – it took up all my free time and required almost no input from them. The modern equivalent of my parents seem to be forever ferrying their offspring to piano lessons or hockey practice and helping them with school projects or mucking out their pets.

Dad loved to identify birds when we were out riding horses or when driving the car. On occasion, we would be taken to bird reserves or places that he knew were habitats for rarer species such as nightingales. He enrolled me in the Young Ornithologists' Club, the children's arm of the Royal Society for the Protection of Birds, to try to foster an interest in birds. I took little notice as a child, but something did stick. Nowadays I often alarm my business partner by watching red kites (Dad's favourite bird) when we are driving along the M4 on the way to see a client for our equine osteopathy practice. These totemic birds were rare in the 1970s and we would drive from our home in Shropshire into the mountains of mid-Wales in search of them. Since they were introduced into the Chilterns in the 1990s, they have successfully spread and now it is my delight to see some almost weekly, even quite close to my home in Wiltshire. They always remind me of Dad.

He taught my brothers to shoot and fish (his brother Michael had been an excellent shot, representing Cambridge University in the highly coveted Queen's Prize at Bisley) and introduced them to skills (such as tractor driving) designed to encourage them to go into farming. My older brother, James, took up this challenge and found himself running the farm at the age of 20 (while completing his agriculture degree in Newcastle-upon-Tyne, 250 miles away) when Dad died. My other brother, Robert, went down the wildlife route, becoming a zoologist before changing course and working around the world for the British Council – still recognisably his father's son in his choices. My sister, Kathy, also lived the international life, working as an English teacher in Egypt and Hong Kong among many other adventures.

Dad's 'can do' attitude pervaded my upbringing, and still today it rarely occurs to me that things might be too difficult or scary or dangerous to attempt. Only sometime later in the planning process might I think – hang on! How can I possibly do this? People occasionally say to me 'You're so brave' when I tell them of my solo travels, but it is not brave to do something that you are not afraid of. Somehow I was brought up not to be fearful and I treasure this gift. It's more like courage blindness, where you have no idea that what you are doing is brave until someone else tells you so. It saddens me to see people who are prevented from trying new experiences by the tyranny of their own fears. Equally, when I see someone overcome a phobia of water to jump into a deep pool, or a person who is scared of heights climb a long ladder, I am impressed – that is bravery.

And yet. And yet, Dad never tried to enthuse us about China. He clearly held the Chinese in high esteem, commenting: 'The Chinese are thoroughly independent and compel one's respect.' One would think that after several years' positive experience in China and being an admirer of the Chinese, he might have... encouraged us... told stories... mentioned it?

I notice that earlier I wrote 'my father died in 1981' as if it were just another day. Evidently I have learned the art of understatement from my father. He was diagnosed with emphysema in 1979. I had just begun my A level course in biology and decided to look up this strange word in one of my textbooks and find out what it meant. What I read put me into a state of shock. Words such as 'terminal', 'untreatable', 'breathlessness ultimately leading to heart failure and death' congealed around my own heart. Medical terminology is elegant and concise but it has no sentiment. It cannot express how the patient is going to feel, how he will look to his family, what the experience will be like as his physiology descends into chaotic and disastrous imbalance.

The emphysema sufferer is in the peculiar position of being able to get enough air in, but has considerable difficulty getting it out again, leading to hyperinflation of the lungs. In between the in-breath and out-breath, oxygen uptake is compromised due to reduced surface area and excessive mucus production in the alveoli. Alveoli are the gas exchange units of the lungs and look like little bunches of grapes. In emphysema, the cell walls break down ('epithelial ruination') so that each bunch becomes one big grape, with a smaller surface area and reduced elasticity. The alveoli both produce more mucus than normal and have a lower capacity to clear it. This means that the sufferer eventually drowns in mucus or their heart packs up from the effort of trying to force blood into the resistant lung tissue.

Textbooks agree that it is a smokers' disease, but Dad didn't smoke, apart from the occasional after-dinner cigar. It's also known as 'farmer's lung', but who knows if wartime events set in train a cascade that led him to being vulnerable to lung dysfunction when he began farming at the age of 46. According to traditional Chinese medicine, anxiety and sorrow both damage the lungs. The English word 'anxiety' comes from a German root, 'angst', meaning narrow, referring to the narrowing of the bronchial passages. Suppressed grief for all of those friends and colleagues lost in the war, and for the stoically borne losses and suffering since, may have weakened Dad's lungs. Whatever the cause, it seems cruelly ironic that an 'action man' should suffer a condition that primarily limits action. Dad's brother Robert developed a muscle-wasting disease in his hands and had to give up his surgical work and retrain as a radiologist. My mother-in-law, a novelist and poet, gradually lost her words due to progressive aphasia and was eventually unable to read, write or speak. Either God has a warped sense of humour or you can 'wear out' the parts of yourself that you need and use the most.

A combination of the time in which they were raised (Dad was born in 1914, Mum in 1927), their education and their military backgrounds meant that both of them were stoic and undemonstrative. It seems that the generation who lived through the Second World War learned quiet suffering and acceptance of hardship and loss. I suppose Dad's diagnosis was just another thing to be borne. Burdened with the devastating knowledge about my father's prognosis, though, I had no skills or experience in talking about it. I didn't know if my parents knew that the prognosis was certain, even if the timing wasn't. Dad showed no sign of being upset. He carried on as best he could over the next several months, as his lungs slowly robbed him of the ability to do anything. I never talked to him about it at all, between diagnosis and death. After a year or so we had to adapt the house so that he could sleep downstairs, and as the end approached it was very clear what was happening. Not a word passed between me and either parent about this pink, puffing elephant in the room. Kathy was living in Egypt, Robert was living in Kenya, and they kept in touch but did not gather for a 'deathbed scene'. I carried on with my A levels, my riding and all my usual activities and thought I was doing splendidly well at coping with the situation, just like Dad always had.

Dad died on a Saturday afternoon. Mum spent the last hours with him at the hospital, while I mowed the lawn. She arrived home and we just sat close to each other on the sofa and cried our separate tears. We decided to drive up to the Stiperstones, a rocky outcrop on the aeon-worn Precambrian hills of south Shropshire with a brooding beauty and spectacular views of Wales to the west and England to the east. It is a place of violent weather, ankle-breaking footing and ravens showing off their aerobatic skills in the buffeting winds. On an August afternoon you can spend several hours picking wild bilberries, sometimes enough for one small pie. On this July day, it was a glorious sunny afternoon. We fought our way against the robust summer breeze up to the ridge. Why? To do something, to see the horizon, to feel the beauty of death's sweet release, to feel the Earth's embrace, to see life carrying on regardless, to avoid thinking, talking and experiencing what had just happened.

A week after Dad died I went to Kenya for a month to visit my older brother, Robert, who was studying Nile rats there for his doctorate. Dad had planned the trip and no doubt thought it would be a good eye-opener for me and a proper adventure (it was). Perhaps it's wishful thinking to believe that our relationship would have developed as I became an adult, but at least I could have interrogated him a bit! The more I have investigated his story, the more heartbroken I have become that I can't ask him about it directly. The research has also ignited in me a desire to know more about my family history in general. Ancestor worship is a very Chinese trait, but I think we could usefully incorporate it into our own culture. In the West we tend to venerate youth, and while youth is beautiful, wisdom, if it comes, comes with age. As Mark Twain said: 'When I was a boy of 14, my father was so ignorant I could hardly stand to have the old man around. But when I got to be 21, I was astonished at how much the old man had learned in seven years.'

The day after my return from Kenya I went to France for my gap year job as an au pair near Paris. I spent no time at home until Christmas, when I returned for a short break. On the first day, I set a place for my father at the kitchen table. Because I had been away, the reality of his death had not sunk in at a conscious level. My body did express grief, however, in that I had no periods for six months after his death. So this man did mean a lot to me, but it took a very long time to process his loss. It is now decades since he died and I have become thoroughly accustomed to his absence, but I bitterly regret not having known him and feel that I have not completed the grieving process. Perhaps one never does.

I loved my childhood and was generally happy, but I now realise that both my parents were rather emotionally closed and distant. By the time I came along, I think Dad had decided to maintain strategic control of our lives but to delegate actual childcare to Mum. He tended to shut himself away in his office, doing the farm admin while listening to classical music. I would try to get closer to him by helping out on the farm and riding to hounds together, but I think his concerns lay elsewhere. He did encourage me to be adventurous, while simultaneously working on the assumption that I would go into nursing or teaching and then marry a farmer, give it all up and have children. An odd juxtaposition of ambitions for me.

He did allow us to follow our own path, however. I understand that he was not keen on my brother Robert's career in zoology and had tried to steer him towards farming. Dad never criticised, but he did once question Robert about it, when he was embarking on the fieldwork for his PhD. Robert's explanation that this might lead to an academic career and that, furthermore, he was earning the equivalent of a junior officer's pay seemed to satisfy Dad. When it came to my turn, I had a fairly low opinion of my academic capabilities and was determined that I would leave school at sixteen and go to catering college. My parents didn't interfere or try to dissuade me; they just accompanied me to the interview, where the principal of the college helped me to realise that my academic capabilities were in fact considerably greater than necessary for this career choice. I decided to stay on at school, at no great loss to the world of catering.

On the physical plane, we had everything we could have wished for, and our parents deeply imprinted their values in us. They were very sociable and hospitable and deeply loyal to their friends and family. My mother at 90 still meets regularly with her old school friends, and Dad always remained close to his army friends and cared for his mother until his death (my grandmother outlived her three sons and three husbands, dying at 101 in 1992). But it never occurred to me to share confidences with them or to seek emotional support. My mother's postnatal depression meant that she was effectively unavailable to me emotionally from birth, through this debilitating illness, for a crucial period in infant development. I learned early to look after myself. Throughout my childhood I was quite compliant and competent, and so I was largely left to my own devices by both parents. Traditionally the baby of the family is the overindulged one, but sometimes they can be the opposite, especially if they are a 'good girl' who can safely be ignored to deal with other, more pressing demands. My self-sufficiency equally meant that I learned little about the internal worlds of my parents. While I discovered more about my mother as a person as I grew older, Dad went too soon. I was left hungry for a bigger piece of my father.

Long after his death, on a visit to my mother, I asked to have a look at the original letters that Dad had written home about his escape from Hong Kong. The '20th-century Great' remark had been buzzing round my brain like an increasingly insistent bee. Mum delved into her bureau and found a large brown envelope that proved to be a treasure trove of documents. There were military reports, numerous letters, diaries, photographs, a map of part of Canton province, correspondence with a military historian, telegrams, letters of congratulation on the award of his Military Cross, and Chinese travel permits written in Mandarin. My filing instinct snapped to attention. This lot needed sorting out before I could even think of piecing together my father's story.

The next step seemed to be to get the documents transcribed so that I could look at them properly. A friend was able to help out and made an impressive job of interpreting my father's handwriting. As I proofread the documents, I began to realise the enormity of what my father had done. There is something about handling documents written by the deceased that is incredibly moving. Buyers of memorabilia are the public face of this effect, with artefacts of the famous changing hands for vast sums. For me, seeing Dad's handwriting and reading his letters and diaries both ignited a desire for a greater connection and heralded howls of despair for the lack of it. I was furious – how dare he die without sharing all of this with me? I began to realise that reading his story was not enough – I wanted to go to China and retrace his steps. Maybe that way I could get underneath the surface that he had presented to me, figure out what made him tick and fill in some of the tantalising gaps in his letters. I was at the beginning of a long and daunting journey.

Why had it taken me from age 18 to my late forties to seek out my father? Maybe it was the right time. At first I was occupied with completing my education and establishing my career and, while I was subconsciously attracted to older men who reminded me of Dad, it didn't occur to me that I could develop my relationship with him posthumously. A marriage breakdown and change of career took up most of my thirties. A combination of factors then led me to thinking more about Dad. The TV show *Who Do You Think You Are?*, which helps celebrities to trace their ancestors inspired me. The stories were always interesting and the programme showed how it was possible to research family history. From 2009, the 70th anniversary of the beginning of the Second World War began to feature in the news and TV documentaries.

On a more personal level, I had been living in Wiltshire since graduating as an osteopath in 1999. I chose the area partly because it was familiar – my grandparents had lived there since I was a baby and I had visited regularly. My grandmother was kind enough to offer me a temporary home, enabling me to move out of London without having to find accommodation first. I found horses to ride at a point-to-point yard near Warminster and enjoyed watching them race at Larkhill, my father's old stomping ground. I have a sketch of him riding at Larkhill by the artist C.J. Payne, known as Snaffles, almost falling off after the last fence, with the caption: 'For 'eavens sake Captin, stick to 'im.' (Mum says that this incident followed a big night out at the Hunt Ball and he was sleep deprived and hung-over. This didn't stop him from racing but it hampered his chances of winning.) Many of my patients in Warminster were retired military men, and conversation sometimes fell to my father's history in the army, especially because of his local connections. I met my husband in 2006 and we married in 2010, so on top of living in one place for several years and feeling happy in my work, I felt more settled generally. Perhaps, having slowed down a bit, I was able to notice the gaping hole in my life where Dad should have been?

Since he died, I have had a fantastic relationship with Dad. He never interrupts, never argues, never judges or disapproves. What follows is the story of how he and I got to know each other properly, 30 years after his death.

2

Hong Kong 1941

My father joined the army as a Gentleman Cadet in 1932 at the age of 18. I suspect that he may have been drawn to the prospect of an active life of adventure, preferring that to years of studying for an office-based career. He was commissioned as an officer in 1934 and sent to Hong Kong in 1937. The British colony of Hong Kong at that time comprised Hong Kong Island, the Kowloon Peninsula (the downtown area on the mainland), the New Territories (a hilly area north of Kowloon dotted with villages and bordering China) and numerous nearby islands.

Dad joined 8th Heavy Brigade, Royal Artillery, and assumed command of a Chinese troop on its formation in 1938. (The appendix at the end of the book shows the command structure of the Royal Artillery during the Second World War.) He was assigned a Chinese interpreter to help him train this troop, Cheung Yan-lun (known as Andrew), who was to become a lifelong friend. Cheung was born in Wuhua, Guangdong Province, China in 1914 and came to Hong Kong in 1928. He too made his way into China from Japanese-held Hong Kong in 1942 and reported to Guilin, where he was selected as interpreter by Colonel Jacobs-Larkcom, head of the British Military Mission there, and helped to train the Nationalist army. When Guilin fell in 1944, Cheung was airlifted to Chongqing with the remaining British forces. He returned to Hong Kong after the Japanese surrender and raised eight children.

In 1940 Dad was appointed to the Hong Kong Singapore Royal Artillery (HKSRA), but by the time of the Battle of Hong Kong in December 1941 he was based at HQ China Command, Hong Kong. In late November 1941 my father had been promoted to Brigade

Major, which he felt very good about, regarding it as quite a step up the career ladder and a recognition of his intellectual abilities. At this time there were rumours and false alarms about the imminence of war with Japan, but it never seemed to come to anything. Dad comments on the last-minute change of plan for the defence of Hong Kong following the arrival of two Canadian battalions in November 1941:

> For the past two years the intention had been merely to deny the use of the harbour to the enemy and to hold the island at all costs. It was realised that it was impossible to hold the colony in sufficient strength to enable it to be used as a Naval Base. No attempt was to be made to hold the mainland or Kowloon. The arrival of the Canadians entailed great changes in this plan. In addition to the island, Devil's Peak Peninsula was now to be held at all costs. The 'inner line', a great belt of pill boxes and wire, constructed in the time of General Bartholomew [Commander 1935–38], on the northern slopes of the ring of hills encircling Kowloon, was to be held in force by three Battalions for about six weeks, whilst the island would be held against any attack from the sea by the Coast Defences.

General Gordon Grimsdale, British Military Attaché in Chongqing (then spelled Chungking), who would later be Dad's boss, held strong views about the wisdom of protecting the colony:

> As long ago as 1934 I started a campaign to persuade people that Hong Kong was not worth defending. The development of air forces had already shown that, as a naval base, Hong Kong was quite useless. It would never be possible, in the small space available, to construct sufficient aerodromes, for use by an air force large enough to take on the potentially strong hostile air forces, based on many aerodromes in nearby China. At the best, Hong Kong could only be used as a temporary naval anchorage... 'But' said my opponent, 'think of the prestige we shall lose.' I am indeed convinced that it was this wretched word 'prestige'

which over-ruled all other arguments. Useless for me to point out that if war came, we should lose far more prestige by a short and unsuccessful siege, than by voluntarily deciding not to try the impossible. And, as I also pointed out, after the war Hong Kong would belong to whoever won the war. I had much reason to remember my arguments when I arrived at Chungking fourteen days after Hong Kong fell; the majority of Chinese were not prepared to let me forget how much prestige the loss of Hong Kong had cost us.[1]

Churchill evidently felt that it would be better for Hong Kong to fall into Japanese hands – to be recovered later – than to fall into Chinese hands, from which it might never be reclaimed. He certainly never expected that Hong Kong could be held and refused to 'waste' extra resources on its defence. After receiving a request in January 1941 to strengthen the garrison, Churchill noted:

> If Japan goes to war there is not the slightest chance of holding Hong Kong or relieving it. It is most unwise to increase the loss we shall suffer there. Instead of increasing the garrison it ought to be reduced. Japan will think twice before declaring war on the British Empire, and whether there are two or six battalions at Hong Kong will make no difference. I wish we had fewer troops there, but to move any would be noticeable and dangerous.

The implied disregard for human life in this strategic thinking seems shocking now, but with a war being conducted on many fronts around the world against a variety of enemies, I suppose brutal decisions had to be made.

Oliver Lindsay, military historian, comments:

> For political and moral reasons Hong Kong had to be defended. Many Chinese would have been seriously discouraged from continuing their weary and interminable

---

1. From the private papers of General Gordon Grimsdale, held at the Imperial War Museum, London

struggle against Japan, if Britain had lacked the courage and determination to resist and had abandoned the colony to the mercy of the Japanese before they had even declared war. Such a sordid act of appeasement would also have shaken the neutral Americans, who were then strengthening their forces in the Pacific while critically assessing Britain's determination to fight on.[2]

On 26 November 1941, the American Secretary of State had handed to the Japanese ambassador a demand for them to leave China. This was the final trigger for the Japanese to prepare for war with the Western powers. The battle of Hong Kong began on 8 December 1941, a few hours after the Japanese attacked Pearl Harbor on the other side of the Pacific, and at the same time as attacks on Singapore and the Philippines, and the invasion of Malaya (the peninsula, with Singapore at its tip, that was a British protectorate at this time) and Thailand. The Japanese objectives seem to have been to neutralise American military striking power in the Pacific and to ensure continuity of supply – Oliver Lindsay told my father many years later:

> After moving into French Vichy Indo-China the US, UK, Dutch etc. put trade barriers and embargoes against the Japs which prevented them getting oil, tin, rubber, etc. Their imports of oil were cut from 80 million barrels in 1940 to 8 million in 1941. They had the choice of losing face by withdrawing from Indo-China and South China, or securing these prizes by war!

My father kept a diary during this period. He was always a good trencherman and his diary is liberally peppered with details of his meals, but he also writes about the events of the day. This is fascinating to me, as he rarely spoke of his inner world or even of his outer world. He writes well and entertainingly and it is a pity that he never wrote a book himself. His diaries were gold mines for me, along with his letters home to his parents and closest friends. In quoting his writings I have not altered any spellings or grammar except where he

2. Oliver Lindsay, *The Lasting Honour: The Fall of Hong Kong 1941* (London: Hamish Hamilton, 1978), 201

mentions names that I now know to be misspelled, or Chinese names that have changed spelling with the current version of Pinyin (Chinese in Roman script) and refer to people mentioned by other writers. Reading his diary for the last weeks before the outbreak of war, there is a constant undertow of threat beneath the day-to-day mundanities, but it is a distant and abstract threat. Remember that his diaries and letters were written in war, when any document could be considered a security risk and so much had to be written in code or left unsaid.

Even on the eve of battle, Dad's diary indicates that there was still no sense of its imminence:

> Sunday 7 December 1941: Yesterday afternoon I went down to the airport for a flying lesson. I thought it went rather well and was very disappointed with Baugh [Flying Officer Norman Baugh] for not letting me go solo. After it got dark we went into the bar and met some of the CNAC [China National Aviation Corporation] pilots. They had about a dozen planes leaving for Nam Yeung that night. The first two Douglasses went off at about 7.15 and were expected back shortly after nine.
>
> Baugh and I had intended going out together to dine. First of all we went up to his mess for a wash. When we got there we found there was a flap in progress. A message had just been received from the RAF Singapore putting them on No.1 state of readiness. 'Horrid' Horry rang up [Colonel Lance] Newnham to find out if he had had any further news, but was told that headquarters far from having had any fresh cause of alarm, were thinking of relaxing their precautions. All the same to be quite sure I rang up my office to find out whether I was wanted. George Cross, who was on duty at the time, seemed quite offended and assured me that all was quiet, and that he could deal with any situation which might arise.
>
> About this time the two Douglasses which had left earlier in the evening returned to the aerodrome long before they were expected. For some reason they had turned back. One landed in such a hurry that it broke its undercarriage.

There was an air of expectancy and excitement in the mess where I stayed to dinner as Baugh was now confined to barracks.

As I went home after dinner everything seemed quiet and normal. There were the usual Saturday night crowds in the main streets and on the ferries. Hong Kong was illuminated as usual. This morning when I went to the office, I found that the situation had worsened. I don't really believe that anyone thinks that it will come to anything. We have had so many flaps and lived in a state of tension for so long that we have become blasé. We live only for the day when the rather annoying precautions that interfere with our private amusements are once more considered unnecessary. This is more serious than most. The Hong Kong Regiment have been ordered to get their ammunition onto their mainland positions.

The Allies were woefully unprepared for a land-based attack and were extremely poorly supported at every level. They were 15,000 men (including the two battalions of Canadians who had been sent as reinforcements at the last minute) against over 50,000 Japanese. As Edwin Ride says[3]:

> The Japanese were overwhelmingly superior in artillery and had complete control of the air. They had a well-prepared intelligence system. The Japanese were a homogeneous force of highly trained troops with battle experience in China.

My father was also impressed and surprised by the Japanese forces:

> The Japs pulled a gigantic surprise on us. We had no idea that he was as good as we found him to be. Before the war we looked down upon him, considering ourselves more than his match both in physique, training and equipment. To our consternation we found him better than ourselves

---

3. Edwin Ride, *BAAG: Hong Kong Resistance 1942–45* (Hong Kong: Oxford University Press, 1982), 4

in all respects. Certainly the Troops he brought against us were magnificently fit and hardy. Both their fieldcraft and night fighting were first class. His cooperation between the arms was excellent. His Infantry never seemed to be without adequate close support. We hated his heavy mortar and, though I believe that it has been more bark than bite, it did the trick against us even if it might be ineffective when used against more seasoned troops. Whatever his troops may carry on the march his assault troops in battle only carried very light equipment. They were dressed in KD [khaki drill] usually with netting sewn over the upper portions, I suppose for holding garnishment; a steel helmet also covered with a net, rifle, ammunition, bayonet, some hand grenades and an iron ration. He seldom seemed to wear leather boots usually rubber soled hockey boots with a separate big toe. Officers usually carried glasses and a large leather map case. To our amusement they invariably wear swords. Their morale was magnificent.

However, the British might have been better prepared for a land attack, as Dad observed:

Saturday 24 January 1942: Shortly before the war started I read in the Manual of Coast Defence that history has shown that land frontier has been the weakness of every besieged fortress. Hong Kong has reiterated this saying. Our seaward defences were immensely strong. The enemy made no attempt to attack us from that side, but our defence against a land attack was quite inadequate. Three Battalions had to hold a front of eleven miles, spread out on such a front there could be no reserves and no real defence in depth.

Initially the Japanese air force knocked out the Allies' capability for air defence and reconnaissance, before ground troops began to push south from the Chinese border. Dad's account of the battle was hair-

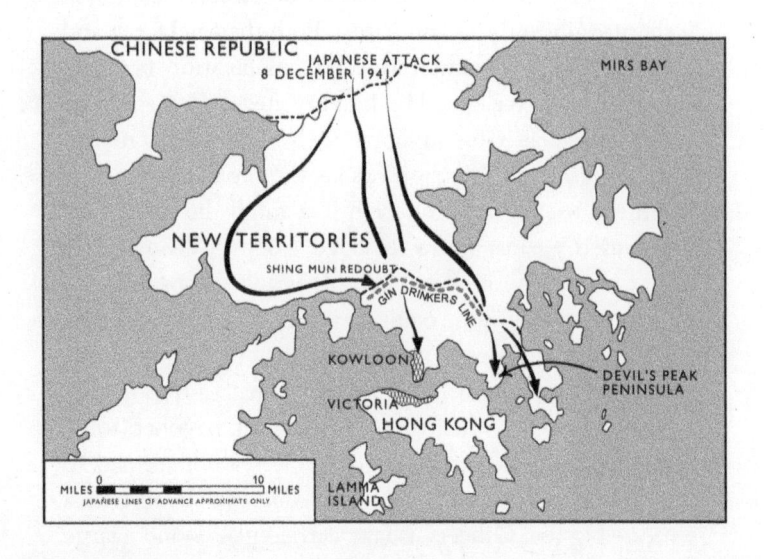

Battle of Hong Kong 8–25 December 1941.

raising and poignant. I had to keep reminding myself that he was only 27 at the time:

> Wednesday 10 December 1941: About 8.00am [on Monday 8 December] the first Japanese bombers came over. They did a lot of damage at the Aerodrome, destroying 7 CNAC planes, The Clipper, most of the RAF planes and the two Walruses. They were unopposed. The volunteer AA [anti-aircraft] platoon had drawn no ammunition, I suppose because the day before was a Sunday. The gunboat supposed to be in the seaplane anchorage was being used for something else. The Japs made rapid progress down the Taipo Road, and by the evening we were back in Shatin. HQ were gravely disappointed with the Stanley guns [on Hong Kong Island]. They have shot too big a line, boasted that they could get almost to Taipo [a village 15 miles to the north in the New Territories], in actual fact they

can only reach about 1500 yards beyond Shatin Station [in Kowloon].

The lack of air cover combined with very limited troops defending the mainland meant that the Japanese made rapid progress through the New Territories, now a region of wetlands, parks and mountains in Hong Kong, north of Kowloon.

> Thursday 11 December 1941: I tried hard to sleep but it is an unpleasant feeling to lie still, while periodically in the distance you hear the first whisper of a coming shell, rising in a crescendo to shriek and ending in a tremendous crash. There is the feeling that this one may be going to get you. However after a few have exploded harmlessly, so far as you are concerned, you become quite fatalistic.

The mainland was lost by 13 December, when the Allies were forced to evacuate their last stand, the Devil's Peak Peninsula, to the east of the Kowloon Peninsula:

> Yesterday there was a tremendous battle on the Devil's Peak Peninsula. Twice in the afternoon we were asked to put down big concentrations of 6" Howitzer 9.2" guns on enemy advancing to the attack. We beat them off and by evening were still holding our original line, but the General [Maltby] decided that the peninsula must be evacuated. We got the guns across safely, but the lighters to take the mules were sunk and the entire lot, about 100, were lost. We must have very badly weakened the Japs yesterday because the final boatloads of men only got away shortly after dawn this morning. I believe Thracian (our only destroyer) and the MTBs [motor torpedo boats] only left the Lyemun Pass [a channel separating Kowloon and Hong Kong Island] at 7.00am.

The Japanese General Sakai asked for surrender on 13 December. He was refused. Dad describes the demand document:

About 9.00am the Japs sent across a boat with a white flag demanding our surrender. I saw the demand itself shortly afterwards in the intelligence office where the interpreters were busy translating it. It was a scroll, unfolded, right to left about a foot wide and 10 feet long. There were three of them working on it, it was spread out between them. There was plenty of room for each to work on his own portion.

There followed three days of bombardment of the Allied positions on Hong Kong Island.

Tuesday 16 December 1941: For the past three days the Japs have been shelling us very heavily indeed. Mt. Davis have had the worst of it. One of the AA [anti-aircraft] guns has been knocked out. About 11 men were killed when the enemy scored a direct hit on one of the shelters. A dud shell hit the muzzle of the upper 9.2" gun and it appears to be slightly bent. The plug gauge bore will no longer pass through it. A shell (9") came in through the old canteen along the passage into the plotting room and came to rest under the command exchange. The lights and the ventilating plant have been put out of action. We are only through to them by one line which goes through their Regimental HQ at Felix Villas which they have had to move twice.

Courtlands [a hotel where Dad was staying] has been lucky so far. It is very close to the Peak Tramway which the enemy base succeeded in putting out of action. The houses all round have been totally knocked about. At breakfast this morning the base of a 150 millimetre shell came in through the window and landed under the table. Buzz [Dad's dog] is standing up better than I expected. He is puzzled, rather startled but so far not really frightened.

On my way back to HQ I nearly fell into a bomb crater. There was the usual blackout. I stopped the car when the road surface didn't seem quite right, got out to look and found the front wheels on the very edge of a hole about twenty feet across and ten feet deep. It was a small car and fortunately I was able to squeeze by on the right hand side.

General Sakai demanded surrender again on 17 December after this punishing shelling of Hong Kong Island but, again, the British refused.

> Today the Japs sent over another demand for surrender. They claimed to have destroyed by bombing or shellfire every military objective in the colony. If we still refused to surrender they threatened to bring down the place about our ears. The demand was summarily rejected.

From 18 December a fierce battle raged for control of the island:

> Friday 19 December 1941: The Japs landed last night, at Sai Wan, Lyemun Magazines and North Point. I suppose it was obvious they would land there from the amount of artillery preparation they have carried out in these areas. For a long time we refused to believe it in the Battle Box [the underground command centre]. There have been so many false alarms from this area that the attitude was rather 'Those bloody windy buggers! At it again.' They took Sai Wan Redoubt [a redoubt is a defensive fortification, in this case just up the hill from Lyemun Fort, where the Japanese landed] during the night. Bompas made a counter attack and retook it but most of his troops melted away and he was pushed off again. By daybreak we had to evacuate Sai Wan 6" Howitzer position. The Japs were up on the top of Mt. Parker and beginning to trickle down into the Ty Tam Valley. Then we had to evacuate Parker How position; after that came news that they had captured most of the guns in the Ty Tam Valley and were attacking Wong Nai Chung. It looked as if Ty Tam Gap would go at any minute, so the CRA [Commander Royal Artillery] ordered the destruction of the guns at Collinson, D'Aguilar, Bokhara and Chung Am Kok. The men had to

go to Stanley for use as infantry. The controlled mine fields in the Tathong and East Lamma Channels were blown up.

The island bisects neatly into a western half and an eastern half. The road that runs from north to south down the middle goes over a pass between the hills called Wong Nai Chung Gap. The Allies had to hold the Gap to have any hope of retaining control of the island.

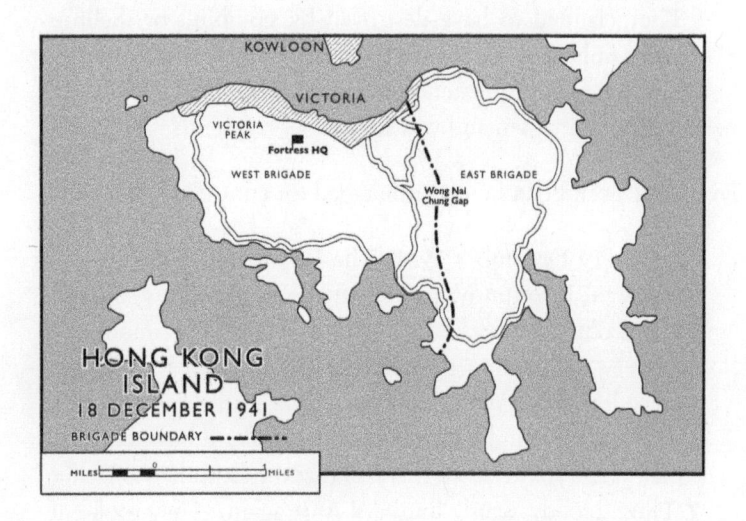

Hong Kong Island as at 18 Dec 1941.

Friday 19 December 1941: I rang up to ask Jack Fox what the position was at Wong Nai Chung. I could hear the machine gun fire down the phone. He had been manning one himself. 'Tell Pat' he asked me. Quarter of an hour later I rang up again, this time I got Tim [Temple]. He said that they were surrounded and fighting a tremendous battle with small arms: 'What else is there to do' he said in a rather humorous, resigned tone of voice. That was the last we heard of them. Wong Nai Chung was taken. It was the key point of the island.

Jack Fox, Tim Temple and all of the infantrymen were killed at

Wong Nai Chung. With hindsight, this would have been the time to surrender to avoid further loss of life, but the Allies were determined to continue, against all odds.

> Ted Hunt came in this evening. He had led a counter attack against Wong Nai Chung and had recaptured it almost single-handed. As he got near the enemy his Battery just melted away. Though the gunners are steady under shellfire, they will not face the enemy at hand to hand fighting. I don't really blame them. They have had very little training in the use of infantry weapons and so few of our young officers can make themselves really understood in their language. Jack Fielden was killed in this attack and Colonel Yale badly wounded. Ted could tell us nothing of Tim Temple, Geoffrey Proes, or Jack Fox. Ted is looking very wild and woolly. He is wearing an extraordinary assortment of uniform, he has 3 or 4 day growth of beard and is carrying a Tommy gun which he swears is the finest weapon ever invented. He has had no sleep for the past two days. The CRA had ordered him to go back to Stanley and rest. About this time news came through that the Japs had reoccupied Wong Nai Chung. Just as Ted was leaving I warned him of this and told him to go round by Pok Fu Lam but he replied 'Bugger the Nip I am going back that way anyhow'. And with that he dashed up the stairs out of the Battle Box.

Hunt was killed that night. Fierce fighting raged for the next few days as the Allies obstinately refused to admit defeat.

> Wednesday 24 December 1941: I have shot Buzz. Up to now the bombardment has only puzzled and startled him; it has never really frightened him, but yesterday and today he has been terrified by every exploding bomb or shell. It is obvious that very soon we shall all be dead or will surrender. He is better off out of the way though I don't suppose I shall have another dog his equal.

It is typical of Dad to comment so matter-of-factly about these nerve-shredding events. He never mentions fear or anxiety and seems to have quickly adapted to battle conditions with a rather Chinese fatalistic approach. Confucius recognised that not all outcomes are controllable by oneself in particular or mankind in general. Rather fate, or Heaven's Command, is ultimately in control. Dad was never sentimental about animals even when he had a close bond with them. Horses and dogs revered him as their master and seemed to respond well to his authoritarian style. He obviously had a special bond with Buzz, his 'once in a lifetime' dog, perhaps. How hard it must have been and yet merciful to end his suffering – Dad would have regarded it as his duty, I'm sure. He clearly felt that his own death was imminent, in the fighting or at the hands of the victors after surrender. In that circumstance, shooting his dog was the only way he could be certain of Buzz's welfare. Had victory for the Allies been in prospect he might have tried to calm the dog, in the hope that the prolonged fireworks display would soon be coming to an end. Perhaps he felt he couldn't express sadness about his dog when so many colleagues and friends had also lost their lives in the battle.

In the same extract he went on to comment, admiring a kindred spirit perhaps:

> After lunch I had my hair cut. I was greatly impressed by the barber, a Chinese. Shortly after he had started there was an air raid. A bomb landed nearby which put out the electric lights. He sent for a coolie to hold a candle and carried on, quite unperturbed.

The Governor of Hong Kong, Sir Mark Young, surrendered the colony to the Japanese on Christmas afternoon, 1941, at the Japanese headquarters in the Peninsula Hotel, Kowloon. Major General Maltby, General Officer Commanding, wrote in his despatch, published in *The London Gazette*, 27 January 1948, but written in Sham Shui Po camp in Hong Kong shortly after the battle:

> This advance by the enemy along the line of Gaps [or passes], the possession of these Gaps by him, thus giving

him an open line of advance to the Central District, the fall of Bennets Hill, the isolation of the forces in Stanley, the deployment by the enemy of such superior forces and armament, the exhaustion after sixteen days of continuous battle with no reliefs for any individuals, our vulnerability to unlimited air attack, the impossibility of obtaining more ammunition for the few mobile guns I had remaining, the serious water famine immediately impending – these were the factors which led to the inevitable conclusion, namely, that further fighting meant the useless slaughter of the garrison, risked severe retaliation on the large civilian population and could not affect the final outcome. The enemy drive along the North Shore [of the island] was decisive.

Dad later had dinner with the Japanese Commander, General Kitajima, during his stay in the prisoner of war camp at Sham Shui Po. He and his boss, the Commander Royal Artillery, Brigadier MacLeod, were taken to the Japanese Commander's house on the evening of 7 January 1942. Dad's fluency in French proved useful as the conversation was conducted in French through the Japanese Camp Commandant, Major Nakazawa. They seem to have discussed the battle, as if it were a game of cricket that victor and vanquished were amiably reviewing, over a good meal and a glass of whisky. Dad's enthusiasm for food was no doubt heightened by the lack of food in the POW camp. He wrote that this was the only square meal he had during his incarceration. Most of his fellow POWs suffered starvation rations for the next several years. He describes the meal with the Japanese general in detail:

> He gave us a good meal, a pretty fair attempt at a European dinner. We had tomato soup, rissoles of bully and crab, followed by fried meat loaf, cold ham with asparagus and mayonnaise sauce. I astonished everyone by eating almost an entire loaf of bread. The general drank white port, his staff tawny port, the CRA and myself had neat Johnnie Walker.

In a report about the dinner meeting, it is clear that the Japanese were surprised by the British lack of defences on the mainland:

> At a later date Major J.P. Crowe, RA, the senior surviving officer of the Mainland artillery, was taken round the Mainland positions by General Kitajima. The General again expressed surprise that we had so few guns upon the mainland. At Shing Mun he told Major Crowe that he was amazed that so few troops were allotted to the defence of the Redoubt, which he considered to be the key to our position. He had made preparations for a whole battalion supported by his entire artillery to attack the Redoubt. The advanced company reported to him that it was very thinly held and had begged him to allow them to make a surprise attack, which he had rather unwillingly permitted but with, for him, most happy results.

3

Escape

The allied troops were unsure about what would happen following the surrender, but being held on the island made escape a near impossible prospect:

> Friday 26 December 1941: I am trying to make up my mind whether to make an attempt to escape or not. On the whole I think not. Chuck Bramble tells me that the island is busy with Jap troops. So far as I can see the only way out is to get to Shikko [on the island's east coast – now spelled Shek O] or Little Sai Wan [on the north coast] and then take a sampan [a flat-bottomed wooden boat] to the mainland. But I rather doubt whether there are any available. The Coast Defences have sunk so many there can only be a few left. The owners of those that remain would probably cut the throat of any white man as a reprisal for the tremendous destruction we have wrought amongst the fishing fleet. I don't feel like getting my throat cut alone, I prefer to die, if die I must, in company. I have asked several people to make an attempt with me. Baugh says he is still feeling badly knocked up. MacAlister is toying with the idea of escape but seems unwilling to come with me. Others, whom I think would be good companions, say that they are married and must think of their families.

Fortunately, the Japanese decided to transfer all their military prisoners to the mainland barracks at Sham Shui Po in Kowloon:

> By going to Sham Shui Po one great obstacle to escape

(the crossing to the mainland) would be behind us. Should I take food across in the hopes that I would be able to make a quick getaway, or should I take clothing in preparation for a long stay? I was undecided and made a compromise. I took a little food but a lot of clothing.

Thursday 8 January 1942: [On 29 December 1941] we were landed at the wharf near the Police Pier. Slowly we straggled past the YMCA, the Peninsula Hotel and up Nathan Road, most of us wearing overcoats, being the easiest way in which to carry them. We all had heavy bundles of kit and bedding. It was a hot day and we became damned tired. Large numbers of Chinese lined the streets. In the past our attitude towards the Chinese had been arrogant to say the least of it. I feared, now that we were defeated, marching to a prison camp, that the Chinese would remember past insults and take the opportunity to humiliate us still further by jeering at us and throwing rotten vegetables or eggs. However, they were strangely and apparently sympathetically silent.

Another escaper, Gunner Whitehead, made a similar comment about the Chinese lining the streets of Kowloon:

The Chinese lining Nathan Road looked on impassively. There was no hint of pity or scorn or anger at our having let them down, just that dour stoicism that through centuries of hardship has become a national trait of these people.[1]

Tony Hewitt describes the barracks at Sham Shui Po that had now been commandeered as a prison camp:[2]

Situated about three miles from Kowloon, the camp consisted of a cluster of small, low wooden huts squatting on

---

1. J.S. Whitehead and G.B. Bennett, *Escape to Fight On: With 204 Military Mission in China* (London: Robert Hale, 1990), 40
2. Anthony Hewitt, *Bridge with Three Men: Across China to the Western Heaven in 1942* (London: Jonathan Cape, 1986)

reclaimed land close to a smelly slum and a fetid, typhoon, junk anchorage. There was no sewer in the area and the faecal stench was nauseating. Pungent Chinese cooking odours blew into the camp along with the fetor of rotting fish and bad meat from open stalls.

It was an unhealthy place for prisoners and they were to suffer from the diseases associated with poor sanitation in addition to their other troubles.

As soon as he arrived at Sham Shui Po camp, Dad began planning his escape. Many of the senior officers were against the idea of escape and discouraged it, but Dad saw it as his duty and evidently took no notice, even when others tried to escape and were immediately recaptured. In the early days of the camp everything was quite disorganised, with no roll call or proper facilities for the prisoners. This may have encouraged Dad to think that an escape might go unnoticed and that getting out of camp would be a reasonably simple matter:

> Thursday 8 January 1942: I went out to reconnoitre possible means of escape. The camp was a real shambles. In the period between our evacuation of Kowloon and the Japanese occupation, the Chinese have gutted the place. All doors and windows have been removed for firewood. All the taps in the wash houses have been taken for the brass. There are no buckets left in the latrines, the wiring has been torn out of the huts for the copper. In Jubilee buildings they have even broken up some of the baths in their efforts to get off the taps, many of the lavatory pans are broken but in any case are useless as there is no water. I was astounded to find that most of the wire on the northern side of the camp was broken down, The Chinese had pinched the posts for firewood. I was elated – there was a golden opportunity to escape.

Australian Colonel Lindsay Ride, the Senior Medical Officer in the camp, escaped from Sham Shui Po camp with three other men on 9 January 1942. Ride had been a professor of physiology at the University of Hong Kong since 1928, after studying medicine at Melbourne and Oxford universities, and ran the field ambulance service during the battle. He could see from the outset that there was a very high likelihood of outbreaks of dysentery, cholera and other infectious diseases and that the necessary supplies to treat them would not be forthcoming. He estimated that, combined with undernutrition, the casualty rate might be as high as 60 per cent by the end of the summer.

Ride felt that the best thing he could do was to escape so that he could alert the outside world to the plight of the prisoners and so bring in help. He invited various officers to join him, but most were against the idea of escape and thought it too risky. Eventually his loyal Chinese student, Francis Lee, and two university colleagues who were lieutenants in the Hong Kong Naval Reserve, D.W. Morley and D.F. Davies, agreed to come. Lee was the lynchpin of the plan, as a native Chinese who could move more freely in the occupied territories and obtain help of various kinds. He arranged a sampan to pick up the party from the camp after dark on 9 January 1942. They succeeded in getting away from Sham Shui Po camp but then spent a couple of days getting lost in dense fog in the New Territories. Eventually they headed north-east and, with the help of Chinese Communist guerrillas, made it across Mirs Bay into China, only narrowly avoiding recapture by the Japanese.

The support provided by these Communist guerrillas represented the start of an important relationship that Ride depended upon when he set up the British Army Aid Group (BAAG) in March 1942 in Shaoguan. BAAG's aim would be to help prisoners to escape and to smuggle in essential supplies and news to the prison camps.

The poor fate of the prisoners was also clear to Dad as the Japanese established their regime over the first couple of weeks:

> The Japanese have just started issuing beans. These are a great improvement to the diet even though we only get enough to give each man a couple of tablespoons once a day. When they were first issued there were great arguments as to whether they should be germinated or not. The arguments in favour of germination (vitamin C) seem to

me so obvious that I really think X [another staff officer] must be insane as he opposed. The silly little man even argued with the doctors. Some of the troops don't like it. They say it makes the beans hard! But unless the Japanese give us more meat and vegetables we are in for a poor time. Already they have almost closed down the traffic over the fence. Relatives and Chinese girl friends are still allowed to bring parcels of food but these are examined and handed over by the Japs themselves. Ordinary trade has stopped. They have shot several Chinese who have been caught selling stuff to us. They are afraid of messages being passed into the camp.

Although actually getting out of the camp seemed quite easy, surviving a journey through occupied territory without getting shot or recaptured would be another matter. Very few men did escape from the POW camps and they invariably had a rough time of it. The Japanese were not the only potential opponents, as Dad observes:

We had both seen and heard much about the work of the 5th Columnists, and I had heard that when the Japanese took Canton [now known as Guangzhou], treachery and bribery were the chief reasons for the fall of the city. As a result we thought it was impossible to trust any Chinese, particularly in or near Hong Kong and that if we were unfortunate enough to meet one unexpectedly, he would betray us. We had also heard that there had been considerable guerrilla activity north of the border, but we imagined that there were probably Freelances over whom the Chinese government would have no control; that the term 'guerrilla' was a euphemism for 'bandit', and that if we fell in with any of these we should be murdered.

In typical military fashion, Dad considered all the options for escape. As the fence was not much of a barrier they could have walked out, but there were Japanese sentries everywhere, well-lit streets and a curfew in force. The camp was next to the sea, and bypassing the most heavily patrolled land around the camp by escaping across a short stretch of water looked a much more achievable route. They would then have a much better chance of returning to land, slipping unnoticed into the backstreets and up into the scrub-covered hills of the New Territories. Hiring a sampan would have meant trusting a Chinese – Dad thought this too risky, but Captain Tony Hewitt did escape successfully with the aid of a sampan. Although they could wade along the water's edge and then get up into the hills, their silhouettes would have been highly visible at low tide – the only feasible time to attempt that route. They could steal one of the sentries' rowing boats at night and make a getaway, but it was uncertain whether the sentries left the oars in the boats. The only other option was to make a raft and swim for it.

One of Dad's original companions for the escape baulked at the absence of any safe option and withdrew. It was difficult to find any willing companion – married men thought it irresponsible, others were sick or wounded and most just thought the whole prospect was too daunting. Anyway, we were bound to win the war soon and then everyone would be freed, wouldn't they? Dad comments on morale in the camp in those first few weeks of internment:

> It is curious how morale varies in the camp. The Middlesex and the RAF are good. They are still disciplined men and their officers are not allowing them to go to seed. The Indian Gunners are good. They keep their area of the camp decently clean and what is more do PT every morning. I have been joining them. On the whole the British Gunners are dreadful. They never were well disciplined and now their officers have little control over them. They sit about, do nothing and complain that the conditions are quite incredibly dreadful. The Volunteers are really good but the worst of the lot are the Scots and the Canadians. For a time there were Canadian Officers living in the same room as ourselves. At night they never stopped reminiscing. Their conversation was one long 'do you remember'. I am glad they have left. Morale varies with the current rumours. If

we could only get really authentic news it would be a great help.

The role of creating an orderly society in maintaining morale was not fully recognised at the time. Particularly for military men, perhaps, a command structure and a sense of law and order helped to secure the camaraderie and cohesion needed in such a desperate situation – otherwise it was every man for himself, with disastrous consequences. Dad hints at this in his remarks, along with the importance of living in the present moment. The Canadians' habit of reminiscing was not just annoying but unhealthy in that environment. It was hope for the future that was in short supply – in the form of news and the prospect of escape. Laurens van der Post[3] comments on his experience in a Japanese POW camp, where his attitude was to prove invaluable to his fellow internees during two and a half years of incarceration:

> Out of sight of heart and mind of their world, as prisoners were naturally predisposed to think, and even in their dreams, unconvinced that saving intervention from without was possible, it [instinct] had a decisive element of reassurance for me and in due course for all. Whatever chance remained of survival, it proclaimed, depended on a creative attention and positive response to the daily trifles of imprisonment, living an imperilled 'now' as if it were a safe and assured 'forever'.

Although my father doesn't expand on the role of the officers in determining morale, other writers mentioned that the senior officers were against the idea of escape, rather obliging the men to resign themselves to incarceration for an unknown period. While acceptance of their plight was necessary in some ways, this attitude may have unintentionally robbed the men of an essential component of their survival strategy. In Havers' book about Changi POW camp[4], the author comments:

---

3. Laurens van der Post, *Yet Being Someone Other* (London: The Hogarth Press, 1982), 318
4. R.P.W. Havers, *Reassessing the Japanese Prisoner of War Experience: The Changi Prisoner of War Camp in Singapore 1942–45* (London: Routledge, 2003), 33

A central tenet of POW existence, certainly in the way in which the experience has been represented, is that of the role played by the hope of escape in the lives of those held prisoner. Escape for a POW is both a practical and a psychological refuge. POWs necessarily spend much time thinking about their release. Escape is the only way in which a POW can shape his own future and therefore exercise an autonomous influence over his predicament. Escape, in whatever form, is the single decisive expression of self-determination that a prisoner can make.

One might be critical about the senior officers' negative attitude to escape from Hong Kong, but obviously escaping from POW camps in the Far East was rather different from escaping in Europe. The geography was unfamiliar, transport links were poor and, of course, disguise was impossible, even if you could speak the local language. There was also the issue of how escaped prisoners would be treated by the Japanese if caught and the threat of severe reprisals against POWs left behind, for which escapers might feel responsible.

Prevailing medical orthodoxy was that imprisonment actually protected combatants from mental illness, I suppose by removing them from the perils of battle. 'Barbed Wire Disease' was only described after the First World War, acknowledging that incarceration in its own right was detrimental to psychiatric health, regardless of how the prisoner was treated. However, the evidence from studies of First World War combatants didn't really percolate through the military hierarchy until late in the Second World War. Military health researchers Edgar Jones and Simon Wessely noted differences between military captives of the Japanese and Germans:

> In June 1945, Brigadier T.F. Rodger, consultant psychiatrist to South East Asia Command, reported that 'British prisoners of war recovered from Japanese hands showed fewer psychiatric symptoms and a much more stable and satisfactory reaction to their captivity than prisoners of war from German hands' and considered this finding 'due in large measure to the contempt which British soldiers were

able to feel for the Japanese and the absence of any feeling that the enemy was a man of a similar outlook and cultural background to themselves'.[5]

This statement seems extraordinary to us now, ignorant and racist, but we have to remember that the prisoners' only knowledge of the Japanese was most likely the treatment they were receiving, which has been criticised by many commentators as inhuman. Colonel Tokunaga, in charge of Sham Shui Po, was described by survivors as sadistic, cruel and hot-tempered. Demonising their captors as a form of self-preservation might well have been an important coping strategy.

In addition, the very high mortality from brutality, privation and disease (as much as 32 per cent in Far East POWs, compared to 4 per cent among European POWs) was thought to imply physical and mental resilience in those who did manage to survive incarceration by the Japanese.

Clearly, Dad was determined to escape, despite the odds against success, in the face of opposition from his superiors and colleagues and at some risk to those he left behind. To add to his concerns, Dad was given alarming news just as he was preparing to leave:

> Next day I was very badly shaken by Colonel Newnham, who had been giving me most invaluable information and advice about the portions of our route through the New Territories that I did not know well and in particular about the best places to cross the frontier [into China]. On the morning of the 27th January when I went to see him, he told me that the HQ of the 7th War Zone had moved North from Waichow [now spelled Huizhou], to exactly where he did not know; he believed Waichow to be in the hands of the Chinese guerrillas and advised us to steer well clear of it as it was nearing Chinese New Year when we might be robbed of everything we possessed including our boots. On hearing this I refused to go. I, in common

---

5. E. Jones and S. Wessely at the King's Centre for Military Health Research, London, 'British Prisoners-of-War: From Resilience to Psychological Vulnerability: Reality or Perception', *Twentieth Century British History*, Vol. 21, No. 2, 2010, pp. 163–183

with 99% of those in the camp, knew nothing of the interior of China, which in my imagination was peopled by a race of unfriendly bandits, who might possibly welcome you in times of peace if you had plenty of money to spend and could afford an escort of soldiers; but I thought that two people, fleeing from the Japanese, unarmed, with no money, and hardly speaking a word of Chinese, would not stand a dog's chance. The idea of travelling through such a country for an unspecified length of time, to an uncertain destination, without a map and without friends, appalled me.

However, next morning Baugh suggested that we could get the bandits on our side if we could offer a reward to anyone who brought us safely to General Yu Han-mou [in charge of the 7th War Zone]. I remembered that there were missionaries in Waichow and I thought if we could get to one of them, their mission would be a haven in which we could rest and refit for a few days, in which time we would find out the exact whereabouts of the 7th War Zone HQ. Accordingly Colonel Newnham made out two chits, both written in Chinese; one offered $300 reward to anyone who brought us safely to Yu Han-mou HQ; the other offered $15 reward to anyone who brought us safely to one of the missions in Waichow. This we only intended to produce at the city gates.

Colonel Newnham did not himself escape from Sham Shui Po and instead became a key communication link between BAAG and the prison camp. In June 1942 he was transferred to the Argyle Street camp (along with the other officers), also in Kowloon, and continued to send secret messages to BAAG.

Heartened by the idea of rewards for safe passage, Dad's party set about making a raft, using whatever they could lay hands on:

> Our first raft was made of two fir poles about 4" in diameter and about 8 feet long. On these were lashed four pieces of board about 15" long and about 6" wide. The whole thing

was so arranged that with a few cuts with a knife it would fall to pieces. We had decided to make an attempt on the night 31 Jan/1 Feb. Two hours before we were due to start, as I lay in bed trying to get what rest I could, memories of hydrostatics learned at school passed through my mind. I began to calculate, in my head, the displacement of our raft and the position of its metacentre. Gradually the unpleasant certainty came to me, despite all my wishful hoping to the contrary, that our raft was barely adequate for the load it had to carry and furthermore would be most top heavy. These forebodings were realised in full when we put it in the water. We abandoned the attempt for that night.

At last, Dad, his friend Flying Officer Norman Baugh and Captain I.B. Trevor – a Cantonese speaker who agreed to come at the last minute – set off at 11.20pm on the night of 1 February 1942. This seems to have been a popular night for escapes. A party comprising Sergeant Danny Parrott, Mike Jacobs, Gunner Reg Lewis and Gunner John 'Taff' Whitehead left a little later, as did Captain Tony Hewitt's party (with Major Douglas Scriven and Pilot Officer Eddy Crossley). It was full moon – while making the actual getaway risky, it would light their way when they had to travel at night across the New Territories, safer than risking being seen in daylight.

Dad had made a second raft, wider than the first, on which they loaded supplies for the journey. This included some food, a basic medical kit, a compass, some cash and a few clothes. They stepped out along a breakwater, which was about 1 metre under water at the time, and then swam, dragging and pushing the raft between them. They landed 50 minutes later, cold, wet and exhausted, but had to keep going to escape serious danger. Whitehead and his colleagues set off a little later but waded through the mud rather than swimming. Whitehead's party were spotted and shot at, their silhouettes being visible, as Dad had predicted. Only three of them made a successful getaway while the fourth, Reg Lewis, dashed back to the camp in a hail of bullets, one of which ricocheted off the mess tin he was carrying on his back and broke his collarbone. He was smuggled into the camp sick-bay and survived the war, despite being one of the prisoners shipped to Japan.

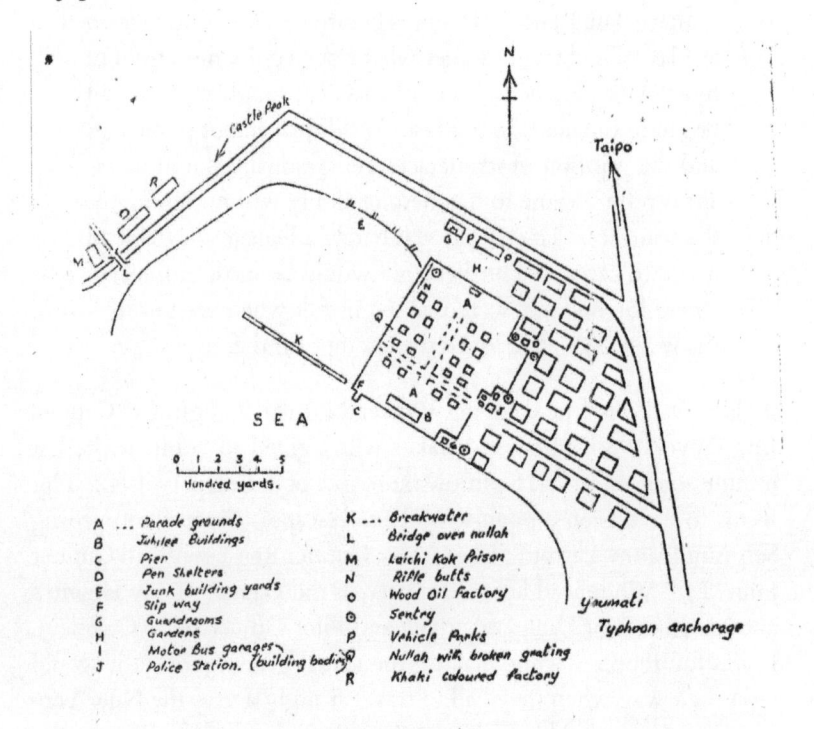

Sham Shui Po Camp, showing the escape route taken by Dad, from the slipway at F, along the breakwater at K to the bridge at L (a nullah is a drainage ditch).

This was the most dangerous part of the journey. At any moment the escapers might be recaptured or killed. The camp Commandant, Colonel Tokunaga, had made it quite clear to his prisoners that there would be punishments for escapes, including of sick or wounded men in the camp. The Japanese had 'a system of reprisals, not stopping short of the death penalty, for recaptured prisoners or for any fellow prisoners who seemed to have helped in preparing an escape'.[6] They didn't shoot prisoners; it was either beheading, bayoneting, strangling or being buried alive.

---

6. M.R.D. Foot and J.M. Langley, *MI9 Escape and Evasion 1939–45* (London: Biteback, 2011), accessed at Imperial War Museum, London

Escape

Against this concern was the hope that prisoners would have a morale boost when they learned of successful escapes. Whitehead reports, however, that shortly after they left, three beheaded corpses were shown to the prisoners and named as Whitehead and his companions, recaptured and executed. Proof of their identity was given in the form of Whitehead's pay-book, supposedly found in 'his' pocket. This had a hugely deterrent effect on other plans for escape and, during the whole term of imprisonment, only 33 men ever escaped from Sham Shui Po.

If any escapers had a serious injury (quite a likely event in this terrain at night), their chances of making it into free China would have gone completely. Successfully crossing the New Territories would take immense courage and luck, but reaching the border would not be the end of their troubles. The position of the Japanese in Guangdong province was constantly changing, advancing and receding unpredictably. They were taking an enormous risk, but perhaps they felt it was preferable to the unknown risks of staying in camp. Indeed, in 1942 there was a diphtheria epidemic in Sham Shui Po camp, on top of dysentery, malnutrition-related illnesses, parasitic infestations and so on, along with appalling quotidian discomforts and brutalities from their guards. In the first seven months 107 men died, and by September 1942 a majority of the more than 1,800[7] prisoners there were unfit to escape.

Many British POWs were shipped from Sham Shui Po to Japan for slave labour from September 1942 onwards, but others were moved into the camp and it remained in use until 1945. One of the boats carrying prisoners to Japan (the *Lisbon Maru*) was torpedoed and sank off Shanghai, with more than a thousand men losing their lives: drowned trapped inside the sinking ship, shot by the Japanese soldiers on board or dying subsequently from exhaustion. A few years ago I happened to meet one of the POWs who was sent to Japan. He had been 'lucky' enough to be forced labour in a peanut-processing factory – the peanuts undoubtedly keeping him alive until his liberation.

Dad's party broke up the raft and snuck up Golden Hill into the New Territories, with the full moon lighting the way. Just before

---

7. Oliver Lindsay, *The Lasting Honour: The Fall of Hong Kong 1941* (London: Hamish Hamilton, 1978)

dawn they came to the Shing Mun gorge and descended to find a place to rest:

> Despite the fact that the hill is very steep, the undergrowth was so thick that we found even going straight down hill was hard work whilst a lateral traverse across its face needed tremendous exertion.

Lying up by day and travelling by night was the safest plan, from a military perspective, but the terrain proved difficult to navigate at night and was physically draining.

He complains that one of his companions had 'no night sense' and was frequently stumbling. I have some sympathy for the poor chap! But Dad knew that this was the most dangerous section of their journey. They had to reach the border undiscovered by the occupying Japanese or it would be certain death. He had spent much time in the New Territories, had a map and a compass and was a keen mountaineer, so it was obvious to him both why and how this challenge had to be met.

> We started off again at 6.45pm [from Needle Hill] but despite my reconnaissance of the path in the morning, I lost the way and had to retrace our steps several times before we struck the right path and got to Grassy Hill. We found our compass of inestimable value while we were wandering in the mist. It began to rain. The path down to Leadmine Pass became very slippery; we each suffered several heavy falls. By the time we reached the bottom we were cold, wet and bruised.

The party continued doggedly on and by 5 February were very close to the border at the village of Lin Ma Hang.

> We were rather discouraged by our rate of progress. In four nights, over country I knew well, by our map we had only covered about 25 miles. We had hoped to average at least 8 miles per night. From this point onwards we would

be in completely unknown country. Though from the map it was nothing like as mountainous it would be considerably easier for us to lose our way.

At this point, Captain Trevor rebelled. He had found the going extremely tough and was less able to cope with the night hiking than the others. He had also found the food indigestible and was getting weak as a result. Tall and gangling, with greying hair and a toothbrush moustache, he was ill at ease in uniform. He had worked for the Kowloon–Canton Railway for several years and was fascinated by the history, language and culture of China. By comparison with his soldier companions, he was unfit and unused to 'night manoeuvres'. As the Cantonese speaker, he decided to go into Lin Ma Hang and ask for a meal to be brought to their hideout. A feast of chicken, rice and lettuce was duly brought, but that evening other, less welcome, visitors arrived:

> At about 6.00pm a party of about six or seven Chinese came to our hideout, gave us Chinese clothes and told us to go with them. They were armed and led us South West over a small pass where we were challenged by a guerrilla sentry armed with a rifle who appeared on the hillside as if from nowhere. We came to a small village, were taken into a farmhouse and told to wait until their leader came. Whilst we waited we were visited by a constant stream of curious visitors to whom we had to recount the outlines of our story. Some were filled with admiration, others were frankly incredulous. As time went on and still no leader came we became uneasy, suspecting that it was a trap and that they had really sent for the Japanese. After a couple of hours two Chinese arrived; one with a bad tempered and shifty expression who appeared to be the leader of the gang, the other spoke English and had been a steward on a British Freighter and knew Liverpool well.
>
> For a time they refused to believe that we were escaped prisoners but thought we were Japanese spies. We had with us packs, food, some equipment and watches. All these

they viewed with the greatest suspicion, particularly the watches. Of course when the Jap catches any of them their valuables are immediately removed and their heads are usually chopped off; so I don't really blame them. They could not understand how it was, if we really were prisoners, we had been allowed to keep all these things.

They refused to believe that we had swum out of camp. 'How is it' they asked, 'that your packs and clothing are dry?' We explained to them that we had carried them on a raft, but they could not believe that the Japanese would allow us the opportunity to build such a thing. They were only convinced when they found that the shorts in our packs were still wet and tasted salt. They were further convinced when Trevor found his military identity card with his photograph and I produced my pass to enter Kai Tak aerodrome.

They took from us for 'safe custody' our knives, our watches and as much money as we produced, explaining that if others found it they would be much safer in their keeping than ours. The shifty looking man who appeared to be the leader suggested that Trevor should 'give' him his spectacles and his fountain pen. We could hardly refuse. As soon as they finished examining our belongings and were satisfied as to our bonafides they agreed to give us a guide to take us to the nearest Chinese forces which they said were at Kong Nam. We were very surprised to hear this [as this village was thought to be in Japanese hands]. Then they gave us a really good meal of roast goose, fresh peas in the pod, whitebait, soup and some other vegetables.

This testing but ultimately fortunate encounter with guerrillas then led to the party being guided north over the border into China. They continued to travel at night as they were still in Japanese-controlled territory.

At 01.00 hrs Feb 6th we were woken up and started on our journey through the Japanese patrol area to Pokut [following the railway line]. Our guide Yap Fong-kiu led us northwards at a tremendous pace. We crossed the border stream about 2 miles east of the narrow gap at the northern end of Messines Ridge. Once we were challenged by Chinese road guards but our guide gave a satisfactory answer. We crossed the Sham Chun–Wong Kong [Shenzhen–Henggang] road which was in good repair, appeared to be in use by motors and had a telephone alongside. At about 03.30 we arrived at a small farmhouse near Pokut. There we were given excellent food, a bath, put in a back room and kept the whole day. They washed some of our clothes for us. Throughout the day we had a stream of visitors most of whom could speak no English; they just sat and stared at us for hours, but those that did talk kept Trevor very busy.

At last they could travel by day and were able to witness streams of Chinese refugees fleeing from Hong Kong along the Kowloon–Canton railway line, which had been torn up. They presented themselves to Chinese government military posts along the way, invariably receiving a warm welcome as Allies and escaped POWs, dining at sumptuous banquets and gaining assistance with their onward journey.

We left Pokut at 03.00 hrs on the morning of 7th Feb. We crossed the railway just north of the village. The track had been torn up, the rails were at the side, but the sleepers had disappeared and the embankment appeared to be used as a road. This night our guide did not carry arms as he had done the previous night, as he said he had no authority from the Chinese government to do so, and that we were now going into territory administered by it. After crossing the railway our guide considered that we were out of danger, but we were given an unpleasant fright by a party of about 30 coolies carrying goods from Hong Kong who came upon us from behind as we were sitting resting by the side of the road. Until we identified them there was a moment of extreme alarm. At daybreak we came to a small village where there were a large number of refugees from Hong Kong. We pushed on, were given a meal at the next village by a Chinese who was a friend of our guide, and were then taken to Kong Nam Market where we met an officer of the Chinese civil government and a junior officer in the uniform of the Chinese army. We were again given a great welcome, taken to the principal restaurant, given snake wine to drink, a bath, a shave and a haircut.

They plodded on up the railway line, and the weather turned colder. At Tong Ta Hao [Tangxiazhen] they learned terrifying news that stopped them in their tracks:

About 3.00pm [on 8 February] news was received that a Japanese force retiring from Waichow had occupied Shek Ma Hau, a village about eight miles north of us. The Chinese garrison commander was uncertain of their intended line of withdrawal. The Japs could either go due west to Shek Lung or else south down the railway. As a precautionary measure he and most of the inhabitants decided to evacuate the town. First, we returned to the restaurant where we had another enormous meal 'in case we shouldn't get another'. Then, together with the troops, we went to a German Mission house about two miles west of the town. We arrived about the time of evening prayer and were amazed to be near a Chinese choir singing a hymn to the tune of 'God Save the King'. During the night a report was received that the enemy were almost on us. For some minutes there were scenes of considerable confusion. Fortunately it proved to be a false alarm.

After getting the all-clear, the march to Huizhou continued with a miserable couple of days walking in the rain, being forced on long detours where bridges had been destroyed. They eventually arrived in Huizhou (then Waichow) at dusk on 12 February 1942.

It took us two days to get to Waichow. Both days were cold and wet. On the second day we marched about 25 miles. We had started rather late so as evening came, remembering how we had been welcomed in every other village, we trudged along the road wet and cold but buoyed up with the visions of the meal we would eat and the bed we would sleep in when we got to Waichow. However, we were sadly disappointed. The Japanese had only recently left Waichow after making a raid on it; there was little food, and four houses out of five had been burned or were merely heaps of rubble. The magistrate plainly considered us one more damned worry. We were sent off to the Italian Mission which was being run by a couple of Chinese Priests. The mission house had been badly knocked about by bombs. There we met some other escapees [Whitehead's party] who had left after us but had used a less circuitous route. We got a meal of a sort, and a single blanket for a bed. It was bitterly cold; the actual bedsteads were plain boards with no mattress; we slept two in a bed to try and keep each other warm, but we really only kept each other awake by our violent shivers.

The town had been occupied by the Japanese for three years before troops were withdrawn for the attack on Hong Kong. It was now controlled by the Nationalist government and it would be a source of help of all kinds for their onward journey. Huizhou was also the destination for Captain Hewitt's party and Gunner Whitehead's – they all knew that, whatever their ultimate destination, Huizhou was the hub that they had to reach first. In peacetime, its main role seems to have been as a centre for smuggling between Hong Kong and China.

After the surrender of Hong Kong, the Japanese returned to Huizhou in January 1942 to raid the supplies of grain held in godowns (warehouses) in the town, but were beset by Communist guerrillas and then repulsed by the Nationalist army. Furious at this defeat, they redoubled their efforts and destroyed much of the city in early February 1942, and raped, tortured or killed most inhabitants who hadn't evacuated, before being driven out again on 8 February. It is a wonder that the Allied refugees who wandered into town just four days after this attack could be given any support at all. Dad arrived just before Chinese New Year (on 15 February in 1942 – it varies with the lunar cycle), and was amazed to see that they celebrated and let off firecrackers in the usual way. Had my father arrived in Huizhou a week earlier, I might never have been born.

I find it hard to imagine a more challenging experience than negotiating treacherous terrain in the dark, in wartime when your 'allies' are as likely to murder you as your enemies, towards a destination that you don't know how to reach and where you have an uncertain welcome awaiting you. As a European you stick out like a sore thumb: tall, white and with light-coloured hair, resembling the white horse of England among Chinese ponies. Always assuming that your efforts are not stymied by accident or injury. At the time, Dad had no wife or children to consider and he obviously felt fit and well, but this was still an act of great bravery, as well as showing exemplary planning and practical skills. These are skills he passed on to us in due course – more gifts that I am grateful for.

4

China's War

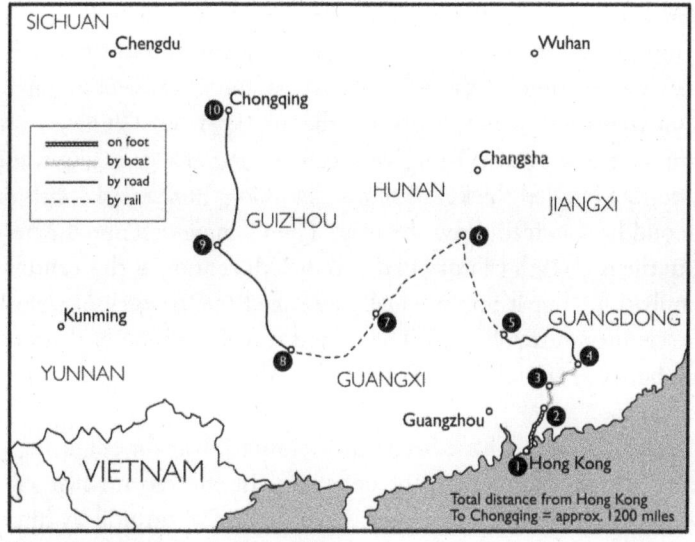

Major John Monro's Escape Route 1942
Town Name [present day] 1. Hong Kong 2. Waichow [Huizhou] 3. Ho Yuen [Heyuan] 4. Longchuan 5. Shaokwan [Shaoguan] 6. Hengyang 7. Kweilin [Guilin] 8. Hochee [Hechi] 9. Kweiyang [Guiyang] 10. Chungking [Chongqing]

Major John Monro's route across China, 1942.

My father's route was a crazy zigzag across the map. Why on earth did he go the way he did? Some of it was explained by the terrain – mountain ranges uncrossed by road or rail links, or river valleys where he took a boat. Intelligence reports from the Chinese army about the location of Japanese troops also played their part. I now realise that at this time the Japanese were trying to connect their occupied areas in Guangdong with Vietnam, to secure supply lines. The whole province of Guangdong, and neighbouring Guangxi, were liable to attack. But my O level in Modern British and European History was no help in understanding what was happening in China in 1942 when I first puzzled over the escape route. I didn't even know that Chongqing was the capital of China during the war and home to Allied Command, and so an obvious destination for a British Army officer.

I started reading about China's modern history and slowly got to grips with what was going on and why during the Second World War. It is a far too complex subject for me to do justice to here, and in any case I am an osteopath and not an historian. However, a brief overview of some of the relevant events and characters might help to set the scene. If you happen to be an expert on Chinese history I am sure that you will forgive me, knowing that it is like wading through a tangled thicket of thorns, in a bog, in the dark, with only the odd lit match to show the way. The Chinese describe the period from the mid-19th century to the mid-20th century as the 'century of humiliation', but it might equally be called the 'century of chaos' or the 'century of revolution'. The period was also a time of sharp contrast between complacent, traditionalist China and energetic, innovative Japan.

China and Japan have been at, or close to, war for centuries, and many would say they're not done yet. In the second half of the 19th century, China was kept in a rolling boil of turmoil by internal uprisings and rebellions, disintegrating state control and international clashes. (This state of affairs is a much-repeated theme in Chinese history from the earliest recorded times. The 'Romance of the Three Kingdoms' fable, set in the turbulent years of the end of the Han dynasty and the start of the Jin dynasty, AD 169–280, famously begins: 'The empire, long united, must divide; long divided, must unite' and ends a thousand pages later with the reverse: 'The empire long divided, must unite; long united, must divide'.) China had maintained its policy of remaining closed to outside influence while Japan had shrewdly judged, in the 1860s, that opening up was the way to economic success. By the end of the 19th century, China was far behind its neighbour economically, politically and militarily.

The first Sino-Japanese War, in 1894, was a conflict over control of Korea, fought by the Japanese with a modern army and navy, against a Chinese force armed with a well-established superiority complex and some sneers of contempt. Almost the only Chinese ship that wasn't sunk was the Marble Boat, a lakeside pavilion in the shape of a pleasure barge in the grounds of the Summer Palace, restored at vast expense in 1893 by the Dowager Empress Cixi. In 1895 China was forced to sign the Treaty of Shimonoseki, recognising the independence of Korea, agreeing to pay huge war fines to Japan, ceding Taiwan and parts of Manchuria and allowing Japan access to China's major ports, including Chongqing, far inland on the Yangzi River.

A brief resurgence of the Qing court followed, with the first years of the 20th century seeing radical change in every aspect of Chinese life and rapid development of infrastructure, much of it paid for with international loans and investment. The death of the formidable Empress Dowager Cixi in 1908 ultimately led to the fall of the Qing dynasty and the founding of the Republic by revolutionary leader Sun Yat-sen in early 1912. The First World War years were marked by political chaos in China, with frequent changes of leadership that allowed Japan to win a sly victory. By 1914 Japan and other foreign investors had US$1.6 billion[1] invested in China and they wanted to protect their assets. Japan signed a secret treaty with the Allied powers in 1917 giving them Germany's rights in China (in the event of Allied victory) in return for naval support. At the Versailles Peace Conference in 1919 the Japanese also announced that they had agreed with China's premier, in 1918, huge concessions in Shandong province on China's north-eastern seaboard. China had contributed 100,000 men to the Allied war effort and had expected a reward at the Versailles conference, but the Allied heads of state confirmed the legality of Japan's covert and coercive deals and China was forced to concede. Apart from the details of the Versailles treaty, this turn of events was

---

1. C.F. Remer, *Foreign Investments in China* (Macmillan, 1933), quoted in *The Search for Modern China*, 3rd Ed. J.D. Spence, (London: Norton, 2013), 268

symbolic of Japan's emergence as the dominant power in East Asia in the eyes of the international community.

A student protest against the terms of the Versailles treaty, in Beijing on 4 May 1919, was part of a wider uprising against the Chinese government's international and domestic policies. The date became shorthand for a revolutionary movement that was anti-imperialist and anti-feudalist, and it is commonly regarded as a pivotal moment in the development of modern China. May the Fourth also serves as a key date in relations between China and Japan, which Japan remembered when they devastatingly bombed the wartime capital, Chongqing, on 3 and 4 May 1939, reiterating the humiliation of China's government from 4 May 1919.

Throughout the 1930s the Nationalist government was engaged in niggling disputes or uneasy coalitions with the Chinese Communist Party (led by Mao Zedong), and this took their collective eye off the threat from foreign invaders. If the government focused its attention on the Japanese, then the Communists would take advantage and try to spread their influence. If the government focused on keeping the Communists at bay, then the Japanese took advantage by pushing further into the interior. The Nationalists lacked the resources to fight on both fronts. Furthermore, despite pleas to Western powers, China remained without any international support to fend off the Japanese invasion. They received limp communiqués offering condolences on their predicament and heartfelt good wishes, but no support or resources. (In my experience, Whitehall has a knack for this kind of behaviour. When I was a management consultant I had to interview a senior Whitehall mandarin for a project I was working on, and he concluded by saying 'We will be pleased to offer you every possible assistance, short of actual help', accompanied by a generous smile and a warm handshake.)

Japan invaded Manchuria in 1931, when China remained less a united country than a random grouping of territorial warlords. Japan by now regarded itself as a major power, seeking a land grab to meet their needs for resources for further expansion. Through the 1930s Japan's economy grew around heavy industries, producing many of the supplies that would be needed in war. Politically, Japan was increasingly militaristic and aggressive and saw China's emerging unification as a provocation. Chiang Kai-shek, who had been the Nationalist leader of the Republic since 1928, knew that his military forces were extremely weak and unprepared compared to those of the Japanese, but he was driven by the urge to protect China's sovereignty at any cost. Japan's skirmishes in central China began to take on a more serious tone, and in July 1937 a battle near Beijing, known as the Marco Polo Bridge Incident, tipped the two countries into war. At a meeting with his government in early August 1937, Chiang offered a stark choice: 'Do we fight or shall we be destroyed?' He hastily called a truce with the estranged Communist Party and legalised the Red Army, bringing apparent but gossamer-thin unity to China's armed forces so as to improve China's chances against the Japanese.

By October 1937 the Japanese had forged southwards and taken control as far as Shanghai, China's most important port, where Chiang had deployed his most able forces but suffered 250,000 casualties during the prolonged battle (more than 50 per cent of his best troops). The Japanese continued inland towards the capital, Nanjing (then known as Nanking). Nanjing had deep cultural resonance for the Chinese, having been a capital at various times since the Ming dynasty. The city had no strategic importance for the Japanese but its capture was a potent symbol of their dominance. The 'Rape of Nanking' in December 1937 and January 1938 followed the fall of the city. Perhaps it was motivated by the Japanese wanting to proclaim their absolute power over China's beautiful heart. The Japanese forces were in a fury about the delay in their anticipated victory over China and vented their anger on Nanjing's population. It was a crazed slaughter of over 200,000 civilians, a sickening rape (often followed by barbaric murder) of thousands of the city's women and girls, and a comprehensive destruction of property on a scale that was returned with interest to the Japanese with the atomic bombings in 1945. It is widely known in the West, but it is a small island of awareness in a vast sea of ignorance about Japan's wartime activities in China, a country that has justifiably been called the 'Forgotten Ally'.

My father was writing in 1942 when news reports would have provided some context to his adventure. However, even then, the media were focused on the major events of the war, with events in China only a sideshow. In the first half of 1942 it was Japan's advance across South East Asia that took priority – the shocking loss of Singapore, attacks in the Dutch East Indies and the horrifying assault on Burma. In the second half of the year Allied attention shifted to the North African and Russian theatres.

In the post-war years, China's role in the war was effectively removed from Western public consciousness altogether. Chiang Kai-shek was prescient when he said: 'When the KMT [Kuomintang, the Chinese Nationalist Party] exists, the nation exists, I shall exist; when the KMT vanishes, the nation vanishes, I shall vanish too.' The coincidence of three factors in the late 1940s and '50s led to a near total amnesia: the focus on the Cold War; China's disappearance behind a Communist 'bamboo curtain', effectively cutting it off from the rest of the world; and Mao's erasure of the Nationalist contribution. Recently I asked a Chinese student, who was helping me with my Mandarin, about Chiang Kai-shek. She said she had never heard of him. For many of the younger generation, Chinese history began in 1949.

It was late November 1937 when Dad first arrived in Hong Kong and so the atrocities at Nanjing would have been his introduction to the Japanese at war. The following few years in the lead-up to the attack on Hong Kong must have brought further alarm, as the Japanese continued their acquisition of China's key ports. Dad realised that Hong Kong was in their sights, and the weakness of the Chinese government's response to Japan's advances would have added to his unease. However, he, like most in the British army, thought the Japanese army inferior, despite their successes in China, and this led to a false sense of security.

The Nationalist (Kuomintang) government was forced to retreat, first to Wuhan and then, in October 1938, to Chongqing, and make its temporary capital there. Japan continued to make successful advances into southern China, meeting relatively little resistance from the Chinese army. China's ports and trade routes were of huge importance to Japan, and in October 1938 they took Guangzhou, China's major southern port. By this time, Japan controlled most of the economically vibrant and agriculturally richest areas of China, as well as its key ports. Humiliated by these significant defeats, Chiang's deputy and arch-rival, Wang Jingwei, entered negotiations with the Japanese to seek peace. The Japanese world view was that Japan and China could create a joint force against both Communism and Western Imperialism. Chiang utterly distrusted the Japanese, though, and in December 1938 he ended the peace process, declaring that it was a path to China's enslavement and Japan's dominance in Asia. By November 1939 the Japanese had also taken Nanning, completing their set of major Chinese ports.

China was forced to consider an unlikely alliance with the Soviet Union. Chiang Kai-shek was vehemently anti-communist, but he hoped that if the Soviet Union entered the war with Japan, he would have potent back-up. The USSR, however, unexpectedly signed a non-aggression pact with its ideological enemy Germany in August 1939, effectively making them allies of Japan. At the same moment, luck seemed to be on Chiang's side when a fierce battle over Mongolia between the Soviet Union and Japan in the summer of 1939, known as the Nomonhan Incident, ended with Japan's defeat. To Chiang's frustration, however, the battle led to a non-aggression pact between the two countries, eventually signed in 1941. Chiang's hopes were dashed. The final nail in the coffin of his hopes for a Sino-Soviet alliance came when the USSR invaded Finland in the winter of 1939/40, leading to calls by Britain and France for their expulsion from the League of Nations. Chiang refused to exercise China's right of veto on the motion, and Stalin bore a grudge towards Chiang ever after.

When war started in Europe in September 1939, China's predicament fell even further down the agenda of the Western powers. Japan continued to make inroads and in July 1940, when the Battle of Britain was in full flight, Japan asked Britain, who occupied Burma until 1948, to close the Burma Road. Constructed in 1938, the Burma Road connected the port at Rangoon (via a rail link to northern Burma and then by road) with Kunming in south-west China, and represented China's last international supply route. Churchill agreed; having just witnessed the fall of France and with invasion of Britain imminent, he reasoned that opening up a front with Japan was suicidal. The Nationalist government was now dealing with a civil war with the Chinese Communist Party, international war with Japan, no accessible trade routes into the country and, to make matters worse, agricultural harvests were poor in 1940 and 1941. On top of all that, between May 1938 and August 1941 Chongqing suffered 218 bombing raids, resulting in 11,885 deaths[2], mostly civilians. Chongqing was almost defenceless against this aerial bombing. In 1940 the Chinese only had 37 fighter planes left, while the Japanese had almost 1,000 planes in China, mostly 'Zero' long-range fighters.[3] The Americans eventually came to the rescue with a hundred P-40 Warhawk fighter planes, but much damage had already been done.

China's economic situation at the time was paradoxically described by a British analyst as 'hopeless but not serious'.[4] At a macro-economic level China was too big to fail, but at local level the story was very different. One of the BAAG agents in Guangdong province reported the horrifying realities of life (somewhat later, in June 1943):

> The death rate from starvation is steadily rising. Newspaper reports say that thousands are dying daily, but although this is an exaggeration, the truth is bad enough. From informant's own personal observations he knows that in Toishan district the number is at least one hundred on an average. In a short journey from Toishan to an outlying village, he saw eight unburied corpses. The worst feature is cannibalism. Human flesh sells at $5 a plate. Parents leave their children at certain recognised points, where they are seized and butchered by the human flesh vendors.[5]

In late 1941 there was increasing tension between the US and Japan over Japan's expansion ambitions in South East Asia. With the attack on Pearl Harbor in December 1941, China suddenly became of interest to the West and support was at last forthcoming, a small rent for using China as an Allied base. China was regarded as a weak and subordinate power, but given that the Chinese had successfully held back

---

2. Rana Mitter, *China's War With Japan 1937–1945: The Struggle for Survival* (London: Allen Lane, 2013), 4
3. J.D. Spence, *The Search for Modern China, 3rd Edition* (London: Norton, 2013), 417
4. quoted in Ride, BAAG: Hong Kong Resistance 1942–45, 113
5. Ride, *BAAG: Hong Kong Resistance 1942–45*, 113–114

the might of the Japanese military under extremely difficult circumstances and with precious little help, their resolve and bravery seem to me unquestionable. The Allied powers, though, saw China mainly as a useful pawn to divide the attention of the Japanese. Almost half of the Japanese army was kept busy in China right up until 1945, to the Allies' great benefit. They also had to admit that China's obstinate resistance against the Japanese was the only thing preventing Japan from creating a bloc consisting of Japan, China and Indo-China (now South East Asia), which would have been a serious threat to the Allies' interests in the Far East.

China had geography on its side, but there was a long-held distrust and dislike of the Chinese in the US and Britain, and China lacked the bargaining power of the USSR. In Christopher Frayling's book *The Yellow Peril: Dr Fu Manchu & The Rise of Chinaphobia* (London: Thames & Hudson, 2014), he analyses the influence of Arthur Sarsfield Ward, a former clerk of Irish-Birmingham stock who gained international fame as Sax Rohmer, creator of the bestselling Fu Manchu novels and propagator-in-chief of the yellow-peril myth. Between 1912 – publication date of the first Fu Manchu story – and 1959, Rohmer peddled fantasies about ruthless international Chinese conspiracies to his millions of readers. At the height of Rohmer's fame, Fu Manchu stories were to be found in public libraries, cinemas and the book collections of liners carrying westerners out to China, ensuring (in the words of one such young traveller of the 1920s) that they 'knew all about Chinamen; they were cruel, wicked people'. In fact, Rohmer/Ward never visited China.

Dislike of the Chinese goes back further in the USA. In the latter half of the 19th century, starting with the California gold rush, many Chinese left desperate conditions in feudal Qing-dynasty China in search of riches in America. They were encouraged to do so by American entrepreneurs, with flyers being widely distributed offering well-paid jobs and amazing opportunities. The reality better resembled slavery, mainly back-breaking work in the gold mines and on the railroads. Mostly men came, intending to send money back to their families and ultimately to return home. As they weren't planning to assimilate into American society they chose to keep to themselves and to maintain their culture intact. The result was the development of 'Chinatowns' in the big cities of the west, with 300,000 Chinese living in California by 1880.

The self-segregation, the strange language, the habit of the men to wear their hair in queues (hair is grown long and is often worn in a plait, while the forehead is shaved), the unusual foods they ate and their unfamiliar customs and religious practices were met with distrust and distaste. It wasn't difficult for the Chinese to be villainised and feared as the ultimate 'other'. The existence of the Triads and a seedy underworld of crime didn't help their public relations. American racism towards the Chinese was particularly vicious. White Anglo-Saxon essentially Calvinist Americans in the late 19th century embraced the theory of 'Social Darwinism' – a ghastly, pseudoscientific abomination that claimed that the superior race, the fittest, was the one with wealth and power. The Chinese, working amazingly hard for low wages, must, by definition, be inferior, if not subhuman. Their extreme foreignness and willingness to work for a pittance ultimately led to the passing of the Chinese Exclusion Act in 1882, preventing further immigration. It wasn't repealed until 1943, by which time China had been a supposedly equal partner in the Allies for over a year.

While it is true that China was a somewhat corrupt and disorganised mess in 1941, the attitude of the major Allied powers towards China was unjustly negative, tainted by fantasy and ignorance. The Chinese had every reason to distrust the Allied powers, especially Britain, after the opium wars of the 19th century, which led to China ceding the island of Hong Kong to Britain, and to the 'century of humiliation' (1839–1949), which marked the nadir of China's status as a world power after the previous twenty centuries of mostly glory. In the 17th and 18th centuries, the balance of trade had been entirely in China's favour – silk, tea and porcelain were exported to Europe in great volumes, while almost no European goods entered China. Britain sought to redress this balance by exporting opium from India in mind-blowing quantities, especially from 1820 onwards. At this time, Britain's access to China was limited to the port of Guangzhou. After a humiliating defeat of Chinese forces in 1842, the Treaty of

Nanking was signed, first of the 'unequal treaties', allowing Britain access to five major ports (including Shanghai) and ceding the island of Hong Kong. A supplementary treaty was signed the following year, giving Britain 'most favoured nation' status, which meant that any concessions negotiated by other countries had to be given to Britain too.

Over the next decade, Britain's imperial ambitions expanded, accompanied by the hubris of power. On a trivial pretext, Britain went to war with China in 1856. France was also expanding its empire and joined Britain against China, supposedly in response to the murder of a French missionary. Together they overthrew Guangzhou and installed a more agreeable governor and then advanced to Tianjin (then known as Tientsin). In 1858 the Treaties of Tientsin were signed, opening up more ports, allowing freedom of movement through the interior, giving access to missionaries, granting residence for diplomats in Beijing and legalising the importation of opium. In 1860, the culmination of the animosity between China and the British came with the burning of the Summer Palace in Beijing, after which the emperor fled and the entire Qing dynasty rule began its slow decay. This embarrassing defeat was ratified under the Convention of Peking, which confirmed the terms of the treaties of Tientsin. The unequal treaties the Chinese were compelled to sign were eventually repealed in January 1943 at the instigation of US President Roosevelt.

Dad has a talent for brevity and understatement, which sometimes serves to make his narrative more like a cryptic crossword puzzle than a story. He says nothing about how he knew which places were en route. Given the unpredictable movements of the Japanese advance, it was prudent to avoid explicitly stating their route and thereby risk jeopardising others' escape. His map only covers the first part of the journey as far as Huizhou, and he doesn't mention navigation beyond that. I believe that his faithful friend and interpreter, Mr Cheung, helped him to identify a safe route through the New Territories, but this only accounts for the first 30 miles of the journey.

I now know that Huizhou (previously Waichow), a city in Guangdong province, was the nearest point of contact with the British

Military Mission in Free China. Despite the uncertainty about the whereabouts of the Japanese and the attitude towards the British of Chinese guerrillas who might now be in charge, Dad and his party were dependent on support to continue their journey. They had to hope for a welcome in Huizhou. On their own they had no money, no food, no map, nowhere to stay and no intelligence on the movements of the enemy.

Major Douglas Clague of BAAG wrote of Huizhou, in a report to the Military Attaché in May 1943:

> Just inside the tropics, the climate is none too pleasant for nine months of the year and the water is famed for its detrimental effect on the skin. There is no electric light and water is normally drawn from river or pond. There is one known European bath in Waichow. Houses are not provided with fireplaces and charcoal chatteys [kilns] provide the only means of heating in winter, fear of poisoning and the headaches resulting from inhaling the charcoal fumes necessitate very restricted use. There is no recreation other than walking and once the rains have set in, as will be seen from the map, the whole area becomes one large lake, and movement from door to door is only possible by sampan.[6]

As well as being a boundary between Japanese and Chinese controlled territory, it was also a boundary between Communist China and Nationalist China. It must have had a rather tense atmosphere. Those terrified and abused locals that had not evacuated the town were probably wondering what hell was coming next and the moribund Allied refugees must have begun to question if they would ever find safe haven.

Beyond Huizhou their route was dictated by transport links and avoiding Japanese-occupied territory. It appears that there was a more or less established path for refugees travelling to Chongqing, by boat up the East River to Longchuan, then by road through the mountains to Shaoguan, where there was a British Military Mission. After that

---

6. From WO208-3498, MI9 reports 1943, held at The National Archives, London

there was a railroad to Guilin via Hengyang, both of which had Allied bases. From Guilin there were road, rail and air links to Chongqing. Tim Luard's book[7] describes a similar journey from Huizhou, with a much larger party who had escaped by boat from Hong Kong on Christmas Day 1941, with the famous one-legged Chinese admiral, Chan Chak. Luard describes the destination options facing escapers, as had been discussed with Chief Staff Officer Lance Newnham:

> They ruled out Canton (Guangzhou) as it was already occupied by the Japanese, and Macao since they thought it likely to be occupied soon (the nearby Portuguese colony was even less well defended than Hong Kong), Burma was too far away, with too many high mountains to cross. They finally agreed on Chungking (Chongqing). Although it too was remote – 1,200 miles away, across some of China's wildest countryside – they believed help would be available once they were in the interior.

As Allied refugees, the escapers were entitled to a small allowance from the Chinese government and freedom of movement, so, once they had succeeded in reaching Huizhou, they knew that they would be provided for. However, it must still have been a daunting prospect to consider the onward journey to Chongqing, 1,000 miles away, when the local population were as destitute as the refugees, food was scarce and transport was unreliable, dangerous and slow. The Japanese were continuing to push into southern China and had their eye on the capital. They were following precisely the same route as Dad, so at any moment there might have been an air raid or even a ground attack. Indeed, later in the war, several of the towns that Dad journeyed through were bombed and captured as the Japanese pushed successfully towards Chongqing. Had he delayed his escape it might have been a short-lived taste of freedom. Dad doesn't reflect on any of this in the letters home that he wrote when he eventually reached his destination. But they were letters to his parents, in wartime, so he

---

7. Tim Luard, *Escape from Hong Kong: Admiral Chan Chak's Christmas Day Dash, 1941* (Hong Kong: HKUP, 2012)

would not have wanted to cause alarm, or divulge secrets, or give any impression of fear or despair.

5

Road Closed and Open

Reading Dad's letters was like having a glimpse of another world with a few breadcrumbs for clues. When I first read them, I really didn't understand much of what he was saying. The names of people and places mostly meant nothing to me, and I found the army acronyms to be indecipherable. It felt like a dead end, a secret never to be told. In any case, China is still a challenge to travel through and it would be fiendishly expensive to go on a non-standard route. If only Dad had gone via the Great Wall, Xi'an and the panda sanctuary!

As the 70th anniversary of my father's escape approached, I reconsidered the possibility of going to China. I am an experienced and reasonably intrepid traveller, used to independent travel, but China seemed to be another order of magnitude, more difficult than anywhere else I had been. I trawled the internet for reputable tour operators who could provide guides and accommodation along Dad's escape route, but they all seemed determined to direct me to the well-known tourist attractions. I contacted my father's interpreter's daughter in Hong Kong and even she said, 'Why on earth do you want to go there? You'd be better off in Shanghai.' If any tour operators could help me, it was at inhibitingly vast cost.

It occurred to me that I should learn some Mandarin if I was planning to go off-piste in China. How would I navigate airports if all the signs were in characters and no one spoke English? What would I do if I got lost? How would I buy anything? How would I explain that I don't eat dog/chicken's feet/fish eyeballs?

Zhongguo, 中国, is the Mandarin word for China and is translated as 'Middle Kingdom'. Often this is interpreted as meaning that China regards itself as the (superior) centre of the world, or alternatively it is simply translated as the Central State. This refers to periods in China's history when a central state has been bordered by hinterlands only weakly under central control or indeed run by rebel warlords. The word Zhongguo theoretically derives from ancient philosophy, implying a harmonious integration of opposites, a balance between competing and dynamic tendencies. Confucius said: 'If zhong he [*literally: middle way harmony*] is reached, heaven and earth will be in place and all things will grow.'[1] Confucius (or Kong Fuzi, 551–479 BC) has gone in and out of fashion over the centuries, but his texts are more or less written into China's DNA and his influence is one of the unifying features of Chinese culture.

Chinese philosophy emphasises an holistic world view – all things are interrelated and interdependent. Relationships, society and spirit are all aspects of an integrated whole that cannot be split. Indeed, it is paradox that allows transcendence of opposites to an integrated whole. We recognise this through the universally known yin and yang symbol, but the language is full of such opposing ideas coming together. The best-known example is 'wēi-jī' 危机, meaning crisis, made up of 'wei' – danger – and 'ji' – opportunity – inextricably linked concepts to the Chinese mind. Traditional Chinese wisdom has it that the closer we come to truth, the more we encounter paradox.[2]

The local university offered evening classes, and I began to learn the language. I have had little difficulty learning French and Italian, but Mandarin was a decidedly different kettle of fish. The difficulties are manifold. We share almost no words in common (cognates), so whereas in French and Italian you might successfully guess the meaning of, say, 'cité' or 'città', the Mandarin word for city has no connection to English whatsoever. To try to memorise words, you have to invent connections – for example, 'shǒu' 手 means hand(s), so I remembered 'show of hands'. Obviously, the Chinese have the same problem with vocabulary in reverse – they remember that the word for 'hello' in French is 'bonjour' by thinking 'bèn zhū' in Mandarin, which has a similar pronunciation but means 'stupid pig'.

---

1. M.J. Chen, 'Transcending Paradox: The Chinese "Middle Way" Perspective' *Asia Pacific Journal of Management*, 19, 2002. p179–199
2. Ibid.

Then of course there is the fact that Mandarin is a tonal language, so the same word can have many meanings depending on how you pronounce it. On top of that, there actually aren't very many words in Mandarin – each phoneme can mean a variety of things depending on the context and, most importantly, the character. 'Zhu', for example, has dozens of meanings, several for each of the four tones, so that you can only be absolutely certain of meaning if you see the written character.

To be literate in Mandarin you need to know about 4,000 characters, which can be used in a variety of combinations to make about 60,000 words. One of my Chinese-speaking friends suggested I use an app called Pleco. As well as being a Chinese–English dictionary, it has an optical character reader. This means you can point your phone at a character or paragraph of text and it translates for you, giving you the Pinyin pronunciation and English meaning. This is a godsend in restaurants and might also prevent you from accidentally buying a T-shirt with 'Idiot Westerner' written on it in characters. English words are chic in China in their own right. On my travels I saw a young woman walking down a city street wearing a white T-shirt with bold black lettering on it saying 'Acne'. I doubt that she knew what the word meant.

Mandarin may be the official language of China, but it is only one of many dialect-languages and strong regional accents that can make spoken communication hard even between Chinese speakers. Those learning Mandarin as a foreign language often encounter blank looks, even after years of hard study. Not exactly encouraging. There are small mercies, however. If you can count to ten and know the word for hundred, thousand and ten thousand, you can say any number in Mandarin. The complicated and tricky verb endings in European languages don't exist. The verb 'to be' is always 'be', not will, was, am, were, would, etc. Even past and future don't really exist; rather, an indicator word is used to identify when something is happening. There is room for confusion even here. The word 'hòu', 后, generally means behind, as in 'hòumian' (后面 behind) or 'hòumén' (后门 back gate) but the word 'hòunián', 后年, means the year after next. In order for the logical consistency of this contradiction to become apparent, you have to understand that the Chinese regard the past as visible, in our sight as it were. The future is not visible and so we must be facing the past (our eyes being at the front of our head) and reversing into the future. Therefore, two years hence is in fact behind us.

Learning Mandarin did start to give me an insight into Chinese culture. The language is thoroughly grounded in nature – many characters are inspired by natural phenomena (pictographs), while others convey concepts that define the meaning of the word in a rather poetic way (ideographs). For example, the character for the word 'xi', 西, which means west, was originally designed to represent a bird in the nest. While there is only so far you can go with pictorial representations of things, even characters that are phonetic are often rooted in layers of meaning. 'Wen', 文, means writing, but really it means any conglomeration of marks or symbols. It can mean veins in stone or wood, animal tracks, constellations (the patterns connecting stars), tattoos, the pattern on turtle shells and even, by extension, literature.[3] So, when a Chinese person sees this character, they are not necessarily just reading a word, or making a sound, they can also immerse themselves in centuries of Chinese thought.

For the first year or so we did not learn Mandarin for 'yes' or 'no', because the Chinese hardly ever say anything so direct. I found all this to be completely charming – and infuriating at the same time. Nonetheless, for a middle-aged westerner with a full-time job, learning Mandarin is not the easiest skill to acquire. The young university students I was learning with soon accelerated past me, and I found I still didn't understand the structure of the language, let alone have a functional vocabulary. Our teacher was Chinese and I think she didn't really understand my difficulties. Rote learning is common in China, and my determination to build a scaffold of understanding seemed to be mysterious to her. Having been educated in a system where criticism was always just the meat in a praise sandwich, I found it demoralising to only ever be corrected.

I don't think Dad learned much Mandarin, but he had enormous respect for Chinese culture, which he learned through living in Hong Kong and then China over a period of several years. By studying the

---

[3]. David Abram, *The Spell of the Sensuous* (New York: Vintage, 1996), 96

language and learning about the history of China, I was trying to substitute book learning for direct experience. By choosing to retrace my father's footsteps, with local Chinese guides, I would recreate a reduced and intensified version of his years of immersion in China. Slowly my understanding of my father was developing, like getting a bird's-eye view over territory where I had only walked a small section previously.

Having transcribed all of Dad's documents and collated them into a single narrative, I wondered if I should contact the Imperial War Museum (IWM) to see if they wanted a copy of my father's story. I was blessed to reach Rod Suddaby, curator of the museum at that time and one of the most astonishing people I have ever met. He was kind enough to show great interest in Dad's story and remarked:

> As the Brigade Major RA, his analyses, both during the battle and following the surrender, as well as after his meeting with General Kitajima, of the performance of the artillery units during the defence of Hong Kong make very interesting reading. Similarly, his description of the planning and execution of his escape with two fellow officers gives a graphic account of the hazards and frustrations that they experienced during the two months which it took the party to get to Chungking.

I visited Mr Suddaby at the IWM with all the original letters, reports, travel passes and so on. The IWM library is particularly interested in personal accounts as they are generally much more revealing than the sawdust-dry military accounts of events. He told me that their research department had never been busier, with family members booking appointments to access the IWM library. As we sat chatting in his office, I wondered out loud if they might also have documents pertaining to my maternal grandfather, Brigadier Howard Greene. 'I spoke to him once,' said Mr Suddaby, and immediately rose to go to his files. Within a minute he returned, holding a letter from my grandfather, dated 1978! It is a pity that archivists are not recognised in the same way that great artists are – Mr Suddaby was a Michelangelo in his world. He helpfully put me in touch with Tim Luard, whose father-in-law had escaped after the battle of Hong Kong, and who had done a similar 're-enactment' of the escape to the one I was considering. Hope rekindled. I was very sad to learn later that Mr Suddaby died in 2013, barely into his retirement.

Mr Luard generously shared the details of his trip with me, but he had been the BBC's correspondent in Beijing for many years and so had already known his way around. He sensibly advised against any kind of official trip, organised with the assistance of the Chinese authorities, where I would get bogged down by bureaucracy and would probably have to attend official banquets and make speeches. He was encouraging about the value of my journey and wished me luck. At this point my mother stepped in and offered to pay for my trip to China. She was very interested in all my findings and was keen for me to retrace Dad's journey. She was in her mid-eighties by then and not up to joining me, but I knew she would enjoy seeing photographs and a written account.

After much email discussion with various tour operators I eventually found an interesting itinerary with a Chinese company called My Odyssey Tours (MOT) that allowed me to retrace Dad's steps and do some sightseeing along the way. MOT were very thorough and clear with their instructions. They were able to help me to get a visa and supported the entire process – I found their whole approach very reassuring. I was cautious about using a tour operator based in China whom I had found online. As it turned out, MOT were faultless from start to finish. Finally, I was all set to make my trip in the spring of 2013. I would spend a few days in Hong Kong and then take the train through the New Territories into China. At last the obstacles were falling away and the road ahead seemed clear. I felt as prepared as I could be and excited at the prospect of learning more about my father and about China.

Paradoxically, I was also becoming anxious. My visit to China was never intended to be a 'holiday', and I suspected that it might uncomfortably stir the sediment of my grief. I realised that I had not grieved properly after Dad's death, when I had been whisked away to Kenya to visit my brother and then went straight to France to start a gap year job. It doesn't matter how much time passes after a traumatic event such as an untimely death. Memory is processed in two parts of the brain – the amygdala processes the emotional aspects of memory, and the hippocampus files it in time and place. Under stress, the amygdala's role magnifies and the hippocampus's role diminishes. You are thus left with the unpleasant emotions, floating free of time, able to spring out at you when triggered, as fresh as the day the trauma happened.

It also occurred to me that the trip might be a failure. Seventy years is a long time and China's development since the war has been phenomenal. Would there really be anything that could connect the present with the past? Was I deluded in thinking that I could share experiences with my deceased father? How would the landscape that I saw mysteriously transmute into a deeper understanding of this man who had died more or less a blank sheet to me?

Landscape can have personal meaning for us – rolling green hills always make me think of home and the Shropshire Hills, for example. But this is only one aspect of our interpretation of landscape. At a deep, evolutionary level we read landscape in terms of navigability or threat or cultivability. In China, landscape is reinterpreted formally in their garden designs and artworks, with deep symbolic meanings for features ranging from rockeries to pools. Dad remarks that he always thought Chinese depictions of hills in their paintings were fanciful until he saw the karst landscape at Guilin. As he journeyed through this *terra incognita* it must have been a delight to have a sudden chime of recognition, as artistic vision translated into solid reality. The unchanged nature of rural China would help me to see the world through his eyes, and perhaps my emotional responses to landscape would be similar to his. I definitely have his mountain-loving gene, his delight in wild flora and fauna and his curiosity about the history and culture behind the built environment.

6

Crossing the Threshold

I wanted to arrange a tour of the battle sites in Hong Kong, but Tony Banham (a Hong Kong-based communications expert and military history writer) happened to be away, so he kindly put me in touch with Martin Heyes of Walk Hong Kong. I was to meet him on the morning after my arrival. I was feeling quite daunted about this trip. I was very uncertain about my connections in China and nervous about being on my own in such a foreign land. I hoped that Hong Kong would provide a bridge, with plenty of English speakers and a familiar environment. I'd also arranged to meet Dad's interpreter's daughter and an old friend from Shropshire who has lived in Hong Kong for years.

About half of my luggage consisted of technology – a laptop, still camera, Dictaphone, video camera, a mobile phone for local calls and a smartphone with Pleco (the Chinese dictionary app), leads, chargers, adaptors... everything I could think of. Dad had had a prismatic compass and a watch. I have a photo of him taken in the Himalayas in 1946, wearing a woolly sweater and scarf, attempting an unclimbed 6,000m peak. No wonder he never thought much of my achievements! I have unconsciously tried to make my father proud all my life, as so many children do. If I'd realised that to impress him I'd have to scale Everest or win the Grand National, I might have let myself off the hook and decided that impressing him was an unachievable dream, focusing instead on developing my own ambitions. I still regret, though, that he didn't live long enough to see how his influence shaped me as I matured.

Hong Kong airport is vast but somehow manages to have a peaceful atmosphere and is incredibly efficient. Everyone I encountered was gentle and welcoming. I'd arranged a shuttlebus with my hotel in Causeway Bay, and this turned out to be an introductory tour of Hong Kong. The sun was setting as we crossed Lantau Island, the sea pearly blue with a blush-pink sky, the hills snuggled up for the night in their fleecy vegetation. Then past the container port – a vast steely patchwork of containers and cranes, before coming into the centre of Kowloon, with its concrete forest of twinkling skyscrapers. Through the tunnel to Hong Kong Island, along the waterfront and then up the Peak a little way to get a better view.

The hotel alarmed me by taking my case off me at the door in exchange for a scrap of paper with a number on it. It took ages to deliver to my room and I rang reception in a flap. Two minutes and two apologetic phone calls later, my case appeared. Everything went smoothly and I quickly got the computer up and running and found to my delight that the plugs were the same as at home, so my plethora of gadgets could be charged without any of the adaptors that I'd brought. I couldn't have had a softer landing.

Wherever I go, I always like to find my way around and learn how to use the local public transport. Hong Kong has an underground train network called the MTR, so I got myself a prepaid pass and set off to meet Martin Heyes. We began our tour at the site of the Battle Box, home of Command Headquarters, where Dad had spent much of his time during the battle. The Battle Box was demolished after the war and the site is now occupied by the British Consulate, but it was helpful to be able to orientate myself. We also swung by Flagstaff House, which had been home to the Commander of British forces in Hong Kong since the mid-19th century, until the Japanese occupied it after the battle in 1941. It was slightly surreal seeing this Classical Greek-style building, with its Doric columns, in the midst of all the modern concrete and glass.

We continued up the hill to Wong Nai Chung Gap, the site of the decisive battle between Allied troops and the Japanese. Tony Banham succinctly describes the last days of battle:[1]

From December 13th [1941], all that lay between the

---

1. A. Banham A., http://www.hongkongwardiary.com/book1thebattle.html.

Japanese and Hong Kong Island was a narrow stretch of water. Armed with good intelligence, they took the opportunity to destroy much of the Island's military infrastructure with shells and bombs. It became a war of counter-battery fire as the batteries on the Island fired back – though many were destroyed in the process.

With all forces back on the Island, there was a reorganization. Two new brigades were formed, East Brigade under Col Wallis and West Brigade under Col Lawson; the dividing line ran due south from the east side of Causeway Bay.

The scale of the shelling and bombing has long been underestimated. The whole north shore of the Island – from The Peak down to the waterfront – came under intense fire. Military areas were hit – Mount Davis Fort, Belchers, Pinewoods; troop concentrations; the pillboxes; institutions were hit – Central Police Station (two killed), Bowen Road Hospital (over 100 hits), the Royal Naval Hospital in Wanchai (over 100 hits), the Bank; and residential areas – rich and poor – were struck with great loss of life.

It must have been deafening, bone-shuddering, with an ever increasing sense of impending doom. In the cold light of day, more than seventy years later, it is absolutely clear that the battle was now over and the Japanese had won. The British were determined to continue against the hopeless odds, however, and many more armed forces and civilians were to die before the inevitable surrender was declared.

By December 18th, the Island was a mess. General Maltby had lost a further 54 dead, many of the pillboxes were useless, and the infrastructure was so badly damaged that it was almost impossible for vehicles to proceed down some of the northern streets such as King's Road. Well before midnight on December 18th the 5/7th Rajputs ceased to exist as a fighting unit. Killed, wounded, captured, or simply isolated, they had been torn apart as the Japanese assault troops charged through them and made for higher ground. By dawn their assault had paused in the west thanks to the refusal of the HKVDC [Hong Kong Volunteer Defence Corps] Hugheseliers [a sort of Dad's Army group of veterans] to let them pass, but their penetration to the south had reached Wong Nai Chung Gap.

The whole of December 19th was dominated by the fighting for Wong Nai Chung Gap. Initially defended simply by Lawson's West Brigade HQ, 3 Company HKVDC, elements of 5AA regiment, elements of the HKSRA, and the HQ of D Company Winnipeg Grenadiers, the battle sucked in A Company Winnipeg Grenadiers, the entire 2nd Battalion Royal Scots, Royal Engineers, and many odds and sods. The Japanese were soon effectively in control, but the day resulted in 451 fatalities amongst the defenders, the majority in this little valley.

On December 20th A Company Punjabis was told to relieve the Repulse Bay Hotel which had come under attack that morning. At the same time East Brigade struck West along the same road. The Punjabis got no further than Shouson Hill, whose commanding peak was already held by the Japanese. East Brigade penetrated as far as the hotel and castle Eucliffe (just to the hotel's south west) before coming to a halt thanks to Japanese forces on Middle Spur and Violet Hill.

On December 21st East Brigade made an individual attack on the Japanese holding Wong Nai Chung Gap. The plan was to drive north to Ty Tam Gap, then head due west via Gauge Basin to the area that now houses Park View. However, this attack was halted by strong Japanese resistance in the Red Hill area.

From then on, the fate of Hong Kong was sealed, and Britain formally surrendered on 25 December 1941. Martin walked me round a 'discovery trail' that brought alive the battle – the tactical errors, the stories of survivors, the history of the Japanese in China and the roles of the various regiments and battalions. I could see that although the Allies had the advantage of familiarity with the battleground, this wasn't much of an advantage in jungly, hilly country with poor lines of sight and plenty of places for the enemy to hide. How terrifying it must have been, especially when the means of communication were destroyed, leaving units isolated and unaware of developments.

While we were surveying the scene over the cricket ground and Happy Valley racecourse, two black kites, smaller cousins to our European red kites, flew overhead. I had the strangest feeling that somehow it was a wave from Dad. Seeing these birds made me feel at home and that Dad was with me on my journey.

None of us knows what happens to us when we die, and this is, perhaps, one of the consolations of grief – we can believe whatever we like. I have had a number of experiences over the years that lead me to believe that we retain some sort of presence after death. This seems to fluctuate such that when you are doing something that resonates strongly with the deceased, they in turn manifest more strongly. This trip to China was all about Dad, and so far it was as easy as wallowing in a warm bath. On a subsequent visit with a more tenuous connection to Dad's time in China, I didn't feel him with me in the same way, and the trip was more difficult.

My reaction to the kites was visceral and immediate and it made me pay attention to the nature of my experiences during the rest of my trip. I realise that my sense of being accompanied may have been a construct of my mind to stave off fears about this challenging journey, but this first sighting was not consciously anticipated or sought. In my career as an osteopath I have had to learn to trust my hands and my intuition with the same confidence that I trust my eyes and my ears. At first you naturally cross-check with more tangible evidence – if I can feel the impression of an impact injury, I quiz the patient about their history, for example – but gradually you accept the veracity of incoming information from all of your sensory apparatus. It's like going from black and white to colour.

While I was in Hong Kong I made a side trip to Lamma Island. My sister, Kathy, had lived there in around 1980 when she was teaching English as a Foreign Language, and I was curious to see what it was like. Her usual style was to choose to live in the most squalid conditions in a low-rent part of town, whether it was Edinburgh or Cairo. I remember her saying proudly that her house on Lamma Island had no electricity. She was always unconventional and took pleasure trying to shock with her attitudes and behaviour, but this was the zeitgeist of the 1970s, ploughing up the status quo and exploring novel ideas.

I assumed that Lamma would be a dump, but I could not have been more wrong. It was far and away the most lovely part of Hong Kong and where I would have chosen to live if I were working there. I walked across the traffic-free island from one village to the other, stopping briefly at a cocktail bar on the beach, and was accompanied by yet another kite. I found my oblivious, soaring companion a great comfort. Visiting Kathy's old haunt also stiffened my resolve. She was a properly intrepid traveller who would quite happily hitch-hike through a war zone with only a toothbrush and a spare pair of knickers in her backpack. I really had nothing to be fearful about on my fully guided, luxury-hotel itinerary.

I transferred from the hotel in Causeway Bay to the YMCA in Kowloon, next to the Peninsula Hotel but about a quarter of the price and handy for the places I wanted to visit. Dad had been marched past these same hotels on his way to Sham Shui Po camp – I don't suppose they have changed much. I then walked into the rather disreputable Chungking Mansions to buy some Chinese currency. It was described in my guidebook as a 'huge, ramshackle, high rise dump' with 'a peculiar odour of cooking fat, incense and sewage'. Regardless, it has the advantage of having about 20 bureaux de change next to each other, forcing competitive rates. Bizarrely, the entrance is on the main shopping street in Kowloon, Nathan Road, sandwiched between Chanel, Louis Vuitton and other such elegant global brands.

The next day I met up with my friend from Shropshire and we drove out of the frenetic city and into the hills. She lives in Stanley on the south side of the island, which is where many civilian refugees were taken for internment. It is a delightful spot nestled on a pretty bay and a world away from the exhausting pace of the city. We visited the military cemetery where almost 700 people are buried. While every single headstone tells a sad story, I didn't really connect until I found the grave of one of Dad's colleagues, George Neve, whom he mentions in his story of the battle to defend Hong Kong. Dad was surprisingly critical of the opportunistic action taken by Neve and his companions. They were all staff officers, responsible for communications and intelligence, and thus rather crucial to the management of the battle:

> Wednesday 24 December 1941: A few days ago Bird, Neve and Boxer went down to look at the position at Aberdeen. While they were there they took it into their heads to lead a local counter attack. Now all three are wounded in hospital. One of them might have done such a thing, but three staff officers together is folly. We went out to the Queen Mary Hospital to see the George Neve/Boxer crowd. George Neve was very cheerful, Boxer was sitting up and looked fit though they told me he had lost a lot of blood. Bird seemed quite chirpy.

Major George Neve, of the Royal West Kent Regiment, died on 23 January '42, having been wounded in battle on 20 December. I don't suppose the healthcare in the POW camp was up to treating wounds or fending off infection. On further investigation I found, to my horror, that some wounded men in Stanley hospital had been bayoneted to death by the Japanese. The injured and sick POWs were a burden, and disposing of them in this way may have been regarded by the Japanese as the simplest, most resource-effective way of dealing with them.

Captain Godfrey Bird was tortured in a POW camp and was awarded the George Medal for bravery. Charles Boxer fared better, but he was transferred to Argyle Street camp and in September 1943 he was arrested by the Kempeitai (Japanese Gestapo) when they discovered a radio receiver in the camp. He was sentenced to 15 years in jail and spent two years in solitary confinement. He was relatively well treated as he knew some of the Japanese officers (including General Kitajima, who had commanded the Japanese assault on Hong Kong), had spent much time in Japan and spoke the language fluently. He was a scholar of early European contact with Japan and had a valuable collection of books on the subject, written in Dutch, Spanish, Portuguese and English. On his release at the end of the war he discovered that his home in Hong Kong had been looted and all his books stolen. On a later official visit to Japan he found his entire library intact in Tokyo at the Imperial Library of Japan.[2] After the war, Boxer became Emeritus Professor of Portuguese at the University of London and died in 2000, aged 96.

Most of the graves at Stanley were for young men who'd died in the last two or three days of the battle. One couldn't help feeling that they died in vain. They may have had a better time of it than those who were imprisoned, however, many of whom did not survive. Many died in POW camps, many more died on the transport ships to Japan and yet more died under the slave labour regime if they did reach Japan. Subsequently known as 'Black Christmas', the surrender of Hong Kong cost the Allies around 11,000 captured as well as 2,287 killed/missing and 1,300 wounded during the battle. Japanese casualties in the fighting numbered 1,895 killed and around 6,000 wounded.[3]

I also met up with Jenny Cheung, daughter of my father's interpreter. It was wonderful to meet someone with such a long association with our family and who could show me another side of Hong Kong. Her father had only died a couple of years before and I was sorry to have missed the opportunity to meet him. Two of Mr Cheung's sons had visited us at the farm in the 1970s, but by the time of my visit to Hong Kong Robert Cheung had passed away and Joseph was working elsewhere. He has since moved to the UK and was kind enough to visit me for a long overdue catch-up. Jenny and I did a bit of shopping in Kowloon and then took the Star Ferry to Hong Kong Island. The Star Ferry is a national institution and is still the most commonly used means of getting from Kowloon to the island, despite the road tunnel that now connects the two. Our sunset ride had a timelessness to it, despite the modern cityscape.

The Chinese have very different cultural attitudes to us. I showed

---

2. From the private papers of General Gordon Grimsdale, held at the Imperial War Museum, London
3. According to Kennedy Hickman, http://militaryhistory.about.com/od/worldwarii/p/World-War-Ii-Battle-Of-Hong-Kong.htm, although it is difficult to find reliable and consistent information about casualties. This tallies with Gen Maltby's Despatch about the Battle of Hong Kong (published by the War Office as a supplement to the *London Gazette*, 29 January 1948, no. 38190).

Jenny a picture of my husband and myself dressed for Royal Ascot. 'Nice dress,' she said, 'how much did it cost?' She also assured me that the tie she had bought my husband for a present was the most expensive one in the shop. I find these sorts of conversations acutely embarrassing, and that mysterious connection between our emotions and our physiology instantly revealed itself pinkly on my cheeks. Later in the evening she took me to her favourite karaoke bar, on the 18th floor of an office block, where I was subjected to amateur singing of variable quality. We were listening to one singer when I innocently asked what language he was singing in. Jenny looked surprised and said 'English!' Abashed, I inadvertently carried on gnawing on the foot that I had put in my mouth: 'Oh, what is this song called? I don't think I know it.' More astonishment from Jenny: 'Danny Boy – haven't you heard of it?' Not sung like that I hadn't. I'm afraid I pleaded jetlag and fled home on the MTR.

Was this jetlag? Grief? Anxiety? A sort of bumpy, burning descent through the opaque atmosphere surrounding Planet Dad? I know that grief is a funny old process, often circular and repetitive, triggered by the oddest details and prone to ambush one at the least expected moments. I suppose I wished that I could have done this journey with Dad alongside me. Perhaps my grief was for the man I never gave myself the chance to know when I was a hormone-driven, unreasonable teenager.

7

Entering the Middle Kingdom

After Dad's party reached Waichow/Huizhou in February 1942, they were obliged to stay for a few days as it was Chinese New Year, when everything grinds to a halt. They met some other escapers from Hong Kong there, who were billeted at the same quarters, a hospital that had been commandeered as a refugee reception centre as well as providing medical services.

> We were given a chilly welcome by the magistrate and sent to St Joseph's Hospital where we met 3 BOR [British Other Ranks: Whitehead, Parrott and Jacobs of the 5th AA Regt], 2 Dutch Naval Officers [Hordyk and Idema] and a HKRNVR [Hong Kong Royal Naval Volunteer Reserve] Warrant Officer [Proulx].

Gunner Whitehead had been under Dad's command for a time before the war, when he was NCO instructor to the Chinese field gun unit. He seems to have been a rather resourceful but pugnacious Welshman. Dad refers to him as 'the famous gunner Whitehead', possibly in reference to an incident when Whitehead was reprimanded unfairly, responded with his fists, ended up brawling with his commanding officer and was court-martialled and demoted to gunner.[1] This made him a hero among the ranks, not least as the officer was also reprimanded for striking a soldier, and the whole episode was sparked by a failure to be ready for kit inspection when Whitehead had been away on other duties. After he and his party reached Huizhou, White-

---

1. J.S. Whitehead and G.B. Bennett, *Escape to Fight On: With 204 Military Mission in China* (London: Robert Hale, 1990), 52–55.

head was recruited to a secret commando unit (Military Mission 204), where for several months he helped train Chinese Nationalists in guerrilla warfare against the Japanese occupation.

Taff Whitehead, Danny Parrott and Mike Jacobs had slipped out of Sham Shui Po at midnight – half an hour after Dad – and waded through a sapping sea of thick, stinking mud to a track leading to the hills of the New Territories. They were surprised by a Japanese sentry, but made short work of him and took off into the night. Very quickly they realised that they were completely exhausted and decided to lie up in some brush near the road, still not far from camp. Two Japanese search parties came looking and almost trod on them in their lair, but they remained undiscovered.

They took a similar route to Dad through the New Territories but risked travelling by day when it was foggy. They were extremely fortunate to encounter friendly, English-speaking Chinese near Tai Po. Whitehead seems to have been well aware of the risk that three British soldiers posed to the Chinese who helped them, and was keen not to overstay their welcome. He had also troubled to learn some Cantonese and so was able to communicate with those whom they met. (Cantonese is the main language spoken in Guangdong province, then known as Canton, and Hong Kong. It has some similarities to Mandarin and uses the same set of written characters, but they are different languages. Mandarin and Cantonese can be compared to the level of difference between French and Italian, say, rather than between different dialects.) When Whitehead's party did meet some bandits, they had nothing worth stealing and were left alone. Whitehead grumbles that officers who escaped had been able to assemble supplies such as a compass, maps, food, money and so on, but he perhaps didn't realise that these items were as much a hindrance as a help, as they attracted the bandits like wasps to honey.

They encountered further friendly Chinese as they neared the border and were led to a Communist guerrilla camp. They were then escorted to the edge of Nationalist-controlled territory and walked on alone to reach Huizhou for Chinese New Year.

Captain Hewitt's party had much more trouble crossing the New Territories. They had hired a sampan to take them across the same stretch of water that Dad swam, but had been seen and shot at in the bright moonlight. They successfully evaded the Japanese but had less luck with the local inhabitants, partly due to carrying money and other valuables and partly due to their incautious decisions. They risked walking in daytime in fog, but when it suddenly cleared they were accosted by villagers, then they were swindled out of their money by conmen, attacked by bandits on Grassy Hill and attacked again on Cloudy Hill after choosing to pass between two villages rather than skirt them. Their luck changed when, after unwittingly revealing themselves by standing on the crest of a hill next to the Chinese border, they were rescued by a band of Communist guerrillas. I wonder what Dad thought when he and Hewitt's party met later – I imagine that he thought they were jolly lucky to survive to tell the tale!

Hewitt's journey on to Huizhou was no easier. This part of Guangdong province was partly occupied by the Japanese and partly under the control of the Communists, whose relationship with the Nationalist government was tense, to say the least. Hewitt quotes a Chinese Communist whom they met as saying:

> We fight the Japanese because they are capitalists and invade our nation, not because they are the enemies of the Kuomintang, who are our enemies also.[2]

The saving grace of these fleeing European capitalist soldiers to a Chinese Communist was that they had humiliated the Japanese by escaping. The Communist guerrillas that Hewitt met knew that neither they nor the Red Army were recognised by the Nationalists and that help was therefore unlikely to be forthcoming from their own government. Chiang's Nationalist government was technically in alliance with the Communist Party but there was profound mutual mistrust and suspicion. It took considerable charm on the part of the British Military Attaché (General Grimsdale) to persuade Chiang (in February 1942) to allow friendly relations with these 'Red guerrillas'. They occupied a sort of no man's land between Hong Kong and the

---

2. Anthony Hewitt, *Bridge With Three Men: Across China to the Western Heaven in 1942* (London: Jonathan Cape, 1986), 99

Nationalist-controlled area and were critical to the success of communications and transit across it. If any further escapes were to succeed and if any aid were to reach the POWs left behind, it would have to be with the help of these 'bandits'.

The Communists had been strong in that part of Guangdong since the days of Sun Yat-sen in the 1920s. Sun was the founder of the Republic of China, bringing imperial rule to an end in 1912. His philosophy was based on three principles – nationalism, democracy and social justice. He is still known as the 'Father of the Nation'. After his death in 1925 there was a power struggle between his young protégé, Chiang Kai-shek, and Sun's old revolutionary ally, Wang Jingwei. Chiang won, partly because he shrewdly married Sun's widow's sister, Soong Mei-ling, and so could reap popularity by being Sun's brother-in-law. Chiang's leadership led to the split between Communists and Nationalists and to civil war. In 1934, large numbers of Communist cadres were ordered to stay behind in Guangdong and spread 'the truth' rather than join the Long March, when the Red Army retreated westward after defeat by Chiang's Kuomintang.

Hewitt and his party really put the guerrillas at great risk, as the guerrillas would have been killed by the Japanese if they were found to be assisting Allied soldiers. They were being escorted through Japanese-occupied territory, where they were also likely to encounter more bandits, and, because of the poor relationship with the Nationalists, they also had to avoid Nationalist-controlled areas, making for a rather circuitous route. By contrast Dad was escorted by Nationalists, walked up the Kowloon–Canton railway line and arrived in Huizhou a week before Hewitt's party.

The escapers now had access to help and an allowance as refugees. Dad describes their sojourn in Huizhou and their onward journey up the East River, heading ultimately for Shaoguan, temporary capital of Guangdong province:

> We were allowed $6 per day for our food which, though it was quite inadequate, was really very generous of the Chinese, as they only gave their own people who were refugees $2 per day. We became very hungry and used to prowl the streets like hungry cats inspecting all the

little street corner food stalls trying to find something both cheap, meaty and filling.

We were there for 5 days as because of Chinese New Year we were unable to get a boat up the East River. Despite the fact the town was in ruins, the Chinese celebrated the New Year in the usual way. For three days innumerable crackers were burned; all the small children ran about with paper bombs which made a tremendous noise.

Finally we got a passage up the river. We travelled in two boats; the leader had a charcoal gas engine and looked like a long floating potting shed, I travelled in a large flat bottomed barge, covered with matting, about 55 feet long and ten feet beam. It looked just like a black water beetle, though inside it was beautifully clean, this was towed behind the leader.

There were about 30 people in the leader which was the smaller of the two boats, and which used to list in an alarming manner as its passengers moved about. In the larger there were about 70 people. As it was only about 60 feet long overall and quite large areas in the bow and stern were reserved for cooking and the crew you can imagine how crowded we were. It was only about 8 feet wide so that when we lay down for the night our legs overlapped. We were literally packed like sardines. Once you were settled for the night it was impossible to move without waking up your neighbours.

This journey up the river was quite the most maddening I have ever experienced. We started a day late because one of the passengers suddenly found that he still had some business to transact in Waichow. Having started we broke down within two hours, tied up at the side of the bank and stopped for repairs. Later in the evening we got going but again broke down shortly after dark. This time the clutch had burnt out and a valve spring had broken. This took 18 hours to mend. The third and fourth days were comparatively trouble free until we broke a valve spring. Thereafter we continued to break valve springs for the next two days until we arrived in Ho Yuen [now Heyuan].

Dad doesn't mention the other risks inherent in this voyage. Hewitt's party also took a boat up the East River but were ambushed by pirates with rifles, forced to pay protection money to an opium-smoking village chief and then attacked by an angry mob while trying to get a shave in a riverside village. They really seem to have had the most dreadful luck. Dad's party met up with Whitehead on the river and they travelled together as far as Heyuan. Dad's colleague Captain Trevor struck up a friendship with Whitehead and helped him with his Cantonese vocabulary.

At Heyuan, they abandoned the boat in favour of sampans, continuing their journey towards Longchuan.

> The sampans were far more fun than the motorboat. There is about a 3 knot current in the East River and going up stream they are slowly poled along. I suppose our sampan was about 35 feet long. We had on board about 20 people. Grandma steered, Grandpa, son and his pregnant wife did the poling. We used to start about 6.30am. They went on without a stop till about 10 when we tied up for the morning meal. At about 11 they started again and went without a break till about 6.00pm where we tied up for the night; during which time we covered about 20 miles. An astounding feat.
>
> After three days we got to Longchuan. From here we intended to take a lorry to Kukong or Shaokwan [now Shaoguan] as it is sometimes known. This is the war time capital of Kwang Tung [now Guangdong] province. Trucks are few and far between in China. Though the magistrate was helpful and sympathetic the official in charge of transport was a fat, self-important nitwit. We had to wait 5 days before we could get a truck. Instead of telling us straight out there was none available he was always saying 'you can go on one tomorrow'. We became fed up as 'tomorrow' after 'tomorrow' came and went.

> When we did get a bus it was a closed truck with two small windows on either side, one behind and one in front with a completely closed back. Inside it was almost 5 feet high. Into this enough luggage was put to cover completely the whole floor to a depth of two feet. Into the space above we crammed 34 people. Some I admit were children but even so it was incredibly crowded and once inside and settled quite impossible to move without deranging someone else. On the move when there was enough draught the ventilation was not too bad, but as soon as we stopped it became stifling and one suffered from a terrible feeling of claustrophobia. The drivers were very unwilling to unlock the rear doors, partly because it was a rather long process and partly because at every opportunity we would jump out to stretch our aching limbs and it took a very long time to put us back in again. To add to our comfort about 50% of the other passengers were constantly car sick.

Whitehead, Hewitt and the other escapers seem to have had a much more agreeable journey to Shaoguan, where they were then billeted in 'flower' boats. When at last he arrived at Shaoguan, Dad spent ten days writing up his reports about the battle, the conditions of the POWs and his escape.

> At Kukong [Shaoguan] we were met by Chinese officials and given a tremendous meal of welcome. Afterwards we were taken to a party of British people who at that time were working in that area. We were put up in houseboats. These are very clean and comfortable and also give you good food. They are the real 'houses of delight'. Strange as it may seem I have never slept in a brothel before, let alone for ten nights.

The 'flower' boats were brothels serving the river trade that travelled between Guangzhou and Shaoguan up the North River, a branch of the mighty Pearl River. From Shaoguan the trade route continued overland northwards to Nanjing and Beijing. A decommissioned flower boat was also the first headquarters of the British Army Aid Group (BAAG), the unit set up by Colonel Lindsay Ride to aid prisoners in Hong Kong. Ride had been sent back to Shaoguan after getting approval from his superior officers, and from Chiang Kai-shek himself, to work with both Nationalist forces and Communist guerrillas to support the prisoners in Hong Kong. Chiang was anxious about this arrangement but he was persuaded that BAAG had no political agenda and was purely humanitarian in nature. On this visit in March 1942, Ride met Dad, the other escapers and large numbers of Chinese refugees. Ride realised that help was needed by the civilian population as well as the internees. He quickly recruited some of the escapers to BAAG. They included Douglas Scriven from Hewitt's party and several members of the Special Operations Executive (Holmes, McEwen and Holroyd) who had evaded capture and left Hong Kong on Christmas Day 1941 with Admiral Chan Chak. Dad was intent on reaching Chongqing and did not reconnect with BAAG until August 1942.

Huizhou is now a city of 4.6 million people and a centre for the petrochemical, electronics and information technology industries. Heyuan and Longchuan are major transport hubs for road, rail and river traffic. Somehow I felt that a trip up the East River might not evoke my father's journey, with such huge changes in the character of the area, so I decided against travelling to Huizhou, which is about 60 miles from Hong Kong. The tour operator advised that getting a vehicle from Longchuan to Shaoguan would not be much less difficult than it was in 1942, so I thought I would head directly from Hong Kong to Shaoguan (about 180 miles), travelling by train via Guangzhou.

Everything in Hong Kong seems very orderly and precise. The Chinese all seem to be travelling to work at 8.30am, so when I took a taxi to Hung Hom station at 7.50, there was no one on the road. I went and waited in a coffee shop (little realising that it would be my last cup of coffee for a fortnight) overlooking the entrance to the international platforms, so as not to miss my moment for joining the queue. But there was no queue. At the appointed hour, the gate opened and people started wandering through to the platform for Guangzhou. The platform signs guide you to the correct spot for the door to your carriage and then you just look for your numbered seat. Modern public transport in China is super-efficient, from checking in, to on-board uniformed stewards bringing you free bottles of water and China SIM cards, to getting through customs and immigration. At least, that is the case on the more expensive high-speed trains. The older, slower trains in more far-flung places are a bit more reminiscent of 1970s' British Rail, as I discovered during my trip in 2015 when I travelled standard class from Kunming to Dali, a six-hour journey. There were crowded carriages (mercifully now smoke-free), hard seats, revolting toilets, mediocre food and lengthy, anxiety-provoking stops in the middle of nowhere for no apparent reason.

We proceeded through the New Territories at a stately pace, which was convenient for those of us wanting to study the topography. Of course, it is largely built up now, with utilitarian tower blocks everywhere (unexpectedly, after we crossed the border into China the tower blocks had more of a nod to the aesthetic, with different colours or decorative balconies or other such flourishes). However, the hills remain resistant to development. How Dad and his colleagues managed to make their way through these very steep-sided, scrub-covered hills at night without serious mishap is a mystery.

With Nancy as my Guangdong province guide, I had a quick tour of Guangzhou, the capital of Guangdong, with huge skyscrapers and wide boulevards to prove it. Modern Chinese architecture still seems heavily influenced by Stalinist ideals of utility and conformity, although showing off technical ingenuity and expressing China's renewed status as a world power are also factors. Aesthetic pleasure doesn't, on the other hand, seem to have much influence. That said, the vast new Changshui airport at Kunming (opened in 2012) is perhaps the exception that proves the rule. A glorious sweep of golden roof extends on either side of the main building so that, as you taxi in from the runway, it gives the impression of a traditional pagoda with a greatly extended bottom layer, opening its arms to you in welcome. Seven steel 'ribbons' run through the building, representing the cultural richness of Yunnan province.

Regardless of your response to modern architecture, China is not a great place to go if you don't like elevators. Most hotels are tall buildings with public spaces on the lower floors and bedrooms higher up. The Four Seasons Hotel in Guangzhou, for example, occupies the top third of a 103-storey building.

The high-speed-rail terminus at Guangzhou South is an enormous building at 168,000 square metres, the largest railway station in Asia. It is an impressive concrete, steel and glass structure with a single span canopy – there are no interior pillars to support the roof. We eventually found our platform for the train to Shaoguan. It took an hour or so to do the journey. We reached speeds of over 300kph, apparently slowed down since there was a massive crash of a train travelling at over 500kph some years ago.

Nancy turned out to be a fantastic guide. She had visited Europe but had not been to England, due to visa difficulties. Her English was outstanding and she was patient with my pathetic attempts at Mandarin. We had breakfast together at the hotel and she ordered for both of us. It was then that I realised that either she wasn't familiar with the European concept of breakfast or she wanted me to experience a real Chinese breakfast. We had congee – a watery rice porridge – with pickled vegetables and a side order of boiled spinach and whole baked sweet potatoes. There was also the special delicacy of thousand-year-old eggs, swimming in some gloopy liquid. The eggs aren't really a thousand years old, but they don't appear very appetising as preserved eggs go black. I do like eating local food wherever I go, honestly I do, but I could barely stomach that lot. To make matters worse, there was enough for six people. A charming custom of the Chinese is always to share food. In restaurants, this means that any dish on the menu is priced for a portion for the whole table and that is what you are served, even if you are dining alone. I picked at each of the dishes and then gave up. Nancy commented on my delicate appetite. She might have had a different opinion if there had been bacon and eggs or croissants on offer.

Apparently, Dad was more of a fan of congee. On a business trip in September 1943, after travelling though Guangdong province by truck and boat, he had to do an early morning walk to reach his final destination:

We started our walk at 7.45am. At the end of an hour and three quarters we stopped at the head of a low pass to drink some most welcome tea and to eat two bowls of congee. I was very hungry and rather hot; it was just the semi-liquid food I wanted.

Shaoguan welcomed me with the comforting, familiar presence of rain. Not heavy rain, just what the Irish call 'a nice soft day'. We went to the confluence of the Wu and Zhen rivers where Dad had stayed on his floating 'house of delight'. There was also a statue, the plinth of which declared, in English and Chinese, 'Shaoguan – the top tourist city of China'. Have you ever heard of Shaoguan before? Seen it on a travel itinerary for China? In my 1,000 pages of the Lonely Planet Guide to China, Shaoguan doesn't rate a mention. Perhaps it's an aspiration.

I was driven to nearby Nanhua (South Flower) Temple, one of the largest Buddhist temples in China, founded in AD 502 by an Indian Buddhist Master. He prophesied that 170 years later great Buddhist teachings would be expounded and that there would be as many enlightened ones as trees in a forest. The monastery was originally named Bao Lin – Treasure Forest. Over the centuries the monastery has been in and out of use, and is currently enjoying revival. When Dad passed by it was also in a period of restoration, after 250 years of disrepair. It is in the most beautiful setting, surrounded by forest and hills and with pools and fountains to create a tranquil mood. Tony Hewitt visited the temple on his way to Shaoguan:

> Inside the gates we passed through a paved courtyard, decorated with peach and orange trees which were in blossom in their huge stone tubs. The Lao Yeh (Venerable Father) gave us a blessing and took us to the main temple to show us the bodies of three embalmed and deified priests, many hundreds of years old, lying there for eternity, in perpetual peace. He showed us old, very old camphor trees, which he said had been dead for many years, dead during all the troubles in China, the revolutions, warlords and civil wars, but when the war with Japan had commenced the tree had

bloomed again. The legend was that when these trees came to life China would again become great and united again, and regain its splendour. In fact, China did become united only seven years later, as the People's Republic.[3]

Buddhism, Taoism and Confucianism are the three main religious philosophies in China, with a liberal sprinkling of Chinese folk religions adding an extra dimension. Mao Zedong's Communist government was officially atheist, and the Cultural Revolution of the 1960s–70s led to the desecration of many religious buildings and the death of many priests, monks and other religious leaders. Six thousand monasteries were destroyed in Tibet alone, and almost all of the documents and artworks were destroyed or removed from the Potala Palace in Lhasa. Since the 1980s there has been much restoration of both the buildings and religious freedom. It seems paradoxical that the camphor trees at Nanhua should spring to life as a mystical portent of unity in China, but perhaps not anticipating that there would be an atheist ideologue at the helm.

We were lucky enough to arrive during prayers, and the monks were chanting to drums and bells. In the temple buildings there are various relics associated with the prophesied Master Huineng (AD 638–713, sixth Patriarch of Chan Buddhism), including a statue of him. There are also highly decorated wooden carvings of 360 arhat figures – the Buddhist equivalent of saints or apostles. They are the only Chinese wooden carvings preserved from the Northern Song dynasty (AD 960–1127).

The ancient buildings and natural landscape helped me to feel a connection to Dad's experience of China. Even the weather was probably much the same. Where Hong Kong is almost completely unrecognisable today, much of China is untouched. It is such a vast country that even the development of megacities and high-speed transport links cannot change the essential character of the landscape. I imagine that Dad might have felt this as a sense of sanctuary when he reached Shaoguan in 1942. The journey through the New Territories must have been terrifying, as well as arduous, and then when

---

3. Anthony Hewitt, *Bridge With Three Men: Across China to the Western Heaven in 1942* (London: Jonathan Cape, 1986), 196–7

they reached Huizhou the city was in smoking ruins. The shifting territorial boundary with the Japanese must have made everyone feel unsafe in this part of so-called Free China – those areas of China not under control of the Japanese Imperial Army – with the visible scars of war on the landscape a constant reminder of danger. But at Shaoguan, implacable China reasserted herself, unbowed and determinedly free.

In the present day, the tranquillity of Shaoguan remains untouched, but it cannot escape air pollution. Wherever I went the views were marred by a veil of smog. When I questioned one of my guides about this, they told me that the poor visibility was due to sandstorms in the Gobi Desert. This was one of many indications that the Chinese media are carefully edited. The Western press usually explains China's smog with reference to the rapid increase in the building of coal-fired power stations. The further west you go, the better the air quality. Yunnan province in the south-west has blue skies and wonderful views. Lichen grows abundantly on the trees, a sure sign of clean air. By contrast, I wonder that visitors ever return to China if all they 'see' is Beijing and Shanghai. In December 2015, smog levels in Beijing hit 40 times the 'safe' level defined by the World Health Organization, and a three-day Red Alert was declared, restricting car use and closing schools and factories. It is thought that air pollution causes as many as 4,000 deaths per day in China, as reported in August 2015.[4]

As soon as I had crossed the border into China, I hit the Great (fire) Wall of China – the immediate cessation of contact with the outside world via the internet. No BBC, no Facebook, no blogs. There are ways of 'climbing over the wall', so I was surprised that my guides seemed to accept the version of events they had been told. No different to readers of the Murdoch press at home, perhaps. That said, the Chinese state is becoming more interested and adept at scuppering the so-called Virtual Private Networks (VPNs) that pole-vault the firewall. It is now the case that it is much easier to install the necessary software outside of China than in it – no problem for visitors but difficult for citizens. China has always been self-contained and has always regarded what is going on in China as far more important than

---

4. http://www.theguardian.com/world/2015/aug/14/air-pollution-in-china-is-killing-4000-people-every-day-a-new-study-finds.

what is going on beyond its borders. China has a long history of trade with the rest of the world but has never sought to build an international empire in the way that Britain, France, Spain and Portugal did. Arguably it didn't need to, being a vast country in its own right, but it may have more to do with national or ethnic character. Just as Britain has long regarded itself as separate and singular, and this perhaps made Brexit inevitable, so China feels both superior and complete in itself. There is an appetite for news from the outside world but it is not as urgent as one might expect.

8

Rosy Cloud Mountain

I stayed at a newly built international tourist hotel designed to cater for visitors to nearby Danxiashan (Rosy Cloud Mountain), which was made a World Heritage Site in 2010. It is the only World Heritage Site in Guangdong province and one of only 52 in China. So, a good idea to build a hotel for international tourists. While the hotel had many favourable aspects – spacious rooms, Western-style bathrooms, good location on the river, impressive interiors – having someone on the staff who spoke enough English to check you in and out would have been useful. I had a hilarious conversation with a receptionist when I got to my room and couldn't get the Wi-Fi to work. Her response to my inability to speak Mandarin was exactly the same as the stereotypical response of the Englishman abroad trying to communicate with a non-English speaker. In my very best Mandarin, I said: 'Hello, can you speak English? I have a problem with the internet.'

In her very best Mandarin, she said: 'No, I don't speak English, but – [long explanation in Mandarin].'

'I don't understand.'

'OK, [long explanation in LOUDER Mandarin].'

'Er... thanks. Bye.'

There were about 40 channels of Chinese reality TV shows but no English-language channels. They did provide a book containing the house rules in English, so I settled down to read them all (it was quite a long list) and enjoy this glimpse into Chinese cultural norms. Rule number 5 caught my attention:

> Lecherous acts, prostitution, drugs taking and trafficking,

smuggling, gambling, wrestling or any other outlawed activities are strictly forbidden.

Well, that put paid to any evening entertainment I might have had in mind! I had thought I might wander the streets looking for someone to bring back to my room for a wrestle. I had an enormous bed but it was like lying on floorboards. This is normal in China. Luckily (or perhaps due to the draconian house rules) I was alone, so I made a sausage roll of myself with duvet pastry, just soft enough to allow sleep. Things have improved since the 1940s though – Dad describes his Chinese hotel room, when he was travelling from Shaoguan to Huizhou on a later journey in September 1943. He never complains, focusing instead on whatever positives he can think of, in a rather Panglossian way:

> It was clean but the bed was the usual affair of boards covered with a mat, with a hollow brick for a pillow and draped by a mosquito net.

Danxiashan Geopark is a unique 290km^2 protected area with the most amazing mountain range of sandstone outcrops – the several-hundred-metre high remnant of a landscape formed 70–90 million years ago that has otherwise worn away. Where the terrain permits there is subtropical forest, now providing safe haven for 23 plants and 66 animals listed as endangered species, as well as a huge diversity of other flora and fauna.

We took a cable car to the top of one of the outcrops and drank in the spectacular view, before strolling along a contour to a lookout pavilion. The authorities have worked hard to provide weatherproof walkways, toilets and kiosks selling drinks along the way. Too sanitised for the intrepid hiker, too brutal for the environmentalist but great for the average punter. You could hike for days in the protected area, and it looks good for climbers too.

The route down was little short of a cliff, with steps that made the Peak Tramway in Hong Kong look like a gentle incline. On the way we spotted a tung oil tree (*Vernicia fordii*) in full bloom – Dad mentions seeing these beautiful trees on his way from Guiyang to

Chongqing, and one of the reasons I wanted to come to China in spring was to see them. They are quite large trees with pendulous white flowers with a pinkish-orange throat, which Dad describes as looking like a cross between a tree tulip and a frangipani. Perhaps in anticipation of his later career as a farmer, Dad noted with approval that tung trees were often being planted on uncultivable hillsides, creating a useful crop for the future and preventing soil erosion. Tung oil, made from the seeds, is still used to preserve and weatherproof wood.

At the bottom of the mountain is a lake, which we had to take a boat across. I was expecting a motorised ferry, but in fact I was delighted with a small boat (capacity: perhaps a dozen passengers), poled by a strong young man. My guide told me that this is the traditional style and may be similar to Dad's experience of being poled up the East River in a sampan from Huizhou. The poler stands at the rear facing forwards and has two long oars that cross in front of him. He gets into a rhythm of shifting back and forth on his feet (positioned as if taking a stride), and with a straight back, using his whole body, he could probably continue for hours, as Dad described.

It had been a very enriching day. As we were speeding back to Guangzhou on the train at 300kph, we passed farmers ploughing their fields with buffalo. It's like being in parallel universes. We all live in a dualistic world most of the time – self, other; mind, body; head, heart; us, them; but we forget that these opposites unite to create wholeness. In Chinese thought, xing (form) and shen (spirit) are united by qi (energy). At the moment it feels as though opposites are only creating conflict in the world – between Muslim and Christian, Sunni and Shia, Catholic and Protestant, Scottish and English, even.

In China this dualism is visible, palpable, ever present. We all know that there are major conflicts in China: with Tibet, Taiwan, the Japanese, the environment, to name but a few. The State is an all-powerful, deeply controlling, almost sinister force, yet, at a local level, people cheerfully ignore it. They can climb over the firewall, carry on their business as usual, disputes are sorted out without reference to state level whenever possible and, on a day-to-day basis, people appear to be free. Western movies are not shown in cinemas but are easily available and cheap to buy on black market DVDs, sometimes under a different name. I was shown some dinosaur fossils and exclaimed that we must be in 'Jurassic Park' to a blank look from my guide. A quick plot summary later, she said of course she'd seen the movie, just not with that title.

I was amazed to find that ordinary people had pictures of Chairman Mao as an object of worship in their home shrines, given that his government was responsible for some of the worst deprivations in Chinese history. The Great Leap Forward began in 1958 as Mao's Five Year Plan to modernise the Chinese economy, through developments in agriculture and industry. By the end of 1958 over 700 million people had been grouped into local communes, where individual ownership was not allowed and people were assigned to work in teams overseen by Communist Party Members. Workers were encouraged to set up local production plants, most famously including 600,000 back-yard furnaces making steel. Initially the plan was a great success, but poor harvests in 1959 and 1960, combined with catastrophically poor-quality steel produced in back yards, and machinery and buildings that fell to pieces as a consequence, led to disaster. About 20 million people are thought to have starved as a result of the Great Leap Forward. Even Mao admitted that he had made an error and resigned as Head of State, though not as Party Chairman.

The Cultural Revolution in the 1960s and '70s was a vanity project of Mao's to reassert his authority and establish his own cult status. He was ably assisted by Lin Biao, leader of the Red Army and an extremely strange man, with a phobia of water that meant he was unable to even look at pictures of rivers or the ocean and that gave him diarrhoea if he heard running water. Together they produced the 'Little Red Book', comprising ideological sayings of Chairman Mao, and shifted the focus of government from economic development to revolution towards a communist utopia. They recruited Red Guards to enforce the revolution, with powers above those of the military or police. The aim was to get rid of 'The Four Olds', namely old customs, culture, habits and ideas. In practice this meant closing universities and even secondary schools, desecrating religious sites and ancient artefacts, terrorising ethnic minorities and persecuting anyone with an education, artists, writers, musicians or anyone who did anything considered 'bourgeois' or 'reactionary'. The numbers who died, either from the diseases of poverty or from torture, have never been accurately established, but probably exceed one million. Few were untouched by the privations of the period. One of my guides, who had been a child during the Cultural Revolution, pointed out some flowers by the path, saying: 'I used to eat those when I was young.' I asked if they were a local delicacy, but he answered, 'No! Starvation was very popular in those days.' His charming sense of humour betrays the stoicism of the Chinese character and the truth of those times for the majority.

However, Mao also brought a disparate, warring country together and founded modern, industrial China. He brought basic education and healthcare to the rural masses. Monster and genius seems to be the conclusion. The Chinese say that he was 70 per cent right, 30 per cent wrong, as if this precise statistic were the outcome of some scientific analysis of Mao's life. Probably we should apply this analysis to our lives and thereby accept that nothing is perfect and that compromise is a fact of life.

China has an enviable record on improvements in health and education over the last 20 or 30 years, on top of its economic success. And yet it is one of the most unequal societies on Earth, with the rural poor falling further behind their urban fellows with every passing year. On the positive side, education in China does reward achievement with the opportunity to extricate oneself from deep poverty. The better you do in examinations the higher you can rise, either in a government job or as an entrepreneur.

The concept of a meritocracy goes back to the very earliest dynasties in Chinese history. The Zhou (1046–256 BC) first introduced civil service examinations based on Confucian texts, formalised as the Zhouli or 'Rites of Zhou'. This book formed a sort of constitution and is thought to have been written about 300 BC. Over the centuries the use of the imperial examination system rose and fell, depending on levels of nepotism and corruption and the willingness to root it out. The examinations were amended and added to as the needs of the burgeoning bureaucracy advanced. Perhaps the golden age of the examination system came in the Song dynasty (AD 960–1279) when emperor Song Shenzong (ruled AD 1067–85) appointed the Governor of Nanjing, Wang Anshi, to his court. Wang introduced an ambitious scheme of reorganisation, the impact of which rippled through the following two millennia. It wasn't until the Ming dynasty (AD 1368–1644), however, that a true meritocracy emerged.

Our word 'mandarin' is not actually of Chinese origin, but was borrowed from a Malay term meaning counsellor or minister, used by the Portuguese from the 16th century as they developed trade with China. A mandarin was a Chinese scholar-bureaucrat, wearing distinctive dress and speaking a distinctive court language – hence the transfer of the term to the language. By the late 16th century, up to 10 million men (about 20 per cent of the population) are thought to have been educated to basic examination level – remarkable, considering literacy levels in Europe at the time. The system retained a strong central focus and atmosphere of ritual. The highest level of achievement was the Jinshi rank, achieved by 0.01 per cent of the population. The Jinshi examination lasted three days and nights and was a great occasion, attracting crowds of supporters and onlookers, and Jinshi graduates were the celebrities of their day. The examinations themselves were rigid and formulaic, and cheating was rampant. The exams were a better measure of accurate memory than of any ability to govern, and allowed no room for innovation in thought or writing style. The system was abolished in 1905, but its legacy lives on.

A typical story of the speed and scale of change achievable through education was told to me by one of my guides, who was aged about 30. She had been born to parents who had government jobs as teachers. They already had two girls and it was illegal for them to have a third child, but they were determined to have a boy. If they kept the third child they would have lost their jobs or had to pay a very large fine. When a third little girl was born, they handed her over to childless relatives who lived in a remote village in the mountains, and kept their jobs. The little girl was cared for by her adoptive parents, but they were extremely poor, with an income of less than US$150/year. To get to school she had to walk an hour before reaching a road, where she could then catch a bus. The family were too poor for proper shoes or umbrellas so, in the rainy season, she struggled through the cold and the mud in homemade shoes and wearing a plastic bag for a hat. She worked hard at school and her adoptive parents gave up all they had to pay for her school expenses. Eventually she won scholarships to university, majored in English and is now a successful tour guide. From rural peasant to urban sophisticate in 30 years. (Meanwhile, her birth parents tried again for a boy and this time they succeeded, paid the fine and kept him.)

The constant sense of feeling held between opposing poles is magnetic in every sense of the word. No wonder Dad found the Chinese irresistible, if maddening at times. From Shaoguan, Dad took the train to Guilin via Hengyang. In 1942 this was a two-day journey. The train was apparently very comfortable but they arrived in Hengyang in the middle of the night.

> We arrived at Heng Yang at 4.00am and with a little difficulty we found our way to the American Mission. Even at this hour they seemed pleased to see us, parked us in the drawing room and told us to sleep until 7.00am which we did. We stayed with them all day having rather a wearing time bear fighting with the children and took the evening train to Kweilin [Guilin].

Currently it is a 10-hour trip on high-speed trains but still only costs £30. I had been persuaded by my tour operator to fly from Shaoguan to Guilin, which I now regret. By the time we'd got the train back to Guangzhou, spent an hour and a half on the metro getting across the city to the airport, hanging around at the airport and then waiting for luggage at the other end, it would have taken much the same time to have gone directly by train. I suppose I would have had to travel alone as my Chinese guides did not seem to be allowed to cross provincial borders. It is quite common to find that tour guides are restricted to a particular area or province (anywhere in the world) – they have to be expert in their local 'patch' and it helps to share out the work.

On a later trip to China in 2015 I did travel alone by train, from Kunming to Dali, a journey of six hours. I chose to do this to follow Dad's departure from China in January 1944, when he flew from

Chongqing to Kunming and then drove up the Burma Road to Dali. I wasn't able to do the journey by road, but I was determined to travel overland.

This train journey proved to be slightly nerve-wracking, not least because there had been a terrorist attack on Kunming station in 2014 when 29 people had been stabbed to death and another 140 had been injured. Airport-style security had been introduced, which mainly served to confuse and delay. The only signs in Kunming station were in characters, I was the only westerner on the train, none of the stations en route had signs to indicate where we had arrived and when I eventually disembarked at Dali there was a huge crowd of people on the forecourt, who surged towards us, shouting loudly and unintelligibly. I silently prayed that they weren't agitating against capitalism or Christians as it seemed I was the only example of either for miles around. They streamed past me, yelling and gesticulating, and I was left in a whirl of dust, hoping that one member of the herd might have my name on a board. Sadly, my guide was not there to meet me, delayed by a traffic jam. Nonetheless, all ended well and I was glad to have seen the country rather than to have flown over it.

9

Expanse West

Guangdong literally means 'expanse east', while Guangxi means 'expanse west'. When talking about directions, we would normally say 'north, south, east and west' and if describing a midpoint between north and east, we would say 'north-east'. In China, the cardinal directions are ordered differently, always stated as 'east, south, west, north' and the midpoint between north and east is called 'east-north'. The Chinese include a fifth cardinal direction – centre (zhōng 中). The character for east (dōng 东) represents the sun rising over a tree, while the character for south (nán 南) represents a tree going into the earth and the fertile, forested south of China; west (xī 西) is a bird in its nest for the night; and north (běi 北) is two people back to back, representing defence against the barbarous and antagonistic north. The character for zhōng represents an arrow hitting a bullseye. Each direction is associated with a colour and a season. East is represented by green and spring, south by red and summer, west by white and autumn, north by black and winter, and centre by the colour yellow (and hence it is also the colour associated with the emperor). East, being the direction of sunrise and associated with the season of spring, is naturally regarded as the first direction.

Guilin is one of the major cities in Guangxi province. The city was an important US Air Force base during the Second World War and consequently attracted Japanese bombing. When Dad arrived in March 1942, the train had to pull into a siding between steep hills to protect it from a threatened air raid. This must have been a familiar occurrence, and Dad doesn't comment on it, instead describing the extraordinary landscape that he now found himself in.

> Kweilin is a pleasant city. Its streets are fairly wide, there are plenty of trees and compared to some places it is clean. The country in that part is very curious. On the whole it is flat but it is dotted about with little hills two or three hundred feet high and about 200 hundred yards in diameter which rise in sheer cliffs from the surrounding plains. Many of these hills are riddled with caves and in fact those near the city are used as air raid shelters. We went into one of the biggest and most famous [Seven Star Cave] and which I believe can hold about 15,000 people.

Nowadays you can wander through the labyrinthine caverns of Seven Star Cave for a kilometre or more, with the stalagmites and stalactites lit up like Santa's grotto. In places you can stamp your foot on the ground and it sounds hollow – there is another layer of caves below. The city is well protected by natural features – two rivers flow around it, making a sort of moat, and the many limestone karst hills form a defensive wall on all sides. There's even a more or less conical hill (Solitary Beauty Peak) in the centre that makes an excellent lookout!

The escapers from Sham Shui Po were en route to Guilin as a port of call on the way to their final destinations. In Whitehead's book, he describes the train journey from Hengyang to Guilin, but says that the train did a sort of emergency stop during the night at a town called Qiyang. The train was boarded by some Australian troops from Mission 204, who led the escapers off the train, presumably for a secret conversation. This is when Whitehead was recruited into Mission 204 commando unit and said his goodbyes to Dad. When Dad eventually reached Chongqing, he reported Whitehead's successful escape from Hong Kong, and Whitehead subsequently received a letter of commendation from Field Marshal Wavell, Commander in Chief, India, and was awarded the Military Medal. At that time, the Military Cross was only awarded to officers, the Military Medal being the equivalent for other ranks. Dad's account says nothing of Whitehead's departure from the train, merely stating that they boarded the night train and arrived in Guilin in the morning.

Mission 204 aimed to train up 'Surprise Troops' in the Chinese Nationalist army to undermine Japanese supply routes and installations. It suffered from serious under-resourcing, and although they usefully trained some Chinese troops in guerrilla tactics, they never really made much impact on the Japanese advance. Their charismatic and persuasive leader and General Officer Commanding, British Military Mission to China, Major General Dennys, was killed in a plane crash in March 1942, which disabled their access to proper funding. The support for them in food and other supplies, which had been agreed with senior Chinese military officials, did not materialise on the ground. The efforts of Mission 204 were seriously hampered by these failings, and they became exhausted from starvation and lack of proper equipment and porterage. The experiment in Anglo-Chinese guerrilla warfare was discontinued in September 1942.

Meanwhile, Hewitt enjoyed the cosmopolitan atmosphere of Guilin, filled with refugees of various nations, journalists, missionaries and businessmen. Through a chance meeting, Hewitt was taken to meet the Commander in Chief of Nationalist forces in Guangxi province, General Chang Fa-kui:

> He asked questions about the fall of Hong Kong, wanting to know in detail the strength of our forces in the fighting. He was critical about the number of prisoners the Japanese had taken in Hong Kong, and even more so about those taken in Singapore. 'Chinese soldiers do not surrender,' he said flatly. I may have looked a little sceptical. To convince me he added, 'China is fighting 29 Japanese army divisions. We have been fighting for five years. We have not been conquered, even by 29 divisions, because we do not surrender. Hong Kong was taken by one division. Singapore by two. Java by one.'[1]

Hewitt continued on to Chongqing, which he disliked intensely, describing it as a 'grim and ugly city', and then flew on to India, stopping off at the Great Eastern Hotel in Calcutta (now Kolkata) before going on to Delhi to take command of 400 men. Hewitt's book includes a scan of his letter from General Wavell, commending

---

1. Anthony Hewitt, *Bridge with Three Men: Across China to the Western Heaven in 1942* (London: Jonathan Cape, 1986), 214–215.

him on his escape from Hong Kong. It is identical in wording to the letters to Colonel Ride and to my father, and written on the same day! General Wavell must have had a busy day congratulating numerous men on their successful escapes from Hong Kong. Sadly, this pleasant activity was not destined to require much of his time, as the trickle of escapers rapidly dried up, with only 33 men ever successfully escaping from Sham Shui Po camp from January 1942 until the end of the war.

From June 1944 it became apparent that Guilin was a likely target of the Japanese, and BAAG were given permission by the British Military Attaché to take whatever action they thought necessary, provided that they kept in touch with central government. Over the summer BAAG evacuated its civilian staff and family members, but as quickly as they were sending people away, more were arriving having evacuated from Japanese-occupied areas in eastern China.

The Japanese were advancing towards Guilin from Hengyang (to the north-east), and in early September 1944 Colonel Lindsay Ride drove out of the city to see what defensive preparations the Chinese army had made in this direction. He drove for 60 miles and didn't see a single Chinese soldier. Alarmed by this open door to the city, a mass evacuation followed swiftly, leaving only a small group to assist the Chinese forces. Ride managed to persuade the British and American authorities that the Japanese assault on Guilin could be delayed and diminished by blocking a narrow gorge to the north-east of the city and by destroying villages and bridges for miles around. This was accomplished in mid-September with the help of American air support, and much to the delight of the local Chinese military commanders. Unfortunately, General Chen of the 93rd Army was to be the scapegoat for the Chinese army's strategic failure to defend Guilin. He was recalled to Chongqing and executed for dereliction of duty. BAAG finally had to withdraw from Guilin in mid-October, but their efforts did delay and alter Japanese plans and, no doubt, inspired fortitude in the Chinese army. The Japanese attacked Guilin on 1 November, and by 10 November 1944 the city had been taken.

The battle of Guilin was part of the Ichigo campaign, in which the Japanese were aiming to drive further into southern China from Hong Kong and Guangzhou, heading ultimately for the border with

Indo-China, where they hoped to build a railway to open up a new supply route. They were also taking control of airbases to limit the Allies' capacity to respond. Between August and December 1944, 100,000 Chinese lives were lost in Guangxi. The campaign failed overall in that by the time the Japanese had taken these vast tracts of territory they were too thinly spread and depleted to make much use of it. The Ichigo campaign succeeded in many ways, though – as well as taking airfields and territory, it showed up weaknesses in the Allied command structure and showed how weak and compromised Chiang's position was. He was too concerned with keeping his best troops for fighting the Communists rather than stemming the advance of the Japanese. Ichigo also crippled the Nationalists in terms of taking territory that was their main food and manpower source (Henan and Hunan provinces) and led to 750,000 casualties. It is estimated that of 1.67 million Chinese men drafted in 1943, 44 per cent died or deserted before seeing combat.[2] The abuses inflicted by Chiang's regime on their own army and population, on top of famine and corruption, meant that by the end of 1944 the Americans started looking to the Chinese Communist Party for support. It was the beginning of the end for the Nationalist government.

My guide in Guangxi province, William, had put a lot of effort into researching the wartime history of Guilin to share with me. We climbed the 300 steps up Fubo Hill in the centre of Guilin to get a bird's-eye view of the city. He told me:

> To the north is Parrot Hill, an important line of defence. The Japanese spent three days attacking that area as they knew how important it was to the defence of the city. To the south is Elephant Hill, where the local Chinese troops placed machine guns and cannon, killing many Japanese troops as they tried to cross the Li River to enter the city.

I could understand how, thanks to the natural defences of the city, the Chinese were able to hold off the Japanese for a surprisingly long time.

---

2. J.D. Spence, *The Search for Modern China* 3rd Edition, (London: Norton, 2013), 427

The thing to do in Guilin is to take a cruise down the Li River to Yangshuo. This takes you through the spectacular limestone karst landscape, consisting of the most unlikely-looking hills dotted about on a flat plain like chess pieces on a board. The hills are given names reminiscent of their shape – Snail, Dolphin, Woman with Baby on her Back, Clutching Hand, and so on. I was overwhelmed by the beauty of the scene even though it was raining, but my fellow passengers were mostly glued to their tablets or phones, or sitting inside drinking tea. On the way we saw a fisherman with a cormorant on a bamboo raft. Dad had had this experience earlier in his journey, on the boat up the East River:

> For the first and only time in my life I saw a man fishing with cormorants. He had three of them sitting on a low raft in the water, on which he also sat looking rather like a cormorant himself.

Yangshuo is a charming tourist trap. On arrival at the dock you are led into West Street, home to a ribbon of taterias (a term I coined in Mexico, to describe small shops or roadside stalls that sell cheap souvenirs) with one or two jewels thrown in. Most interesting was a handicraft shop selling work by local ethnic minorities. Their intricate and numinous textiles were of a delicacy and skill that was mesmerising, and when I chose a table runner but said it was too long, the shopkeeper cheerfully arranged for it to be altered ready for later that day. China is ethnically over 90 per cent Han, but there are numerous minority groups with their own language, culture and dress. Like many other ethnic minorities around the world, they are by turns marginalised, romanticised, disenfranchised, patronised and held up as symbols of human rights magnanimity by the ruling elite. In China, they are growing faster than the Han population as they have not been obliged to adhere to the 'one child' policy. Ironic.

I stayed at the gorgeous Li River Retreat outside town, with a view of the mountains and the river, accompanied by the rhythmic thrum of crickets and the lilting chatter of birds. It was run by a European: finally, someone who understood the need for wine with dinner! The Chinese are not big drinkers. At a restaurant, they will automatically bring a pot of tea and then ask what you would like to drink. Tsingtao beer is commonly offered, but wine is a rarity. Even a request for gin and tonic produces cries of alarm and searches in the depths of cupboards for a can of tonic water, followed by dire warnings that gin is 'strong drink'.

The next morning, William, my guide, asked me, 'Are you OK to cycle through town?' I had spent a couple of years commuting in London by bike so I foresaw no problem with this plan, which would then take us out into the countryside along the Yulong valley. Well, alright then, except that in London there is a Highway Code, which people pretty much stick to, whereas in China even driving on the right isn't mandatory if it looks easier on the left. Turning left requires nerves of steel as there are no lines on the road, no one stops and there are pedestrians, bikes, mopeds, cars, buses and lorries all competing for road space. I don't even know how we got round the roundabout – I decided it was best to stick like glue to William's side and not look at the traffic.

Out in the countryside it was more peaceful and we pedalled along flat, empty roads. We stopped at a traditional house where they allow tourists to take a look around. Looking at the pictures I took, I begin to understand why the Chinese stared at me so much. I suppose that to them I am like a human only much bigger, with ghostly pale skin and weird brown curly hair. When I was catching flights to my next destination, I would text the guide who was meeting me to say that I was on my way. I added that I was tall with curly hair and a red suitcase. I needn't have bothered as I was invariably the only European on the flight and was usually much taller than my fellow passengers. Short of having a flashing neon sign on my head I couldn't have been easier to spot.

Dad had been in Hong Kong since 1937 and would have felt more at home with Chinese people and their customs on his journey across China. This deep familiarity would have comforted him in an otherwise extremely alien situation, giving him a solid sense of security in a constantly shifting, uncertain and threatening environment. The more time I spent in China, the more I savoured the occasional moments of common experience – a bar of chocolate, a native English speaker, a recognised plant. And I wasn't having to worry about an aggressive and powerful enemy! Dad's lack of emotional narrative in his letters and diary entries was part of his way of being, as well as a necessity of war, but, blimey! Didn't he ever give way to terror or despondency?

The traditional house, home to several generations of a family, had a courtyard with a water pump and a soya bean press. Sweetcorn was growing in the yard and vegetables were hanging up to dry, along with coolie hats and laundry. The main room served as living room, dining room and shrine. The shrine consisted of a table with candles, incense burners and a bottle of snake wine on it, pictures of family ancestors and Mao Zedong on the wall and an eclectic selection of souvenirs from around the world – a picture of the Eiffel Tower, a plate from Sweden, a Canadian flag and, ranged around a wall hanging showing an ancestor on horseback, numerous cuddly koala bears. There was also a propaganda poster from the good old days of the Cultural Revolution, showing a smiling Mao with Lin Biao and the famous Little Red Book.

There was a bedroom with a bed actually made of floorboards – no mattress at all, so worse than the hotel, and a basic kitchen. I doubt it would have been much different 70 years ago and it gave me another insight into Dad's experience of China.

Next up was a ride on a bamboo raft, advertised as a nice relaxing way to see the extraordinary karst landscape. The rafts are made of 10 bamboo poles roped together, with a couple of deckchairs lashed on top, floated along by a man with a pole. I settled in for a bit of photography and filming, but shortly we came to a concrete trackway blocking the river. We had to get out, drag the raft across and then set it in the water, about six feet lower than on the upstream side. It got worse: at the next trackway, I was expected to sit in my deckchair for re-entry into the water. We went over several of these water slides, each time the raft sinking about a foot into the water on entry. It was all quite exciting and the scenery was magnificent, even if I did end up rather wet. Dad would have been highly amused by it.

While in Guilin I was reading a book about the Arctic[3] that helped

---

3. Sara Wheeler, *The Magnetic North: Travels in the Arctic* (London: Vintage, 2010)

me understand the context of Dad's youth. He was born in 1914 so would have been an impressionable youth in the 1920s and '30s. This was the era of attempts on Everest, expeditions to reach the North Pole, daring flights across the Atlantic and over the poles. Tutankhamun's tomb was discovered, the *Australopithecus* fossil was found, new depths were reached in the oceans, new heights reached in the atmosphere. Dad had taken a keen interest in mountaineering at school in Switzerland, and after the war he joined an expedition to attempt an unclimbed Himalayan peak with his old schoolmaster, Jack Gibson, who was an acclaimed mountaineer. Dad also rode in point-to-point races after the war and had been learning to fly when he was in Hong Kong. In fact, the battle to defend Hong Kong prevented him from taking his first solo flight. To find himself in the mysterious interior of China in wartime must have been a thrill, an exhilarating opportunity, and the terrors and challenges merely natural partners to the adventure.

The concept of resilience is enjoying a renaissance currently. Robert A Heinlein said: 'Don't handicap your children by making their lives easy.' Over the last couple of decades it seems to me that we have been making children's lives too easy, on the one hand, in terms of tolerating risk, accepting responsibility and managing disappointment. When these skills are not learned in childhood, because the parents take over, it is unsurprising that young people feel overwhelmed when these challenges inevitably arise and their parents are not present. Why are parents so anxious to prevent their children from experiencing difficulty? From learning by their mistakes? We don't even want children to ever have any illnesses, despite their inevitability, generally self-resolving nature and the resilience in the immune system that this experience confers. In our desperation to love them we have stopped asking anything of them or setting boundaries, and we are so afraid of predators that we won't let children explore independently.

Equally, we are overwhelming our children with spurious academic demands (and constant testing) and the tyranny of social media, heaping enormous stress on them. Mental health is becoming one of the biggest problems facing schools and universities. Issues such as low self-esteem, self-harm and depression are at epidemic levels. Child mental health is a social issue, a community issue, not a medical issue with a medical solution. We need to understand the stresses that we as a society place on our children and change to a better model, reducing the stress input and increasing the coping skills for future generations. My parents were far from perfect but they did raise us to be competent adults, albeit in a pre-internet world. Real-life challenges just keep coming throughout our lives, so practise in childhood must help to establish ways of not only coping but of actively enjoying new situations. At this point in my journey I began to forget my worries about travelling in China and started to revel in the opportunity for striking out into the unknown.

10

Mountain Minorities

In March 1942, Guilin represented Dad's entry to Mandarin-speaking China – Dad's party had no Mandarin speakers and they were suddenly at a loss as to how to proceed.

> Luck was with me. I ran into an American Professor of a Chinese university whom I had met in Shaokwan. He managed to fix up some rooms for us in a hotel. I showed him a card of introduction to a Colonel Lee Chin Sum who had the same name as the local General who is really a Marshal of the Chinese Army and commands no less than four war zones – about a third of the Chinese Army. The Professor thought my introduction was to the Marshal and took me off to see him. He was most affable and very interested in my account of our adventures. He sent for this Colonel and ordered him to give us priority passes on the buses from the railhead [at Hechi] to Kweiyang [now Guiyang], our next objective on our journey to Chungking. This was most useful.

I reflected on my father's good fortune as we drove north out of Guilin towards the mountains to explore rural Guangxi and its peoples. Our first stop was a visit to the Longji rice terraces, made centuries ago and still in use today. We were planning to stay overnight in Ping'an village, so I had all of my luggage with me. This was going to be a bit tricky as there was a fair walk from the road up to the mountain village, but I was assured that for a few yuan someone would carry my wheeled 22kg case for me. We set off from the ticket office car park up the steep road towards Ping'an but within a mile came to a landslip that had happened just half an hour earlier. It completely blocked the road, and several vehicles loaded with glum-looking tourists were halted, while a few Chinese were looking impotently at the vast heap of earth and rubble. We asked around and found that it was thought that it would take the rest of the day to clear the road. We were faced with the prospect of abandoning our trip but my wonderful guide, William, knew the area well.

He suggested that we go back down the mountain and take a road up to another village, from which we could walk to Ping'an. We returned to the car park and I handed my suitcase to a surly and grubby-looking man in charge of what one could charitably call a left luggage facility – a room guarded by a dog that would have done well in a 'dog that looks most like its owner' contest. As it seemed possible that I wouldn't be reunited with my case, I travelled onward slightly more heavily laden than usual for an overnight stay. No one else seemed to know about this option and we were the only vehicle on the hairpin-looped, vertiginous ribbon of asphalt that led to Longpu village.

The disappointment of the landslip gave way to the most serendipitous 24 hours of sublime beauty, unaccompanied by bleating flocks of tourists. The walk across to Ping'an, mercifully following a contour, was exquisite. Once again I had a sneaking suspicion that Dad was near at hand, steering events with subtle dexterity. Laurens van der Post found that ocean voyages opened up his internal world through the constant access to uninterrupted vistas, the rise and set of the sun and the blazing clarity of the stars. For me and, I suspect, for Dad, it is mountain scenery that has this effect. The contact with pristine nature, the opening out of views that accompanies ascent, the clean air and the sense of reaching for one's higher self through the climb all contribute to a reflective state.

We were in Zhuang territory, descendants of the ancient Luo Yue people, who were also originators of the Vietnamese people. The Zhuang still practise the Luo Yue animistic and ancestor-worshipping religion. Their chief deity is the thunder god, bringer of the rain that ensures a good harvest. Frogs are the thunder god's children and messengers, and Zhuang rituals include imitations of frog postures in their dances. Another important deity is the water god, regarded as evil, as bringer of flood and drought, and representing the underworld. The middle world, between the sky above and the underworld below, is represented by the ancestor god, who is regarded as the progenitor of the Zhuang people, with his lover the flower goddess. I am struck by the commonality between the beliefs of first peoples around the world, from the Americas to Asia, Europe, Russia and the Bushmen of Southern Africa. Perhaps their common ground is their close communion with nature, from which 'civilised' societies have long since divorced themselves. We met several Zhuang people on the path, the women in dark blue trouser suits and usually carrying woven baskets on their backs, laden with leaves and vegetables.

The mountains were steep sided, with glimpses of craggy peaks in the clouds. The terraces extended above and below us as far as the eye could see, and wild flowers dotted the verges with splashes of colour. There were pines, bamboos and ferns along the way, the fern shoots being a local delicacy that is made into a sort of cake. Eventually we came to a substantial bridge over a small stream. It was a covered wooden bridge, perhaps 10 metres long, with a tiled roof and stone supports. It had the feeling of a community centre rather than a border, though it marked the boundary between the Zhuang and the Yao peoples. There were one or two people sitting on benches contemplating the view. It seemed to be an invitation to peace and community, to sharing and exchanging news and views as well as goods.

The Yao are a diverse minority, with this particular group known as Hong Yao, referring to their red (or rather deep pink) dress. The Yao women in this area only have their hair cut once in their lives, at the age of 18. They keep the hair that has been cut off and add it to their remaining hair, styling it according to their marital status and number of children. Their hair is remarkable not only for its length but also for the retention of its glossy blackness into old age. Two Yao women showed me how they style their hair. First, one of them loosed her hair and let it fall in front of her. They are small people and her hair was easily longer than she was tall. She removed the hank of hair that had been cut in her youth and handed it to her friend. I suppose it was about four feet long. Then she combed out her hair with a simple wooden comb and restored the hank so that the full length of hair from root to tip was about six feet. She wound it expertly around her head, twisting and securing it, combing stray strands until she ended with a bun at her forehead. With a final sweep of the comb, which she popped into the depths of her hairstyle, she completed the job, without anything to hold the hair in place except itself.

When I went to stand between the two women for a photograph, they felt so grounded that it was like being hugged by two trees. I envied these women their connectedness to nature. They seemed like vibrant threads woven firmly into the fabric of the magic carpet of life. In these mountains, life is stripped bare of the buffers that we normally place between ourselves and nature. No wonder the weather gods dominate the local religion and the change in seasons is so acutely observed. Circadian and annual rhythms are the only beats that matter, brutal but comforting in the clarity of their demands.

We reached Ping'an and went to look at the famous 'moon and seven stars' and 'dragon's backbone' rice terraces. The beautiful layers of terracing on these softly rounded slopes must have cost the most colossal amount of labour to construct and maintain. They are functional in that they are the only way to use the slopes for agriculture, but they are also designed with great respect to their appearance. They are works of art, pleasing not just to man but likely intended to please the sight of the gods. The tenacity and determination required to keep them in use reflects their importance to the survival of the local people's traditional way of life. How long will it be before the young generation opt for an easier life in China's cities?

The dark tiled roofs and wooden walls of the village buildings and their placement on the hillside gave them the appearance of strange beasts that were placidly grazing their way up the valley. My hotel was one of these charming buildings, simple but comfortable. It was made even simpler when a thunderstorm overnight knocked out the electricity to the whole village. Luckily, my husband had insisted that I bring a torch to China with me, so I was able to find my way along the dark corridor and stairwell to breakfast. A gas burner had been hastily installed to cook porridge – it was cool up at 800m so hot food was extremely welcome.

After the rain in the night, the morning was bright and fresh. Wisps of mist were puffing up the valleys, and the sunlight on the freshly flooded terraces produced a spectacular effect – as though the paddy had been decorated with mirrors overnight. I have come to expect this sort of thing with my unreasonably lucky aura, or whatever it is, but William was overwhelmed. He'd had a guest who was a professional photographer and had wanted to see exactly this scene, but after a week of dull days had returned home empty-handed. I silently thanked Dad and any other guardian angels who were doing such a great job of giving me the time of my life.

We drove on to Sanjiang to see the Wind and Rain Bridge there. Think *The Bridges of Madison County* with Chinese characteristics. Further into the mountains north of Guilin are numerous remote villages with these iconic bridges. The one at Sanjiang (meaning 'three rivers') is the oldest and most impressive. It was built in 1916 by the local Dong people, who use only dovetail joints – there are no nails or rivets. There are four stone piers supporting the wooden bridge, covered by five adjacent pagodas, decked as always with red lanterns and with seats in the various alcoves for people to stop and gossip or shop. Compared to the dull, utilitarian architecture of modern China, this bridge seemed almost baroque.

The Dong people, who live in the valleys, wear blue tunics and are very friendly and hospitable. I was invited to a banquet that was going on but, fearing that I would refuse more dishes than I would eat, I declined, to prevent embarrassment all round. My husband had visited China on business and had been honoured at various banquets, where delicacies had included deep-fried goose intestines and braised sea cucumber with tendon and chives. It would be extremely rude to just eat the chives. The Dong have some rather strange customs. When they marry, the woman doesn't sleep with her husband but instead continues to live in her family home. She visits her husband on high days and holidays and is expected to get pregnant. She is then allowed to move in with her husband, having proved that she is fertile.

We drove along narrow lanes through tea fields, rape fields and rice paddies, all shoehorned in between steep mountains, to see another local feature – the drum tower. These square pagodas are the equivalent of town halls, where the villagers meet to discuss complaints, settle disputes between families and generally lay down the law. It is considered poor form to have to pass up an issue to state authorities. Nowadays they also contain a TV, and the local menfolk sit watching sport, smoking and drinking beer, while the women work. Some things are universal. It was a long journey back to Guilin and I don't recommend being on the road after dark. At least in daylight you can see the hazards ahead.

We stopped for a comfort break on the way back. For a nation that is fastidiously clean and well-organised, the toilets in China do seem to be a bit of a blind spot. Neither privacy nor hygiene seem to be important factors in their design. At the '3 star' end we have Western-style sit toilets, with doors on the cubicles. If these toilets exist at all, it is in the guise of 'disabled access'. For full 3-star rating there also needs to be toilet paper (rare as hens' teeth), water in the basins, soap (unicorn rare) and something to dry your hands with (not a big deal in a warm country, mind you). Most common is the 1- or 2-star toilet, where some of these things are missing, doors being the most commonly absent feature. The cubicles are usually in a row over a trench, where water runs through periodically to carry away the waste into a collective hole in the ground. Used paper is put into a basket in the cubicle – I'm not against this in principle, if the baskets are emptied frequently. What I do find disturbing is that the cubicles are separated by a wall – no door – and so you have to squat more or less in public. My least favourite is where the wall is only about two feet high, so that when you stand to pull your knickers up, your privates are on parade, as it were.

Dad travelled by train from Guilin to Hechi, along the new railway that was being built.

> We travelled on this for about 36 hours. It is a magnificent piece of engineering. At one place we travelled over a wooden bridge crossing a deep ravine. As you looked out of the carriage it was impossible to see anything of the bridge till you saw its base in the ravine, it gave the unpleasant illusion of being suspended in space. The per-

manent stone bridge was being built alongside and was nearly finished.

The buses only run twice a week and we had to wait at Hochee [now Hechi] for three days. We stayed in a China Travel Association Hotel. All the Hotels run by this company are very clean and good. There the Marshal's passes were most effective and we were given seats on the next bus to Kweiyang [Guiyang]. This time it was a proper bus with numbered seats. It was much more comfortable than the Shaokwan buses. The petrol pump went wrong on the first day so it took us nearly 3 days to do the journey which is normally done in two. It is about 280 miles but it is very steep country. Kweiyang itself is about 5,500 feet above sea level.

I took an evening flight from Guilin to Guiyang. I was slightly puzzled by the appearance of two names on the destination section of the departure board. It said Guiyang (reassuring) and Beihai (of which I had never heard). I couldn't tell which destination we would arrive at first. The plane was delayed by an hour and when I boarded there were only recorded announcements in English – no one on board actually spoke English. After about 45 minutes we landed at… somewhere. There was a large neon sign saying 北海 to tell me where we were but I couldn't read it. I am ashamed of this as 'běi 北' means north (as in Beijing) and 'hǎi 海' means sea (as in Shanghai). I jolly well should have been able to recognise those characters! Fear paralyses the rational mind, I find.

Anyway, it was about 10.30pm by this stage and I was a little alarmed. I asked the stewardess if this was Guiyang, but she said not and insisted that I leave the aircraft along with everyone else. We trudged into a poorly lit and deserted building, bereft of either staff or signs. I would have liked to use the toilet facilities but I didn't dare leave my little flock of fellow passengers. I was the only European, as per usual. After about 15 minutes everyone suddenly headed back down the stairs and out of the building, crossing the tarmac back to our aircraft. Off we went, and another hour or so later we landed at…

Guiyang. Hurrah! It turned out that the stop made the journey equivalent to flying from London to Edinburgh via Paris.

Dad arrived safely in Guiyang and enjoyed being up in the mountains:

> The weather was good and the scenery grand. We stayed two days in Kwei Yang. Trevor, when he had been manager of the Kowloon Canton Railway, had got to know the present Chinese Minister of Foreign Affairs very well. We wired to him and with his influence we got into a fast convoy of trucks going up to Chungking.

Guiyang looked much more modern and sophisticated than I was expecting. It is on a high plateau and is the meeting place for cold winds from Siberia to the west and warm winds from the Pacific to the east. The result? Near constant cloud and fog.

The only remaining sign of old Guiyang is the First Scholar's Tower, perched on the Fuyu (Jade Floating) Bridge over the Nanming River. It was built in 1598 during the Ming dynasty in honour of those who passed the imperial examinations. China's governance has been based on a meritocracy (in principle) since the Zhou dynasty of 1046–256 BC. Various philosophers since have tried to find ways of countering the corruption inevitable in human society, but the basic rule that China should be run by noble men (gāoshàng de rén 高尚的人) rather than by noblemen (guìzú 贵族) continues to this day. The tower was destroyed and rebuilt several times over the next four hundred years. It is a picturesque building, three storeys tall with pagoda-style roofs. Inside there was a photo of the tower from the 1930s. It hasn't changed at all since, but a forest of skyscrapers has sprouted on all sides.

The city is the capital of Guizhou province (meaning 'expensive state'), south-west China. Until recently it was the poorest province in China, poorer even than Tibet. Central government decided that development was needed and has taken a three-pronged approach. Tourism, mainly domestic but, hopefully, international is one prong; the discovery of epic quantities of coal and phosphorus is another; and, finally, fiscal incentives to investors are sweetening the deal. They say the national bird of China is the construction crane! As we drove out of the city, it was evident that there is a massive boom going on here, and I swear the city was a little bit bigger by the time we got back in the evening.

Meanwhile, 45 miles away out in untouched China, we visited Tianlong Tunpu, an ancient town founded 600 years ago, when 300,000 soldiers of the Ming dynasty were told to stay put after a battle and bring their families to join them. Today it is occupied by another one of the minorities, the Miao people. The life stage of the women is easy to identify – young women wear no headband and have a full head of hair. When a woman marries, she wears a white band and plucks the hair from her forehead, and when she becomes a grandmother she wears a black headband, again with the hair plucked from her forehead.

Onward to Asia's largest waterfall at Huangguoshu, 100 miles south-west of Guiyang. As Ted (my Guizhou guide) said, 'If Niagara is a strong man, then Huangguoshu is a slim girl.' It's fair to say the waterfall is not huge at 80m high and 100m wide, but it is beautiful. It was first discovered several hundred years ago by Xu Xiake, the Chinese Marco Polo, who described it poetically:

> The sprays burst apart like pearls and jades and the foams rise like a mist. The waterfall is with such a momentum that even the couplet 'a screen of pearl released from hooks / or silk that hangs on faraway peaks' cannot describe to the full its majesty. I have seen waterfalls that are much higher and more precipitous, but never a waterfall with such a width and magnificent.

To get to the waterfall you pass through sculpture parks, bonsai parks and a statue of Xu Xiake. The Chinese tourist board has really gone to town on it. Perhaps in search of the ultimate unique selling point, this is what they say about it:

> Huangguoshu Tourist Resort features beautiful natural environment, refreshing air (with over 28,000 negative oxygen ions per cubic centimetre according to the statistics

of the provincial environmental protection department), a pleasant climate (with the annual average temperature at 16°C), long historical and cultural tradition, and complete supporting facilities. It is an ideal resort for amusement, rehabilitation, sightseeing, and 'lung-washing'.

If I'd stuck to the beaten track I'd have missed some amazing and wonderful sights. However, the Chinese do like to add concrete walkways (why should you change out of heels to look at a waterfall?) and plenty of coloured lights (think Christmas lights on London's Oxford Street). It's another fine contrast: on the one hand the signs don't say 'Keep off the grass', they say very gently 'Make the little grass smile by going round about', while on the other they think nothing of brutally carving up natural features in the name of tourist convenience.

It was time to head to Chongqing. Although it is the place where my father spent most of his time in China, I had little enthusiasm for my visit because I knew that Chongqing had been bombed to smithereens in the war and there would be almost nothing to see to connect with Dad's time there. Also, it is now a huge industrial city that is a major economic development area, rather than any kind of tourist destination with interesting sights to see. I knew that, if he were with me on this trip, Dad would scarcely recognise the place.

11

Wartime Capital

Dad managed to join a convoy of trucks to take him and his colleagues to Chongqing.

> It took us two and a half days to get to Chungking. Again the scenery was magnificent. We were travelling at the best time of year; all the tung oil trees were in bloom. They have a pretty flower like a cross between a tree tulip and a frangipani. The first day out I developed a pain in my stomach, the second day it was dreadful but I had none of the other symptoms that I usually have with a disordered stomach. By the evening after a horribly jolty trip in the truck I had a temperature. A Chinese doctor came to see me. He diagnosed appendicitis. However, after an aspirin and a good night's sleep I felt better the next morning. We arrived at Chungking about midday 31st March 1942, just two months after we had left Sham Shui Po.

When Dad finally reaches his destination, he barely remarks on the scene that greeted him. He also fails to convey any sense of ongoing jeopardy, even though Chongqing, as capital city, was frequently attacked from the air. Between 1938 and 1943 Chongqing was repeatedly and comprehensively bombed by the Japanese, killing thousands of civilians and destroying many buildings. Dad's sole comment on the city's plight:

> At one time or another most of the city has been bombed flat. When it has been rebuilt they have taken the opportunity to build fine wide streets but, having no cement or

tar available, you can imagine how disgustingly slimy and muddy they become in wet weather. Though the main streets are kept clear of refuse and human ordure, the paths and alleyways are not. Mothers bring their children out of the house and hold them over the gutters when they wish to relieve any and all of the calls of nature. Kitchen refuse is just thrown on the nearest heap of rubble. The city swarms with rats of a portliness that has to be seen to be believed.

Edwin Ride[1] describes Chongqing in less than glowing terms:

> The administrative centre of Free China was the western province of Szechwan [now Sichuan], protected by high mountains on its eastern boundary as if built by nature for a wartime base. The Nationalist Government had for three years conducted its business from Chungking, capital of Szechwan, which clung precipitously to the hillside and was said to have a summer worse than Calcutta and a winter that perpetually wrapped the city in cold fog. Chungking had already been so heavily bombed that there was hardly a house that did not show damage. Air raid shelters honeycombed the Cliffside; and with its universal grey camouflage paint, its improvised structures of cheap brick, matshed and bamboo, it was at the time one of the ugliest as well as the noisiest and busiest cities in the world.

Chongqing means 'double celebration', but I think that spirit must have been killed in the bombing. A painting in the museum there showed the nightmare it must have been, with burning buildings, ruins everywhere and the streets crowded with people searching for loved ones, food, water... Han Suyin, a British-trained Chinese midwife, writes very movingly of the appalling conditions in Chongqing in her book *Destination Chungking* (London: Penguin, 1942):

> The whole city smelled of burning and ashes and, mixed with that, the sour, penetrating reek of decay. Where

---

1. Ride, *BAAG: Hong Kong Resistance 1942–45*, 108

demolition bombs alone had fallen, the bodies of those killed by blast and falling walls, buried for days in the wreckage, were horribly decomposed when uncovered and smelled far worse than those who had been burned to death.

The public [air raid] shelters are all at the foot of the hills; they consist of ramifying tunnels, seven or eight feet wide, wet, dark, and suffocating. The walls drip moisture; the floor is mud underfoot; there are no seats. People stand hour after hour, packed together; a few bring stools or folding chairs. After half an hour the stench is fearful. The only conveniences provided are one or two open buckets outside the entrance for the men. The children relieve themselves like little animals. It was in such a shelter I spent that first day from ten in the morning to four in the afternoon – six hours.

Dad's appendix continued to trouble him, and in April 1942 he was flown to India to have an appendectomy at the British Military Hospital in Murree (now in Pakistan). He stopped off in Calcutta on the way. Gunner Whitehead's companions, Parrott and Jacobs, were also flown via Calcutta on their way home. They happened to meet Dad there, all staying at the Great Eastern Hotel, which seems to have been more or less an army quarter. Another couple of escapers – Lieutenants Gordon 'Tich' Fairclough and Phillip 'Jumbo' Passmore – were also passing through, and all the Hong Kong veterans had dinner together, before Dad left for Delhi (the next leg of his journey).

The Great Eastern Hotel had been going since the 1840s, when Calcutta was home to the headquarters of the East India Company, and in its heyday had hosted many a celebrity guest. Mark Twain described it as the 'Jewel of the East'. Passmore, Fairclough and Lieutenant 'Jock' Wedderburn RA had escaped Sham Shui Po a couple of days after Dad, using a sampan, after a raft they had made proved too heavy and sank. Jock Wedderburn stayed on in Chongqing, and he and Dad were good friends.

Dad took some time off to recuperate from his ordeals, spending some quiet time fishing for trout in Kashmir both before and after his appendectomy in May 1942. In those days, the concept of convalescence was alive and well – Dad was in hospital for two weeks after his operation and was then expected to rest for a while – but it has since faded into oblivion. The pace of modern life demands that you get back to work as soon as you can lift your head off the pillow. I frequently ask my patients to rest a little before resuming normal activities, to allow their body a chance of completing the repair process. The body has an energy budget, some of which it spends on daily necessities and some of which is available as 'disposable income'. When the immune system rises to the challenge of an invasion, or a fractured bone needs repair, or an adrenaline-fuelled supreme effort has been made, the body can go into 'debt'. A prolonged physically or emotionally stressful event needs a corresponding rest to repay the debt.

On 27 June 1942, Dad received notice of his Military Cross (MC) while he was at his fishing camp. His diary entry is typical of his understatedness:

> Had a congratulatory letter from Wavell on my escape. Ditto from Hartley [General Alan Hartley, Deputy Commander in Chief, India] telling me I had been awarded M.C. Very surprised. Moved camp to a position which I hope has less mosquitoes.

Dad returned to Chongqing in August 1942, having been appointed Assistant Military Attaché (AMA). The British Military Attaché and his assistants formed the link between the political and military arms of the war and were based at the embassy. Dad seemed to spend quite a lot of time travelling through Guilin during the time that he was based in Chongqing, where he was an AMA from August 1942 to December 1943. His visits were partly due to the American Air Force bases being in Guilin and partly because it was the headquarters of the British Army Aid Group (BAAG), for whom Dad acted as liaison with Allied Command.

He flew in to Chongqing from India, landing at the airfield that was then in the centre of the city. General Gordon Grimsdale, British Military Attaché, describes the approach:

> The 'aerodrome' in use at Chungking is a small shingle island in the middle of the river Yangtze. The runway is just under 800 yards long. It is a somewhat nerve-shaking experience to land here for the first time. On either side are hills up to 500 or 600 feet. Just above the island the river bends and, in order to clear the hills, the pilot has to follow the river valley for some distance. As he approaches the landing strip he is thus losing height and coming into land whilst on a turn. He has to lose height rapidly in the last few hundred yards, since there is a high tension cable strung across the river half a mile above the island and which he must make certain of clearing. From the island one is ferried across a narrow branch of the river to the mainland and is then faced with a steep climb up some 400 steps to the city level.[2]

It seems that the adventure was not over on landing, and Dad's daily life sounds like quite a challenge:

> I live on the south bank of the Yangtze; my office is on the north bank. There is quite a good ferry service across the river; most of the day it is a double service but at about 5pm – rush hour – being a free and democratic people, one of the ferries goes off duty for its evening meal; when it comes back the other goes off. Often at this time of day I have had to wait an hour or more before I could get across. In the morning I usually go across in the Embassy Sampan. Now that the river is very low and very fast – in places it has a current of about 8 knots – this can be very exciting. We go down the river at a tremendous pace till we get into the outside edge of a large whirlpool known as the 'Dragon's Mouth', where we get caught in a back eddy and swept right across the river almost to the opposite bank.

A week after arriving, Dad was waiting at the ferry to cross the

---

2. From the private papers of General Gordon Grimsdale, held at the Imperial War Museum, London

Yangzi River on his way home from the office when he witnessed a commemoration of Chongqing's dead:

> The Chinese were floating tiny lanterns down the river representing the spirits of those killed in the past year. The current is about seven knots but they went by in an endless stream for over two hours.

He does admit that there were some difficulties associated with life in Chongqing:

> The foreign community live scattered all over the city and fairly evenly divided between the north and south bank. We don't entertain or visit each other very much. Going out to dinner always seems to necessitate a crossing of the river and/or a very long walk up and down the endless flights of steps in this city. Car transport is almost non-existent except for the very rich Chinese. We manage to have a station wagon to take us to and from the office and the ferry but there is no petrol for anything else. The result is we only go out for dinner when it is a duty or else to a host for whom we have great respect and liking.
>
> Everything is astonishingly expensive. My messing costs me over £1 per day. Butter in tins is about £5 a pound. A small bottle of ink costs about 15 shillings and a single aspirin tablet is two shillings and six pence and a Leica camera about £3,000. How I wish I had managed to bring one with me from Hong Kong! A bottle of whisky, if you can find it, costs about £20 and European cigarettes work out at about two shillings and six pence each! I have just had my shoes resoled for £4 and 15 shillings.

Inflation became a huge problem as the war progressed, feeding ever worsening levels of corruption as well as impoverishing living conditions for the Chinese people. The Nationalist government's response to its magnifying costs was to print money, with predictable results across the economy. The poor agricultural harvests and limited production of goods in general added to the inflationary pressure. An Indian government representative in Chongqing, Krishna Menon, illustrated the effect of inflation on purchasing power: in 1937 100 Chinese dollars bought 2 cows; by 1940 it bought one calf; by 1943 100 dollars bought one chicken and by 1946 it bought an egg.[3]

A typical description of wartime Chongqing is reported in *China and ANU* by William Sima:[4]

> The city's population swelled from a pre-war level of 475,000 to more than 700,000, many of whom lived in densely packed, riverside hovels rife with disease and malnutrition... 'Wartime accounts of journeys into Chungking typically describe a sense of despair and horror provoked by the visitor's initial view of the working class districts along the shore,' writes Lee McIsaac in his study of modern Chungking.

Dad seems to have been unmoved by this:

> The newspaper accounts of the hardships of life in Chungking to my mind are greatly exaggerated. It is true that the climate is foul, prices astronomically high, the amenities of civilised life few and facilities for recreation almost non-existent; but it has its compensations.
>
> I like being here and manage to enjoy myself. I get £1 as living allowance while I am here; I am on Indian rates of pay which are mostly better than British rates. I am employed upon probably the most interesting job I shall ever be called upon to do, and it is a pleasure to work under my current boss, General Grimsdale, the Military Attaché. I live in a comfortable house, we have a good wok and the food is good even if it is expensive.

Gordon Grimsdale (1893–1950) had worked in military intelligence

---

3. Krishna Menon, *Twilight in China* (Bombay: Bharatiya Vidya Bhavan, 1972) quoted in Diana Lary, *The Chinese People at War: Human Suffering and Social Transformation, 1937–1945* (Cambridge: CUP, 2010) 121

4. William Sima, *China and ANU: Diplomats, adventurers, scholars* (ANU Press, 2015)

in the Far East since 1927, before being posted to Chongqing in January 1942. Joseph Alsop, journalist and Washington insider, had a knack for vivid description. He says this about Grimsdale, with whom he shared US Naval Attaché Colonel Jim McHugh's house in Chongqing:

> General Gordon Grimsdale, the British Military Attaché, was a small, intensely conservative man, as rigid as only British officers can be. He was capable of the violence of a cornered ferret if he felt that his conventions were being undermined. Nevertheless, he was an agreeable man and would remain a friend for many years.[5]

Lieutenant Colonel Lindsay Ride arrived in Chongqing in February 1942, having escaped from Sham Shui Po camp with three other men on 9 January 1942. Ride persuaded Grimsdale to form BAAG as a covert operation, later known as MI9 to connect it to the London-based MI9, its European military intelligence counterpart, which was set up in 1939 to support resistance networks. Its role was to assist escaping prisoners of war, obtain intelligence about enemy activities and to smuggle medical and other essential supplies into Hong Kong for internees.

It was an uphill struggle for a number of reasons. At first, when Colonel Ride set up BAAG, MI9 was not informed and so no resources were forthcoming. This was sorted out by Grimsdale, but then BAAG's work was impeded by the fact that Chiang Kai-shek's Chief of Secret Services, Dai Li (known as 'China's Himmler'), was vehemently anti-British and denied BAAG wireless facilities for communication. Furthermore, the hinterland around Hong Kong was controlled by Communist forces who were anti-Japanese and extremely helpful, but this made it seem as though BAAG was pro-Communist. Colonel Ride begged Grimsdale to recognise the role of the Communist guerrillas. Grimsdale's reply was political and to the point:

> However much we may want to recognise the

---

5. J.W. Alsop and A. Platt, *I've Seen the Best of It* (New York: WW Norton & Co, 1992), 201

guerrillas, to do so at present is I fear outside the bounds of practical politics; the political reaction on the Government here would be altogether too much for HMG [His Majesty's Government] to stomach I am sure.[6]

In addition to these problems at 'head office', there was a deep suspicion among the Chinese leadership that BAAG was really a means of the Brits keeping a foot in the door of Hong Kong. The Americans evidently thought the same, and in fact Wedemeyer, the US Commander in China who succeeded General Stilwell (Commander from March 1942 to October 1944), came up with a plan (code-named operation BETA) for a Sino-American recapture of Hong Kong, which was rather hostile to the British position. Although the plan was approved in April 1945, events had by then moved on and it was never actioned.

Despite these difficulties, BAAG was recognised as providing invaluable intelligence to the US and Royal navies about troops and supplies coming and going from Hong Kong. BAAG also successfully sabotaged the Japanese use of Hong Kong's dockyards by assisting the escape of large numbers of skilled dockers, known locally as 'Mateys'. Over 700 Mateys left the dockyards, interrupting ship repair works as well as the movement of Japanese supplies.

BAAG was initially hoping to encourage and help prisoners to escape, but this proved problematic. Most of the senior officers who were imprisoned in Hong Kong were against escape, deterring many men from attempting it, and, in any case, disguising Europeans in China was practically impossible. Major Clague of BAAG was not impressed by this attitude and sent a message to that effect to Argyle Street camp, where most officers had been transferred, in November 1942:

> A much more offensive spirit must be worked up. To hell with this defeatist attitude. There will be risks but I am

---

6. Edwin Ride, *BAAG: Hong Kong Resistance 1942–45*, 122

ordered by the authorities to tell you all especially officers that your duty is obvious.[7]

Conditions at Sham Shui Po were dire, but were misreported in Britain as being fine, with the men being well fed and looked after, according to the International Red Cross. While I expect that this was to calm families' worst fears about their loved ones, it is just as well that the prisoners didn't see the reports as it would have been dispiriting for them when they were already in despair. Mail would only arrive spasmodically, and later on a lot of it was burned as the Japanese censors couldn't keep up with the flow. One artillery officer apparently only received one letter during the whole period of his internment – from his tailor, demanding immediate settlement of an invoice.

By this time, the state of the prisoners was desperate, with illness, infections, starvation and vitamin-deficiency diseases rendering them incapable of escape. Many men were being transferred by ship to Japan, often to their deaths. Dad knew that, with the threat of reprisals against any prisoners who remained, a mass evacuation would be the only way to get the POWs out of Hong Kong. On Saturday 7 November 1942, Dad met with American Colonel Merian Cooper, General Chennault's Chief of Staff (Chennault was Commander of the China Air Task Force (CATF)), to discuss the possibility of developing a plan to evacuate the POWs from Hong Kong. He says:

> I had a discussion with him and two of his Intelligence officers. He then sent them away and we had a very long discussion upon Hong Kong and the POW in general. He asked me to keep the subject of our discussion secret even from General Grimsdale as he wished to think the matter over.

Cooper (1893–1973) was quite a character. He had served as a bomber pilot in the First World War and then joined the Polish as a volunteer pilot in their war against the Russians in 1920. He was convinced that the 'Communist menace' had world domination in its sights and, dis-

---

7. Ride, *BAAG: Hong Kong Resistance 1942–45*, 144–145

appointed that his own government was not taking on the Russians, decided to do so on his own behalf. He was shot down and spent nine months imprisoned in a Soviet POW camp, where typhoid and cholera wiped out many of the internees; he was tortured and threatened three times with execution and then escaped, winning the highest Polish military honour as a result.

Cooper was a founding director of Pan American Airways and was also an innovative film-maker. He was head of production at RKO Pictures 1933–35 and co-wrote, co-directed and appeared in *King Kong* (1933). Cooper plays the pilot who finally kills the beast. The film was groundbreaking in its use of animation and special effects – it impresses even today. Cooper claimed that the story came to him in a nightmare about a giant gorilla attacking New York. Other notable films (many of them made with long-term friend and collaborator John Ford) included *She* (1935) and *She Wore a Yellow Ribbon* (1949). *The Quiet Man* (1952), a hilarious tale set in Ireland and starring John Wayne, which Republic Pictures only agreed to fund as part of a deal to make the western *Rio Grande*, won the best director Oscar and was nominated for best picture. Cooper was also instrumental in the introduction of Technicolor and Cinerama to film-making.

Colonel Ride was conscious that BAAG had been consuming precious resources with little to show for it and so supported the bold idea. However, GHQ in New Delhi, the British Army's HQ in India, wanted the Nationalist forces to take the lead, failing to appreciate the importance of the Communists in the area around Hong Kong. GHQ also wanted the CATF, under the overall command of General Clayton Bissell (Commander of the US Air Forces in the China-Burma-India theatre) to provide the air power for the evacuation. The CATF had replaced the 'Flying Tigers', founded by General Claire Chennault, who acted as Deputy Commander to Bissell from August 1942.

On Wednesday 18 November 1942, Dad flew to Kunming, the capital of Yunnan province, to discuss the top-secret plan, the mass evacuation of prisoners from POW camps in Hong Kong, with Cooper. He did not mention the covert purpose of his trip, but in his diary he says:

I flew down to Kunming in the same plane as General Bissell. This was unfortunate as I don't want him to know what I am up to and it meant that Cooper couldn't see me.

He described the city in a letter home:

> Towards the end of November I visited Kunming. This is a lovely city though even more expensive than Chungking. It is still surrounded by its ancient city wall. I shall never forget coming in through the North Gate on the evening of my arrival. The city is in a wide valley about 6,000ft above sea level. Unlike Chungking the air is clear and crisp. There is a grove of Eucalyptus trees around the North Gate, which is actually a large square tower. You enter from one side through enormous wooden doors, covered with iron plates and spikes, into a very pretty courtyard containing a few Eucalyptus and Cypress trees and the gatekeeper's house; then you turn sharp left through the actual opening in the city wall. Unlike Chungking where all the buildings are in a drab slate colour and the tiles appear to be made of pounded coke, Kunming has quite picturesque buildings and gaily coloured roofs.

They met the following day, and Cooper asked Dad to go with him to Guilin. There they met up with Colonel Ride to talk through the plan in detail:

> Thursday November 26 1942: Cooper came to lunch today. Afterwards we had a long discussion on the intelligence he required and the steps to be taken to prevent news of American Air Force movements on the Kweilin airfield leaking to the enemy. Finally Cooper, Ride and I went out onto the balcony for a long talk. As a result of this Ride and I stayed up most of the night concocting a plan.

The next day Cooper, Chennault and Dad flew back to Kunming at short notice, with General Chennault himself taking the controls as they neared their destination. Cooper instructed Dad to finalise and write up the plan, to Dad's evident excitement. He sat up all Friday night typing up the plan and then took it to Colonel Cooper.

> We had a very long discussion which opened up most pleasurable prospects for me. I have got to make the plan out again, this time in code.

It is agonising to only have this amount of detail on Dad's 'Great Thought', as he called it, but it was a top-secret plan in the middle of war so it is unsurprising, if tantalising, that there is no further record of it.

In a world war being fought on many fronts, the pressure on resources was enormous. There would be a much better chance of being allocated resources to implement the plan if there were a more compelling political objective than simply liberating some POWs who were unfit to fight.

It appears that Dad's plan was a small cog in a greater plan that encompassed the entire Pacific theatre. Chennault and Cooper were strategic and creative thinkers and believed that the Allies would gain most from using China as a base from which to attack Japanese-controlled ports and Japanese shipping travelling between Japan and the Indies. They had already conducted a number of raids on Hong Kong harbour, and Chennault had been absolutely furious when, in late October 1942, he was forced by General Bissell to abandon a bombing raid on Hong Kong at a moment's notice. Chennault knew that the Chinese forces were exhausted, under-resourced and poorly trained. Better to use American air power to repel the Japanese than to expect ground forces to compete against a superior opponent. But, at this moment in military history, air power was still relatively new and the most senior (i.e. oldest) military leaders were not familiar with it. General Stilwell was US Commander in China, and he knew and loved land-based warfare. He was a 59-year-old infantryman and veteran of the First World War, arrogant and conservative in his thinking. He and Chennault were in constant dispute because of their diametrically opposing views on strategy.

According to General Alison of the US Air Force, in an interview recorded in 1958[8], Cooper's plan (which included Dad's plan) to attack Hong Kong was strategically sound:

> This may have been ambitious, but he felt that a bold stroke like this would wrest Hong Kong from the Japanese and severely limit their capability to fight a war because it would prevent them from supplying the homeland. He felt that under the shield of US air power and with US naval support we could not only take Hong Kong but we could hold it.

In June 1943 BAAG tried to get messages into Sham Shui Po with another plan for a mass escape but, disastrously, one of these messages was discovered by the Japanese guards. Captain Douglas Ford of the Royal Scots (aged 25) was the chief suspect, and he was imprisoned in Stanley jail in July 1943, along with Colonel Lance Newnham (aged 54) and Flight Lieutenant Hector Gray (aged 31). They were all interrogated under torture. Colonel Newnham, who had advised Dad about his escape, together with the other two, refused to implicate anyone else. Colonel Newnham repeatedly insisted that he was entirely responsible for organising the attempted escape. They were severely beaten up, starved, and allowed no exercise and no communication with the outside world.

Finally, all three members of the group were sentenced to death. For 18 days they lay alone in their cells with no medical attention, no hope of reprieve, and forbidden to write a note of farewell to relatives and friends. During this period, the Japanese had hoped to break their nerve, and that the group would divulge more information. They failed in this attempt. The three men were eventually murdered by firing squad on 18 December 1943, after being forced to dig their own graves. All three were posthumously awarded the George Cross for gallantry.

BAAG continued to provide what support it could to the prisoners in Hong Kong, but from the second half of 1944 its efforts became

---

8. Interview recorded by Brig Gen John R. Alison, 29 March 1958, in the private papers of Merian C. Cooper, Box 1, Folder 6, held at the Hoover Institution Archives, Stanford, CA. Alison had been a brilliant and courageous airman in the CATF.

increasingly bogged down. BAAG was headquartered in Guilin and, as the Japanese Ichigo campaign advanced, BAAG was torn between supporting the defence of the city and trying to maintain focus on its mission. BAAG eventually had to retreat to Kunming, much further away from Hong Kong and with 'poor relation' status with the Americans, upon whom they depended for air transport. Relations between the Americans and the British in China were steadily decomposing, catalysed by suspicion, US anti-communist ideology and changes in key personnel. Relations with the Chinese were also very strained, with BAAG's reliance on Communist guerrillas in the area around Hong Kong proving too offensive for the Nationalist government to stomach. The Chinese were also increasingly resentful of Britain's post-war colonial ambitions for Hong Kong, which they had lost following the opium wars. To them it epitomised Britain's view that China was not a world power, nor an equal in the Allied power structure.

BAAG continued with its mission to the end of the Second World War, despite being increasingly marginalised, and was eventually disbanded at the end of 1945. Colonel Lindsay Ride remained in Hong Kong and became Vice Chancellor of the University of Hong Kong. He was knighted in 1962.

In 1943 Dad made a return trip from Chongqing to Huizhou, on Military Attaché business, and remarks on how the British were seen by the Chinese at that time:

> When you [Bren Trevor, wife of Dad's old friend Arthur Trevor] wrote your last letter to me in August 1943 (anyway the last I have received) my stooge had just arrived and I was preparing to retrace my steps down south almost right back to Hong Kong. What a difference there was between this trip and my first journey from Hong Kong to Chungking. Then, in the eyes of the Chinese, the British Empire was completely discredited and appeared to be rapidly disintegrating. I was a destitute refugee, always wondering how I was going to make the next stage of the journey and where the next week's meals were going to come from. This time the North African victories had

shown the Chinese that Britain was still the major world power. I had a first class guide and plenty of money.

I was lucky on the journey itself as between Hengyang and Kukong [Shaoguan] the train was delayed (reason: train before have fall off line) and passed through the Pin river gorges in daylight. The scenery was magnificent. China should be able to go into the tourist trade in a big way when the war is over.

It is indicative of the self-image of the British at the time that Dad describes Britain as THE major world power, not just A major world power. The end of the British Empire was only a heartbeat away and America's rise from the ashes of the Great Depression was well under way. China's emergence as a major world power was only a twinkle in Mao's eye, but these seismic shifts in geopolitics were starting to surface, for those who were looking. Perhaps the middle of a war was not the moment to undermine British national self-confidence.

Chongqing now has special status as an area for economic development. It is home to over 30 million people and is a mess of concrete flyovers, sullen ranks of tower blocks and choking traffic. The smog was terrible and I became more and more unhappy as we drove from the airport into town. Even the opera house was ugly. I think they may have had Sydney Opera House in mind but something terrible happened in translation. Most tourists fly into Chongqing, join their Yangzi river cruise and leave without much more than a glance at the city.

It was good to visit General Stilwell's office and meeting rooms, intact with furniture and equipment of the period, helping me to reconnect with Dad's world. There was a photo of Generalissimo and Madame Chiang, whom Dad had met on a couple of occasions. He tells of a British diplomatic mission in November 1942:

> Madame speaks perfect English; her speech of welcome on behalf of the women of China was a masterpiece; not a word wrong and beautifully delivered. It was painful to listen to the halting and rather tactless utterances our representatives made in reply.

Chiang Mei-ling (1897–2003) obviously cast her spell over Dad, among many others. She was from a powerful family and had been educated at Wellesley College in Massachusetts. She was beautiful, stylish, and a charismatic speaker, successfully courting both press and public opinion in the US and earning the support of powerful friends for her husband. Even Churchill was seduced by her sophistication and beauty when she acted as interpreter for Chiang at the Allied conference in Cairo in November 1943, describing her as 'remarkable and charming'. It had been intended that she would go sightseeing to the pyramids but instead she joined the meeting. Wearing a black satin dress with yellow chrysanthemums and the skirt slit up to the hip, she caused a ripple of arousal when she revealingly crossed her legs.

Dad had a real talent for finding enjoyment when there was really very little to be had, another trait that he has passed on to me. Twenty years ago I went on a week-long charity hike across 100 miles of the Judean desert that involved sleeping with 80 fellow fundraisers in a vast tent. The snoring and farting drove me outside to sleep in the desert cold instead, with scorpions for company. Every trip since has felt like blissful luxury in comparison, but it was fun and the stars were spectacular. Dad clearly immersed himself in whatever pleasures of Chinese life presented themselves, going hiking in the hills around Chongqing in his free time and attending Chinese entertainments rather than restricting himself to the ex-pat community:

> I had a very gay time at Christmas 1942. On Christmas Eve a General Ch'eng Chen invited all the allied officers serving in Chungking to a party. He had prepared a good floor, got hold of quite a decent band and had invited more pretty Chinese girls then I had ever suspected to exist in Chungking, where on the whole they are depressingly ugly. He gave us a good buffet supper and unlimited gin and whisky. This must have cost him a fortune. At midnight there was a firework display; a conjuror appeared and produced from nowhere an enormous bowl containing gallons of water and some fishes. I can't think how it was done; I was standing behind him at the time. Later in the evening a troupe of tumblers gave a performance. In

the upper storey of the house he had organised a fair – there was a fortune teller, a caricaturist, a lucky dip and a sort of shooting gallery. I have been to several parties given by this General. He is a very charming old gentleman and has a very nice wife though she can't speak a word of English.

On Christmas Day the Ambassador had a lunch party and in the afternoon I went to a tea party given by the Generalissimo [Chiang Kai-shek] to all ranks of the allied forces serving in Chungking. It was held in the auditorium of the National Military Council. At one end of the room there was a stage with an altar, or at any rate a table with a candle at each end, over which was hung a picture of the Nativity. On the bare whitewashed walls were painted life-size pictures. That on the right depicted the wise men with the camels approaching Bethlehem; on the left a Chinese soldier with Churchill, Roosevelt, Stalin and the other leaders of the United Nations [the UN had been created by President Roosevelt on New Year's Day 1942] trampled on the prostrate bodies of Hitler, Mussolini and the Mikado.

When the Generalissimo arrived we all stood up. The Chinese national anthem was played after which we all sang a Christmas carol. The Europeans and Americans sang in English and the Chinese in Chinese. This is not quite as bad as it sounds as the Chinese translation has the same metre and is sung to the same tune as the original. This was followed by a speech from the Generalissimo, after which we had some more carols and a Christmas play in 4 acts performed by young Chinese children. It was extremely well done. It was accompanied by carols appropriate to the scenes enacted, sung by a Chinese choir in rear of the stage. I think the children must have enjoyed best the scene depicting the shepherds and their flocks. They had most lifelike sheep, though they had some difficulty driving them off the stage. Their masks were difficult to see out of and they had to be driven carefully past the trees on the stage. In the finale the back curtain was raised to reveal the choir waving the flags of the United Nations. A curious ending. After the play we were each presented with a neck tie with the Generalissimo's monogram embroidered on it. Then we sat down to a very good Chinese tea.

I was marginally less impressed with my Chinese tea. I was very pleased to have finally managed to track down a large gin and tonic in my hotel and thought I'd follow it up with dinner. Sadly, the buffet restaurant was offering chicken's feet, pig trotters, flyblown sushi and the sort of mushrooms that you would assume to be toxic, so I had the complimentary packet of dried peas in my room instead.

12

The Devil in the Detail

When I first discovered reference to Dad's Great Thought, his plan to rescue the POWs in Hong Kong, I had no idea that it would lead me to one of the most extraordinary stories of the Second World War. I didn't realise that he was caught up in a titanic struggle between Chennault and Stilwell that altered the course of the Pacific War, ultimately lengthening it and with uncountable loss of life. As briefly mentioned in the previous chapter, the competing strategies of these two men, which niggled through the second half of 1942 and into 1943, were eventually publicly aired at the Trident Conference in Washington during May 1943.

Since 1940, Chennault and Chiang had been asking for increased air power to rid China of the Japanese and to destroy the Japanese navy. Their reasoning was based on Chiang's desire to restore China to freedom and his concern that his army was too thinly spread, too battle-weary and too under-resourced to continue much of a fight. His hidden agenda was to strengthen his forces in preparation for the inevitable post-war battle with the Communist Party.

General Grimsdale, my father's boss from August 1942 until January 1944, was a fan of Chennault, describing him as an outstanding leader and commander. He agreed with Chennault's overarching plan to defeat Japan by attacking Japanese air installations and lines of communication, combined with attacking shipping near the Chinese coast and disabling the major Japanese-occupied ports. This, Grimsdale felt, would be far more efficient and effective than General Stilwell's determination to have a land war in Burma, intended to reopen the Burma Road and bring supplies into China overland. Stilwell was Chennault's ultimate commanding officer and the two had long been rivals. Grimsdale had a meeting with General Archibald Wavell, Commander in Chief of South East Asia Command (SEAC), where Chennault's plan was outlined. Wavell approved the 'air war' plan and informed the British government of his position on the matter. But Chennault needed the agreement of Stilwell to be able to action the plan. Both men presented their strategies to the Allied chiefs at the Trident Conference in 1943.

It took me some time to gather together the pieces of a multi-dimensional jigsaw puzzle that, when assembled, illuminates history through the prism of the key personalities involved. Books written about Stilwell and Chennault have something of the sports fan's blind allegiance to them. Barbara Tuchman's work on Stilwell[1], written in 1970, is determined that his moniker 'Vinegar Joe' tells only a fraction of his story. Tuchman tends to use emotive language both in support of Stilwell and to cast aspersions on Chennault and Chiang. She even justifies Stilwell's failure to argue his case with Roosevelt, likening him to *King Lear*'s Cordelia, who had no need to flatter because she had right on her side. But the timing of Tuchman's book means she did not yet have access to secret files from the period (US army and government papers are declassified after 30 years, so files for 1943 were declassified in 1973) and likewise had no access to Chinese documents, which were not made available until the 1990s. No matter how thorough her research, she could only have a partially obstructed view. Her book is a great read, though, and she won the Pulitzer Prize for it in 1972.

Joseph Alsop was a lifelong friend and admirer of Chennault, so his memoir is somewhat biased in the opposite direction – but an equally fascinating read. I needed several other sources, official documents, Franklin D. Roosevelt's private papers, military and political histories and such like, to be able to make sense of it all, rather like bringing one of those 3-D pictures of dots into sharp focus. Underlying most of the American-authored books is a barely concealed racism towards the Chinese – they are often seen as inferior, sly and corrupt. This brings to mind the general Western attitude towards first peoples – the Australian Aborigines, the Native Americans, the Inuit, for exam-

---

1. Tuchman, B.W. *Stilwell and the American Experience in China 1911–45,* New York: Bantam Books, 1971

ple – who are commonly denigrated as drunks and thieves. There is little attempt to understand their behaviour or to recognise the role of the colonists in driving it. It is true that towards the end of the war the Chinese army abused the locals wherever they went, taking whatever they needed; they stole supplies from the Americans and traded them; constantly asked for more; lacked much fighting spirit and had few skills in modern warfare. I believe they were doing what they had to do to survive, after years of fighting and in an economically collapsing and fragmenting country.

At around this time, in September 1943, Dad had to retrace his escape route, this time on military business, and remarks on a group of refugees he saw on the boat up the East River from Huizhou:

> The whole of the floor space is crowded with refugees. There is one bunch of six, four girls and two little boys, whom Chan [Dad's interpreter on the trip] informs me come from Canton or Hong Kong and have sold themselves to two older women. They are proceeding to the interior where they will be fattened up and then resold as servants, or for adopted children. At the present moment two of them are almost skeletons.

This gives some indication of the utterly destitute and demoralised state of the general Chinese population in Japanese-occupied China.

To tell the story of the air war/land war argument, I need first to describe the main actors, before explaining how a clerical error led to the catastrophic failure of the strategy to defeat Japan that had been agreed by the Allied Powers in May 1943.

Dramatis personae

Chinese

Chiang Kai-shek (CKS) – Leader of the Republic of China 1928–49. Raised in the Confucianist tradition but converted to Christianity after marrying Soong Mei-ling. Elegant, with great personal integrity and charisma, he was a moderniser concerned with restoring nationhood to China, encouraging social, political and economic development. He was beset on all sides by breathtaking levels of corruption and brutality, which he was unwilling or unable to control. In Joseph Alsop's words, 'Chiang Kai-shek, in my opinion, had the stuff of greatness, but he also had more than the average conflicts of greatness.'[2] In particular, he was hampered by a jealous protectiveness of his own power, which led him to ignore his more progressive advisers in favour of trusted but anachronistic retainers.

Chiang (née Soong) Mei-ling – Third wife of CKS, sister of T.V. Soong, Mme Sun Yat-sen and Kung Ai-ling. A charming siren who hid a steel fist in a silken glove. She captivated Congress with her speech in 1943 and toured the USA fundraising for China. She was Chiang's best advertisement and persuaded the American public that China was their great friend and equal. She persistently lobbied Roosevelt on behalf of her husband. In October 1943, though, she went against her husband's wishes, namely the proposal of her brother T.V. Soong that Stilwell should be replaced. She argued that this would make public the rift between the US and China, when the threat from Japan was still great. This argument persuaded Chiang, and he asked that Stilwell should stay after all.

T.V. Soong – Foreign Minister and brother-in-law to Chiang, and a wealthy businessman. Well liked in Washington but undermined by his scheming sisters, Chiang Mei-ling and Kung Ai-ling. They spent September 1943 chatting up Stilwell and supporting his position. This was primarily to put their brother in an untenable position politically, so as to stifle his ascendency and to strengthen their own power base. He was humiliated when his request for Stilwell's removal was overruled by Chiang and he was then effectively removed from power.

American

Franklin D. Roosevelt – President of USA 1933–45, cousin of Joseph Alsop (see below). Regarded by some as one of the top three US presidents, with George Washington and Abraham Lincoln. Preferred to

---

2. J.W. Alsop and A. Platt, *I've Seen the Best of It*, New York: WW Norton & Co, 1992, 203

use his own private advisers, such as Harry Hopkins and Wendell Willkie, rather than military ones.

General Joseph Stilwell – Chiang's Chief of Staff, appointed in March 1942, and Commander of Allied forces in China. Known as 'Vinegar Joe' for his acerbic tongue and readiness for contempt. Fluent in Mandarin and several other languages, including Japanese. Given the amount of time he had spent in China through the interwar years and his facility with the language, I find it surprising that he seems such a Sinophobe. Grimsdale remarks that 'he frequently spoke to me in the most scathing and disparaging terms of the Chinese'. He did not hesitate to call them 'conscienceless crooks' while at the same time appointing his own son Head of Intelligence as well as having two sons-in-law in his command. A courageous and tactical infantryman with little time or talent for planning and administration, he much preferred to command his men in the field rather than from the office.

General Claire Chennault – An aviator since the 1920s, Chennault 'retired' from the US army in 1937 after being frustrated by his failure to overturn antiquated air warfare theories in favour of his more forward-thinking approach. Air adviser to Chiang Kai-shek from 1937 and Commander of the 'Flying Tigers' (three US fighter squadrons of around ninety aircraft), he was recommissioned by the US Army in July 1942 and the Flying Tigers became the China Air Task Force (CATF) and then, in March 1943, the 14th Air Force. He lobbied President Roosevelt from autumn 1942 onwards with his certainty that he could defeat Japan from the air in China. This led to him being labelled a maverick and being regarded with suspicion by the establishment, as he had bypassed the chain of command. In 1945 he was frustrated again by being removed from useful service by Generals Marshall and Arnold, who bore him a grudge, and retired again.

General George Marshall – Army Chief of Staff, long-standing friend and admirer of Stilwell and had appointed him to Commander in China. Antagonistic to Chennault, whom he considered unfit for command because he believed he had no knowledge of logistics and was too heavily influenced by CKS (according to Tuchman). Described Chennault's air strategy as being nonsense, beyond just bad strategy.[3] He felt that a land war was the best approach and was influenced by Stilwell to believe that Chinese troops could be brought up to scratch to fight the Japanese – a key weakness of Stilwell's plan. Lobbied Roosevelt in the spring of 1943 to adopt a land-based strategy and was then furious when Roosevelt sided with Chennault. Anti-Chiang and the Nationalists to the point where he actively supported the Communists in the post-war Chinese Civil War.

General Henry 'Hap' Arnold – Air Chief of Staff and lifelong friend of Marshall. Not present at the Trident Conference due to having had a heart attack a few days before it began.

Harry Hopkins – Close adviser to Roosevelt and friend of Alsop from pre-war days. 'A most curious man – on one side a passionate social worker, toiling tirelessly to relieve human suffering, and, on the other, fun-loving and raffishly disreputable... Although he cared nothing about money and his clothes always seemed to have been purchased from a pawn shop, he had a great liking for worldly and glittering company, adored pretty women and greatly enjoyed a social drink.' Usually friendly with Marshall, but the Chennault affair caused a rift between them, causing a communication breakdown between the War Department and Roosevelt at the time of the Trident Conference. He was also friendly with T.V. Soong and agreed with him that Stilwell should be replaced.

Joseph Alsop – A Harvard graduate and journalist, he'd also flown with Chennault's Flying Tigers. He effectively became staff officer to Chennault in 1942, although technically employed in the Lend-Lease administration (essentially a US foreign aid fund supplying cash and equipment in support of its allies). He was a cousin of Roosevelt and a key Washington insider from the 1930s to the '50s. He lobbied Roosevelt's key adviser, Harry Hopkins, with eloquent letters in support of Chennault's strategy.

Colonel James McHugh – US Naval Attaché, based in Chongqing. Very much in the Chennault camp, host to Joseph Alsop and close friend of General Grimsdale.

---

3. B.W. Tuchman, *Stilwell and the American Experience in China, 1911–45* New York: Macmillan, 1971
4. J.W. Alsop and A. Platt, *I've Seen the Best of It*, New York: WW Norton & Co, 1992, 197

British

Field Marshal Archibald Wavell – Commander in Chief, India (later renamed South East Asia Command, SEAC) and veteran of the Second Boer War and the First World War. Didn't always enjoy Churchill's support and was regarded by the Americans as dragging his heels with respect to Britain's engagement in China and Burma.

Field Marshal Sir John Dill – personal representative of Churchill in Washington, Chief of the British Joint Staff Mission, a role given to him to keep him out of Churchill's way as they didn't get on. Excellent diplomat. Friend of General George Marshall and together they influenced Roosevelt.

General Gordon Grimsdale – British Military Attaché and General Officer Commanding, British Military Mission in China, Chongqing. He spent 18 years as an Intelligence Officer in Asia before the Second World War.

The Drama

Matters were tense between the Allied powers throughout the war, with the British and Americans mistrusting each other, and each regarding Russia as a friend only in so far as it was their enemy's enemy. China, to Chiang's fury, was regarded as very much the junior and least important member of the Allied power structure. Within China, Chiang's government was seen as weak and corrupt, Mao's Communists were seeking to take power, and economically the country was on its knees. By the end of the war, China was paradoxically 'simultaneously in the strongest global position it had ever occupied and weaker than it had been for nearly a century'.[5] Somewhere between 14 and 20 million Chinese died in the eight years of conflict with Japan, 1937–45.

Britain and America had very different opinions about the Pacific theatre. Roosevelt felt that China was a sovereign nation that would become a major world power in the post-war years. The Lend-Lease scheme was to give $1.6 billion in support of China during the course

---

5. Rana Mitter, *China's War With Japan 1937–1945: The Struggle for Survival*, London: Allen Lane, 2013, 369

of the war. Roosevelt was determined to keep China in the war, to use as a base against Japan's home territory and to divide Japan's offensive efforts. Roosevelt was also influenced by the need to shore up Chiang's government in order for China to fulfil these roles. By 1943 the Nationalist government was close to collapse, which would have been disastrous for the Allies, removing the need for Japan to have a million troops in China. The Chinese army might have been much criticised by the Americans but it was still an effective opponent, obliging Japan to keep troops in China rather than deploying them elsewhere.

The British, on the other hand, saw China as weak and disunited and saw no reason to create an Asian powerhouse to replace Japan that might cost them Hong Kong. The British were also preoccupied with protecting and/or regaining their other colonies, primarily India and Burma, but also Malaya, Borneo and Singapore. Americans wryly referred to SEAC as standing for 'Save England's Asian Colonies'. The British and Americans did agree that a base in China from which to attack Japan was essential. Although the Americans were dismissive of Britain's actions in China, this had in fact been agreed between them – Britain would take the lead in assisting certain countries, such as Turkey, while America would assist others, such as China. Britain's concern was that the Americans were too focused on the Far East and were not placing enough emphasis on defeating the Nazis in Europe.

Stilwell had been foisted on Chiang in March 1942 as his Chief of Staff, and the two had almost immediately started a power struggle, with Chiang wanting support from US ground troops and Stilwell wanting Chinese forces to go to Burma to repel the Japanese invasion. The two men had little time for each other and their relationship was very tense. It was only because Chiang needed Allied support that he tolerated the situation.

Stilwell was an inexperienced General, reckless and arrogant. It is hard to say whom he detested more – Chiang or the British – but he didn't try to hide his feelings, and this compromised Allied co-operation. He had ordered a campaign to retake Burma from the Japanese in March 1942, which was ill-conceived and poorly executed, ending in retreat to India in May 1942 with the loss of 25,000 Chinese troops and 10,000 British and Indian troops. This episode marked the beginning of his obsession with the development of the Burma Road, wanting to extend it across northern Burma to Ledo in India, thereby opening a land supply route into China that avoided the Burmese port of Rangoon. In October 1944 Chiang eventually succeeded in removing Stilwell, after President Roosevelt had tried to make him Commander in Chief of all Chinese troops. Chiang said he would tolerate an American commander, but not Stilwell. British General William Slim's assessment of Stilwell was mixed, but he concluded that:

> He was a first class battle leader up to, I should say, Corps level, and an excellent tactician, but a poor administrator. At higher levels he had neither the temperament nor the strategic background or judgement to be effective.[6]

Stilwell was convinced that the tonnage (everything from hospital tents to spare parts and military equipment) that could be supplied by air was hugely insufficient to meet the needs of the war effort. At the time, only about 5,000 tons per month were being flown over 'the hump' (the eastern end of the Himalayas between Burma and China) from India to China. His plan was to provide 60 divisions (about 150,000 men) of Chinese troops with modern US equipment, train them and then retake northern Burma, connecting with Chinese troops in India, and thus occupy territory on which the new road to Ledo could be built. This was an attractive plan to Chiang, in one sense, as it meant getting his hands on valuable American resources and saved him the trouble of supplying a large part of his army. In another sense, though, he had no desire to send his troops into Burma as he felt this would have no impact on driving the Japanese out of China. Chiang chose the pragmatic option of allowing his troops to be supplied and trained by the Americans. He was desperate for supplies of all kinds to be brought into China – his population and his army were starving and he was seduced by the idea that the new road might bring relief. He made it a condition that his troops would be

---

6. Frank McLynn, *The Burma Campaign: Disaster into triumph 1942–45* New Haven: Yale University Press, 2011, 408

commanded by their own officers, a condition that mysteriously failed to be communicated to the US War Department.

This plan was a potential source of serious friction, with the Chinese regarding American officers as 'advisers' but with the Americans expecting to command the Chinese troops. The Chinese army, furthermore, was not trained in modern warfare; the men were half-starved and exhausted and had no appetite for this fight. Moving this vast number of men, training them, feeding and supplying them in the timescale required was the stuff of fantasy. Also, the Generalissimo had ultimate control of how they were deployed, so he could have vetoed plans and scuppered the entire endeavour at any moment.

Joseph Alsop explains why the Chinese leadership was susceptible to Stilwell's ideas:

> The Generalissimo and T.V. Soong, because they had very little knowledge of the practical aspects of the modern war in which they found themselves, were just as convinced as General Stilwell that the real remedy to the situation was to open a new route into China to replace the Burma Road [now in Japanese hands]. The proposed 'Ledo Road' was the centrepiece of the general's offensive plan. It was Whiting 'Whitey' Willauer [T.V. Soong's deputy and an old friend of Alsop] who convinced me that the road remedy desired by the Chinese and Gen Stilwell was, to put it mildly, a bit simplistic. Only a few minutes work with a slide rule were required to discover that the hundreds of miles of road, most of it through awesomely rough terrain, could not in fact deliver any worthwhile supply tonnage to China. The US army trucks of those days would have needed to carry just about their total cargo capacity in gasoline for themselves in order to make the long transit from Assam [in north-east India] to Kunming.[7]

Supplies for the land war began to be stockpiled in Yunnan, taking up valuable air cargo space that could have been used for bombs and

---

7. J.W. Alsop and A. Platt, *I've Seen the Best of It*, New York: WW Norton & Co, 1992, 206

THE DEVIL IN THE DETAIL

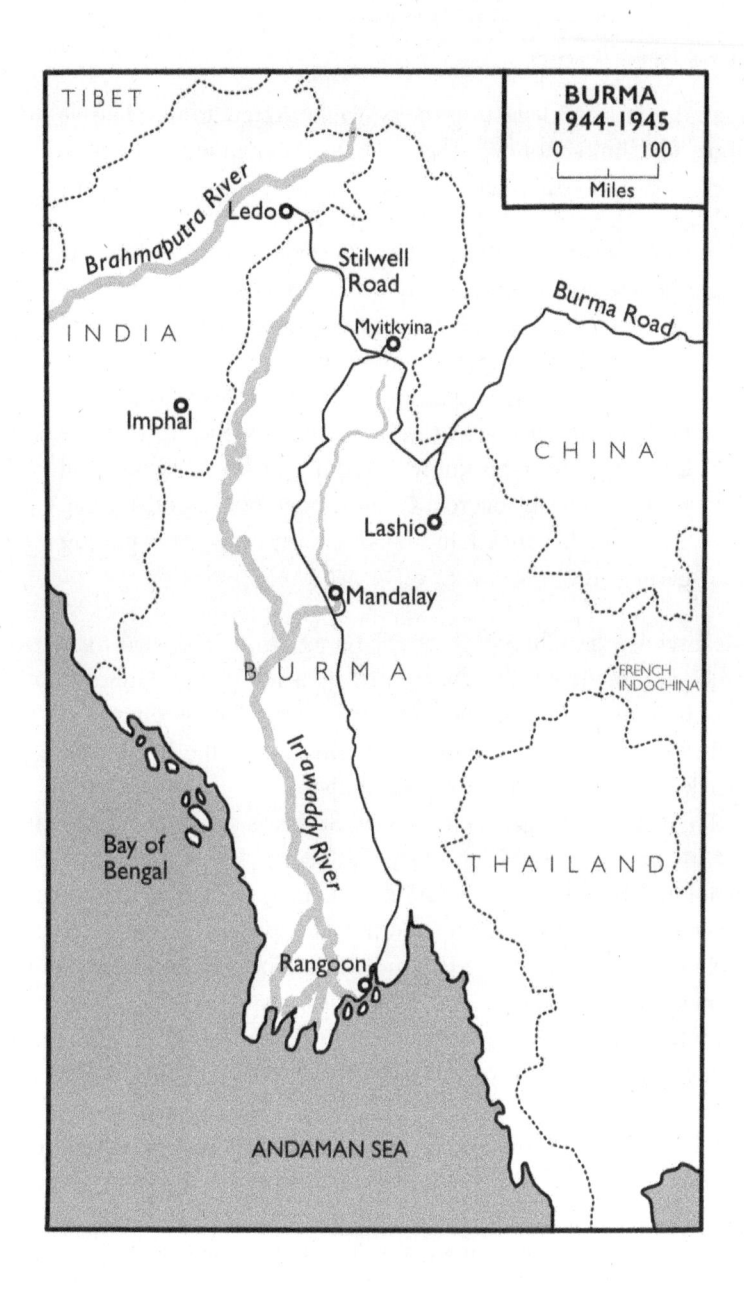

**BURMA
1944-1945**

Map of Burma 1944–45.

ammunition, and deflecting the available aircrew from offensive missions. The limited tonnage that could be flown in was not wisely chosen, as General Grimsdale explained:

> Considerable numbers of large hospital tents were sent; the Chinese could very quickly run up excellent bamboo wattle huts which would have been just as suitable; a lot of carts and harness were brought in that were quite useless for the tiny Chinese ponies that were available; there was even an authenticated case of a complete load of garbage cans. Anyone who knows anything of life in China will realise how valuable to a Chinese household a garbage can would be, but it certainly would never be used for putting garbage in.[8]

Meanwhile, the Chinese troops at Ramgarh in India had their own problems, due largely to the cultural insensitivities of American officers, who didn't respect the authority of the Chinese officers, on top of insufficient tactical training. This meant that the Indian prong of attack on Burma could not be relied upon.

The US War Department was on Stilwell's side, not least because it was run by his old friend General George Marshall. Marshall had appointed Stilwell to Commander in China, and was antagonistic to Chennault, whom he considered unfit for command, feeling that he had no knowledge of logistics and was too heavily influenced by the Generalissimo. Ironically, the British view, expressed by Field Marshal Archibald Wavell, was that it was Stilwell who lacked any appreciation of practical logistics and that consequently his Burma plan was quite unworkable.

Chennault had shown, first with the 'Flying Tigers' and then, from July 1942, with the CATF, that his small fleet was capable of inflicting considerable damage on Japanese shipping, both on the Yangzi River and off the coast. He had made excellent use of his limited resources to

---

8. From the private papers of General Gordon Grimsdale, held at the Imperial War Museum, London, p77

constantly attack Japanese airfields, reducing their capacity for retaliation. This combined approach effectively protected defenceless Chinese cities from air attack, stymied Japanese movements in China (as the road and rail infrastructure was inadequate and inefficient compared to the waterways) and disrupted Japanese shipping that was heading for targets elsewhere in South East Asia. According to Lieutenant General Takahashi, commander of Japanese forces in Central China:

> Considering all the difficulties my armies encountered in China... I judge the operations of the US air force to have constituted between 60% and 75% of our effective opposition in China. Without the air force we could have gone anywhere we wished.[9]

In the autumn of 1942, President Roosevelt's personal adviser, Wendell Willkie, and US Naval Attaché, Colonel Jim McHugh, both reported to Roosevelt that Chennault had a plausible plan for defeating Japan using air power. McHugh went as far as suggesting that Stilwell should be replaced by Chennault (a view he had expressed to Wavell on his way to Washington), which General Marshall responded to with violent outrage, claiming that this indecent proposal did irreparable harm to the war effort in the China-Burma-India theatre.

At the end of 1942, after the discussions with Cooper and my father, Chennault wrote a paper outlining his proposed approach for consideration by General Grimsdale, which included bombing Hong Kong, Guangzhou, Shanghai and other key harbours. Obviously Chennault was in favour of air power, but he included other factors in his analysis of the situation. As well as his history of successful strikes against the Japanese with a very small air force, Chennault was extremely well supplied with intelligence about Japanese movements, through the services of BAAG. This gave him a significant tactical advantage. Also, by this time the Chinese people were stretched beyond their limits and more or less incapable of further fight, and there had been

---

9. Gen CL Chennault – a guide to his papers held at the Hoover Institution archives, Imperial War Museum, London

a build-up of Wang Jingwei's Japanese-supported collaborationist armies, adding to the threat to China's sovereignty. Wang was an old foe of Chiang's and at this time was in charge of a Japanese-sponsored puppet government in Nanjing. The weakness of China and its Nationalist government was reaching a critical moment, as much a threat to the Allies as to Chiang.

Grimsdale approved Chennault's plan and forwarded it to Field Marshal Wavell, his commanding officer. Wavell thought the plan a little ambitious – Chennault famously boasted that he could defeat Japan with just 150 aircraft (and in six months) – but the underlying strategy was sound. Wavell was already opposed to a land war in Burma, and had been convinced by McHugh's preference for Chennault's strategy, so this air-based plan was pushing at an open door.

Roosevelt had long been in favour of the air-based strategy, and had discussed it with Churchill at the Casablanca Conference in January 1943. Sir John Dill had also been present at the Casablanca Conference and was sent to the Pacific theatre in February 1943, with General Arnold, to discuss the plans that had been proposed at the conference. At this stage the plans were not fully formed, but both a land invasion of northern Burma and an air attack on Japan and its shipping had been agreed. Dill and his party visited Wavell in India, on the way to Chongqing. Wavell told them that a land invasion would be unsuccessful without an accompanying seaborne attack on Rangoon. They continued on to Chongqing, to present the plans to Chiang. Dad's diary for Sunday, 7 February 1943 tells of a meeting he had with Dill:

> FM Sir John Dill arrived on Friday. On Saturday he came into the office. He asked a lot of questions about Hong Kong. Saturday night he spent with the Generalissimo. I believe he went this afternoon.

It seems that at this stage the attack on Hong Kong, with the added benefit of liberating the POWs held there, was very much on the agenda, as part of the offensive against Japanese-held harbours.

The Casablanca Conference plan for a China-based air assault on Japan had – rather unwisely – been announced in the press, which the

Japanese had read with interest and responded to accordingly. Chennault was alarmed by the build-up of Japanese ground and air forces in China and wrote[10] to Stilwell to request an immediate increase in fighters, bombers, supplies and personnel to counter Japanese advances and to disable their airbases. Chennault was supported by Chiang, who demanded from the US government an increase in airfreight tonnage to 10,000 tons per month and a further 500 aircraft for the Chinese army. In March 1943 Roosevelt acquiesced, going against the recommendations of his own War Department. Arnold and Marshall were furious at being undermined but were forced to comply. Arnold had been arguing for Chennault to remain under the command of General Bissell, not for him to be effectively given his own private air force! Roosevelt didn't go as far as replacing Stilwell with Chennault, but he did rebuke Stilwell for his condescension towards Chiang. He specifically stated that most of the tonnage should comprise supplies for Chennault.

Stilwell and Chennault were summoned to Washington, D.C. to present to the Allied powers their opposing strategies for the war against Japan, at the Trident Conference in May 1943. They arrived a fortnight before the conference began to have private meetings with Roosevelt. Poor Mr President was between a rock and a hard place. On the one hand he had the War Department, headed by Marshall and Arnold, pressurising him to agree to a land war in Burma. On the other, he had Chiang, leader of the fourth Allied Power, Chennault, his adviser Hopkins and his cousin Alsop all sharing his conviction that the air strategy should prevail.

Apparently, Chennault made a convincing appraisal of his needs for the air-based plan:

> Two groups of fighters, one medium bombardment group (96 aircraft), one heavy bombardment group (72 aircraft), and a reconnaissance squadron, plus reserves for all four categories. The Chinese Air Force would require 80 fighters and 40 medium bombers. Initially 4790 tons a month would permit the operation to get under way (to gain con-

---

10. Private papers of General CL Chennault, Box 8, Folder 14, held at the Hoover Institution, Stanford, CA.

trol over China's air space), eventually building up to 7128 tons a month in the final (bombardment) stage. Chennault did not feel that the Japanese would be any more successful in repelling such an assault than they had been in the past, and if they made the attempt, their efforts in other theaters would be reduced.[11]

Stilwell made a poor impression on Roosevelt, to the point where Marshall felt obliged to personally vouch for him. Roosevelt asked both men what they thought of Chiang. Stilwell spat: 'He's a vacillating tricky undependable old scoundrel who never keeps his word.' Chennault countered: 'Sir, I think the Generalissimo is one of the two or three greatest military and political leaders in the world today. He has never broken a promise or commitment made to me.'[12] Roosevelt had major reservations about Stilwell occupying a role that required tact, diplomacy and negotiation skills when these were clearly Stilwell's chief failings. When Stilwell tried to point out flaws in Chennault's strategy, for example, such as the lack of defences for Chongqing and Kunming against a Japanese ground-based retaliation, he mumbled and fumed and held his head in his hands rather than giving a cogent argument.

Most of the conference was taken up with discussions about the European theatre, but the discussion about the Pacific theatre was interlinked, as the British and Americans had different priorities and agreement had to be reached on strategy for both theatres. Churchill was strongly opposed to war in Burma, saying: 'Going into swampy jungles to fight the Japanese is like going into the water to fight a shark.'[13] The Trident Conference took place just after the disastrous first Arakan Campaign in Burma in 1942–43, when the Allies had been completely wrong-footed by the Japanese and forced to retreat. It had become obvious that the Allied forces were under-trained and unfit for jungle warfare in comparison to their enemy. This defeat was on top of Stilwell's own disastrous foray into Burma in March 1942.

---

11. Maurice Matloff, *Strategic Planning for Coalition Warfare 1943–1944* Center of Military History: US Army, 1994

12. B.W. Tuchman, *Stilwell and the American Experience in China, 1911–45*, New York: Macmillan, 1971

13. W.M. Bagby, *The Eagle-Dragon Alliance: America's Relations with China in World War II*, Newark: University of Delaware Press, 1992, 78

Wavell was present at the conference and made it clear that his preference was for an air-based strategy in China. He was against war in Burma as a means of opening up a land-based supply route. He explained to the meeting the administrative, logistical, command, climatological and medical problems of fighting in Burma. He anticipated a 25 per cent malaria rate per month and didn't expect the road to be openable until 1945.

T.V. Soong represented Chiang at the conference. He too was against war in Burma and asked that the tonnage flown over the hump should be for the air forces. He regarded the war in Burma as having little to do with China, unless it was combined with a naval assault on Rangoon, the port of entry to the existing Burma Road.

Rather than dictate the outcome of the debate, Roosevelt diplomatically put it to a vote. The official outcome of the Trident Conference was that China was to be kept in the war to serve as a base from which to launch a 'sustained, systematic and large-scale air offensive' against Japan. A key harbour was needed, preferably Hong Kong, to supply Allied forces in China, but this would follow after the opening of a new Burma Road, known as the Ledo Road. Thus the overland operation in Burma was seen merely as a necessary precursor, a means of augmenting supplies to China for the air attack, not as an offensive to regain control of the country. The Japanese were far superior at jungle warfare – the better strategy was to bomb their shipping and homeland and win the war that way. Effectively, Chennault's argument had won the day.

Other features of the Pacific strategy involved retaking the Philippines, Taiwan and various islands in the Western Pacific (including the Mariana Islands, from where the atomic bombings were eventually launched), to provide further bases from which to attack Japan and to interrupt Japanese lines of communication. The British hankered after an attack on northern Sumatra as a staging post to regaining Singapore, but there was no American support for this sideshow.

Immediately after the conference, Chennault was urgently recalled to China to repel the latest Japanese attack. On the eve of his departure, President Roosevelt asked to meet with him privately to show him a draft directive to see if it met his needs. Chennault said that it was exactly what he needed and left, fully satisfied with the outcome of the meeting and anticipating a significant increase in supplies to implement an air war against Japan. For some reason, however, the President failed to initial the directive – 'FDR'.[14] This fateful aberration was not corrected. The War Department, led by Marshall, was determined to have a land war and this was their golden opportunity. Nothing that Chennault could do would oblige them to return the directive to the President for signature.

Superficially it seemed that Chennault had won the debate, and certainly the press reports at the time and military history books written since have said as much. Chennault was acutely aware that he had dangerously challenged Stilwell's authority and that Stilwell was now like an enraged bear, ordered to implement, as Chennault acknowledged, 'a subordinate's plan with which he violently disagreed'.[15, 77] Chennault must have been devastated but not surprised when the plan failed to be executed. The tonnage over the hump massively increased (eventually to 50,000 tons per month), but it was used principally to service the needs of the land war, in line with Stilwell's desires. Chennault had difficulty even in reserving enough tonnage to bring fuel for his planes to be able to defend Stilwell's airfield in Yunnan, let alone to attack the Japanese.

T.V. Soong immediately noticed that only the first phase of Chennault's plan (securing China's airspace) was to be implemented. He wrote to Roosevelt on 22 May 1943 (before the Trident Conference had formally concluded) to plead again for a directive to implement the full plan:

> Am I not right in believing that it was your decision to put into effect Chennault's entire plan of operations? You will recall that in his plan's second phase, which should start three to four months from the beginning of the offensive, Chennault will go forward from the attack on the Japanese supply lines and installations in China and sea lanes along

---

14. According to the private papers of General Gordon Grimsdale, held at the Imperial War Museum, London, 83
15. W.M. Bagby, *The Eagle-Dragon Alliance: America's Relations with China in World War II*, Newark: University of Delaware Press, 1992

our coasts, to the attack on the Japanese islands proper with his long range bombers. The priority of 4700 tons monthly satisfies the needs of the first phase; as he has pointed out, to support the second phase a priority of 2300 tons additional or 7000 monthly will be required. ... I am informed that in order to permit the necessary scheduling of air operations and equipment this clarification is indispensable.[16]

Roosevelt forwarded the letter to the War Department, and General McNarney, Marshall's Deputy Chief of Staff, replied, advising the President not to commit to this second phase, arguing that Stilwell would need the additional tonnage for the Burma land offensive.

Stung by their defeat and public humiliation at the Trident Conference, the War Department and Stilwell continually conspired to hamstring Chennault's plans. Like spoiled children who have been made to play their little brother's game, they used every underhand and spiteful trick to sabotage it. They hijacked tonnage for their own purposes and they deliberately prevented ammunition from reaching the Chinese army. Stilwell successfully absorbed much of the increased tonnage that was subsequently airfreighted from India, so that Chennault was chronically undersupplied with the essentials to carry out offensive action, and Hong Kong was not retaken by the Allies. The prisoners' predicament steadily worsened as the war wore on.

General McNarney put the boot in wherever he could. At the end of June 1943, he wrote to Roosevelt's personal Chief of Staff, the military's highest ranking officer, Admiral Leahy, who reported only to Roosevelt, to undermine Chiang. He suggested that China's need of a further substantial loan was exaggerated and that the Chinese efforts at building new airfields were too slow to be useful and anyway dogged by corruption, with black market rates of exchange massively increasing the US dollar cost of these capital projects. Chennault had already explained to the President that the delay in construction of new airfields occurred because 'in my absence the issuance of contrary orders interrupted the work'.[17]

By the end of July, the shortages of supplies, new aircraft, additional

---

16. President's Secretary's File, Series 3: Diplomatic Correspondence, Box 27 – China 1943, FDR Library, accessed online at www.fdrlibrary.marist.edu.

fighter and bomber groups and suitable pilots were making progress impossible. Chennault met with Chiang to explain what was happening. After this meeting, on 30 July, Madame Chiang wrote an impassioned and detailed letter[18] to Roosevelt specifying the shortfalls and identifying what was needed. She emphasised the urgency of the situation, partly in respect of preserving China's freedom and partly in relation to utilising the best flying weather of the autumn months. She did not receive a reply from Roosevelt until September, when his response was drafted for him by General Arnold. It is a masterful example of oleaginous condescension, wrapped around half-promises and regretful apologies about the delays and difficulties that must be expected in war. Floods in Yunnan, pilots being hospitalised, ships carrying supplies being sunk and, of course, the lack of the Burma Road were all employed as plausible excuses for the strangling of Chennault's baby.

Stilwell was replaced in his role as Commander of the US air forces in China by General Stratemeyer in mid-1943, but he too was a friend of General Arnold and was viscerally opposed to Chennault. In December 1943, Chennault wrote ruefully to General Merrill at SEAC,[19] saying that most of the Japanese planes then flying in Burma would not have been flying if the promised increases in bombers and fighters for the American 14th Air Force (the new name for the CATF) had been delivered in July. Japanese airbases in eastern China had not been destroyed, and Japanese planes overflying western China to reach Burma could not be attacked for lack of planes, fuel and ammunition.

The British reluctantly agreed to enter northern Burma from Assam, via Ledo and Imphal, with the American and Chinese troops entering from Yunnan in China. Their objective was to complete the building of a new road from Ledo to connect with the old Burma Road, across almost 500 miles of swampy, sweaty jungle, including 10 major rivers. In the end this took 50,000 men to build, cost the lives of 2,000 of them, and eventually opened in January 1945. At the

17. President's Secretary's File, Series 4: Departmental Correspondence, Box 83 – War, Chennault Claire L, FDR Library, accessed online at www.fdrlibrary.marist.edu.
18. President's Secretary's File, Series 3: Diplomatic Correspondence, Box 27 – China 1943, FDR Library, accessed online at www.fdrlibrary.marist.edu.
19. Private papers of General CL Chennault, Box 8, Folder 18, held at the Hoover Institution, Stanford, CA.

beginning of 1944, more capacious Douglas C-54 transport planes were introduced, and air tonnage increased massively during the year. After the capture of Myitkyina, with its strategically important airfield, deliveries jumped from 18,000 tons in June 1944 to 39,000 in November 1944, and so the justification for the Ledo Road began to crumble. The Ledo Road never achieved the tonnage Stilwell claimed for it and, until the end of the war, airfreight over the hump far exceeded that carried overland. Furthermore, overland supplies had to arrive by ship at Calcutta and then be transported to Ledo via the small-gauge railways, designed to serve the tea plantations of Assam, or the few roads winding up the hillsides. At the time, the eastern side of India had poorly developed road and rail infrastructure, as the British had only expected trouble from the west. It was a six- to seven-day journey by rail from Calcutta to Assam, and the maximum tonnage per day never exceeded 4,000 tons. As time went on, it also became clear that the Chinese forces were not going to be able to evict the Japanese from Burma, but by then much time, effort and life had been wasted.

At the beginning of 1944, China was sliding down the war agenda again, as Allied attention turned back to Europe and Operation 'Overlord', the plan to retake France and push towards Berlin. The attack planned for Normandy meant that amphibious vehicles and air and sea support would all be prioritised for the European theatre rather than for the invasion of Burma from Rangoon. China's role as a strategic ally was losing its cachet, and Chiang's demands for further loans and aircraft were regarded as the grandiose tantrums of a minor despot, rather than the desperate request of an equal in the alliance. Chiang, Stilwell and Chennault were rather left to their own devices, with Stilwell obsessively facing towards Burma, while Japan prepared its Ichigo campaign to extend its reach further into southern China and connect with its captured territories in Indo-China, to Chiang and Chennault's great alarm.

By April 1944, Chennault felt obliged to write again to Roosevelt, identifying the urgent need for more supplies in the face of imminent offensives by the Japanese in China. He clearly understood the strategic importance of preventing Japan from gaining a defensive stronghold in China, to counter its looming losses in the Pacific and South East Asia. He desperately argued for support:

> Owing to the present concentration of our resources on the fighting in Burma, little has been done to strengthen the Chinese Armies in the interior, and for the same reason the 14th and Chinese Airforces are still operating on a shoestring. If we were even a little stronger I would not be worried.[20]

Chennault wrote again at the end of May 1944, confirming that his worst fears had been realised and fearing for the loss of China as an Allied base, which would seriously compromise any hope of victory against Japan. His frustration at his requests and strategic thinking being repeatedly ignored is almost palpable, with fierce underlining, complaints about Stilwell's inaction, and urgent entreaties to the President to act. Another letter was sent at the end of June, with more weary 'I told you so's' as Japan's Ichigo campaign forged relentlessly southward towards Changsha and Hengyang. This letter was accompanied by a chummy note from Joe Alsop, addressed to Grace Tully, the President's private secretary. Alsop says resignedly:

> The worst that the General feared and foresaw has now, unhappily, been permitted to occur. The General feels he should make another report to the President, which I therefore enclose. He is pretty well past caring what happens, but I hope that you can again arrange to have this report, like its predecessors, treated as being for the President's eyes alone. For I judge it will infuriate without educating the rather ineducable War Department, and while every word that the General says is true, the purpose of the letter is merely to bring the President personally up to date, and not to become the subject of official action. That must be taken through ordinary channels.[21]

---

20. President's Secretary's File, Series 4: Departmental Correspondence, Box 83 – War, Chennault Claire L, FDR Library, accessed online at www.fdrlibrary.marist.edu.
21. President's Secretary's File, Series 4: Departmental Correspondence, Box 83 – War, Chennault Claire L, FDR Library, accessed online at www.fdrlibrary.marist.edu.

As far as I can tell, it was mainly Chennault's disregard for the chain of command that explains the War Department's attitude towards him and that precipitated his downfall. In fact, though, Roosevelt had invited Chennault to write to him directly, and, in any case, when he tried to use the proper channels he was repeatedly blocked. Furthermore, the War Department disregarded their own chain of command – Roosevelt, Churchill and ultimately the entire Allied political and military 'heads of government' who had agreed Chennault's strategy – in pursuit of a petty vendetta. The War Department also suffered from stubborn reliance on traditional warfare methods.

Air power was still new and required an entirely different way of thinking. Italian Giulio Douhet is considered the father of air power, and his book *Command of The Air* (1921) is regarded as a classic. He argued that command of the air should be the first objective during war and, having achieved it, subsequent bombing of industrialised and population centres would be so disruptive and destructive that the enemy would be forced to sue for peace. He maintained, over-optimistically, that control of the air followed by strategic bombing could win a war, independent of land and sea power. One of his acolytes, American aviator Billy Mitchell (with whom Merian Cooper had flown), visited Japan in 1924 and saw that they were developing air power with great enthusiasm. He predicted that the Pacific War would start with a Japanese air and sea attack upon Pearl Harbor in Hawaii with an accompanying aerial attack on the Philippines, at 7.30am and 10.40am respectively. In fact, the attack on Pearl Harbor occurred at 7.55am and on the Philippines at 12.45am on 7 December 1941. Mitchell was off by only 25 minutes for Hawaii and less than two hours for the Philippines. Mitchell was later court-martialled for being publicly critical of his own military's sluggishness in developing air power.[22] In a rigid, top-down hierarchy such as the military, novel ideas from the layer below could not easily break through the reinforced-concrete ceiling.

As we know, the land war in Burma went ahead, and the Allies got thoroughly bogged down there until early 1945. There was an increase in the number of US aircraft flying from China, but they

---

22. Evolution of Air Power at http://www.defencejournal.com/2001/november/evolution.htm.

were directed to Burma to provide cover for the ground troops. There were successful air attacks against Japan eventually, but the major offensives didn't start until November 1944, after the Mariana Islands were recaptured and could be used as a base. The introduction of the B-29 bomber in mid-1944 had allowed longer-range sorties against Japan from India, but surely the whole effort would have been much more efficient and effective had Chennault's plan been followed?

Grimsdale despondently says:

> It is now only an interesting academic exercise to consider how long the war in the Far East would have been shortened had Chennault been given even the minimum support for which he asked.[23]

US General John Alison says, in his 1958 interview:

> I think that our failure in the Far East resulted from this personality difference – personality animosities among the leading American and Allied personalities, which prevented a unified course of action and created confusion back at home. There were claims and counter-claims and charges and counter-charges, and I am sure that it was impossible for the American public to understand what was going on. Looking back, it seems to me that you can pin the blame or say who shares most of the blame for what happened in the Far East, I think it would fall squarely on the shoulders of Joe Stilwell.[24]

I expect history is full of these tragedies, of chasms opening twixt cup and lip, of Chinese whispers, of secret handshakes in the crepuscular corridors of power, of triumph turned to defeat by the slip of a pen. But was any such strategic alteration so costly of life as this? For vanity? The Pacific War Online Encyclopedia[25] estimates that there were 70 million deaths in the Second World War, 36 million of them in the

---

23. From the private papers of General Gordon Grimsdale, held at the Imperial War Museum, London
24. Alison, John R. '*Interview*'. Private Papers of Merian Cooper, Hoover Institution Archives, Stanford: CA, 1958
25. Accessed at http://pwencycl.kgbudge.com/C/a/Casualties.htm.

Pacific. Civilian casualties far outweigh the combat casualties, with 18 million Chinese civilians alone estimated to have died. Let's say that of the 36 million total, about half were in the last two years of the war. And now let's suppose the war had finished a year earlier than it did, thanks to the air campaign that never was. If this had happened, Allied troops would have been transferred to the European theatre, probably shortening the war against the Nazis. Maybe as many as nine million lives might have been saved. One can only pray forgiveness of those who died.

13

Onward Journey

Dad left China in January 1944, pausing to drive up part of the Burma Road from Kunming to Dali in Yunnan Province, a distance of about 200 miles, on his way to the Staff College at Quetta, then in India but now in Pakistan. On my second visit to China I stayed in Kunming for a few days, and while it is a lovely city, the old city walls have been destroyed and it looks very different to how Dad would have seen it. Dali, on the other hand, has spread out enormously but retains its walled historic centre and sense of being a meeting place for travellers and merchants along the Tea Horse Road or Chamadao, the ancient precursor of the Burma Road. Dali was an important point on the thousand-year-old trade route between the tea growers of Yunnan province and the horse traders of Tibet. The local ponies can trace their origins back to the Song dynasty (960–1279 AD) and were used for carrying loads along the Southern Silk Road, across the mountains to Iran and the Mediterranean. This part of Yunnan province lies at the eastern end of the Himalayas, rugged and imposing country with a strong sense of frontier. Dad must have felt like he was really heading into the wild west:

> On 31 December 1943 I left Chungking for 10 days leave before coming to this place. I and Norman Standen of the Embassy went to Kunming. We stayed 2 days in Kunming and then took a truck down the Burma Road to Tali [Dali]. Unfortunately 50km out of Kunming the truck ran a big end bearing. The driver managed to cadge a lift back to Kunming to get a new connecting rod. We resigned ourselves to awaiting his return sometime the next day. We

were in a very desolate spot. About half a mile from the truck there was a ramshackle village consisting of a temple and about ten mud huts. The truck mechanic said it was bad bandit country and asked me to get protection from the nearest political head.

Much against my will, as I felt sure I would have to pay through the nose to any guard provided, I and the interpreter trudged two miles to another equally ramshackle village where the local political head was said to live. He proved to be a scrofulous coolie, more likely to be a bandit than a protector. He offered me a guard of 8 men with spears! I refused and told him that I had merely come to notify him that I was in his area. I took care to tell him that the driver had returned to Kunming and hinted that if we disappeared the authorities would know where to start looking for us. He asked us where we intended sleeping and I told him 'at the edge of the road by the truck'. He was horrified and told us it was most dangerous – the district was infested with wolves. I laughed sceptically and thought to myself 'two legged wolves'. However, the laugh was on me as I woke up with a hell of a start in the middle of the night, to hear a pack howling and hunting quite near to us. An eerie sensation.

Dad's fears about the interior of China clearly resurfaced in this wild country, unprotected by the presence of the international community or indeed by any law enforcement agency. He evidently felt that the Chinese would regard him as easy prey and that he would be foolish to take the offer of protection at face value. At state level there was much suspicion and distrust between the Allies, and this seems to have been the case on the ground too. In Chinese eyes, the British were self-serving, arrogant and greedy. The Chinese were also inclined to think the British poor and cowardly soldiers, typically commenting: 'The British are afraid to die.' The losses of Hong Kong and Singapore and the retreat from Burma proved this to be true, in their opinion. Equally, Dad had experienced, at first and second hand, the predations of bandits during his escape from Hong Kong. While the Chinese guerrillas that he had encountered in the New Territories turned out to be invaluably helpful, they had also relieved Dad's party of its valuables – watches, pens, knives, cash and so on. Dad accepted that this was a small price, however, in comparison to the treatment he had feared when they were first introduced to the guerrilla leader.

> Next day a relief truck arrived which took us on without further mishap to Tsuyung [now Chuxiong] where we spent the night with an American missionary. She has lived there with two short breaks for leave for the past 36 years. Think of it, she was in China in the days of the Mandarin Emperors, in pre-republic days. The following day I had to call on the local General so our start was delayed and we did not reach Tali till 7pm.

The number of Christian missionaries in China rose and fell in a parabolic arc, from only fifty in 1860, when the Second Opium War treaties opened China's interior, to a maximum of around 8,000 in 1925, and then declined during the war years before all missionaries were expelled by the Communist government in 1953. In 1900 there were only 100,000 Chinese Christians, after nearly a century of missionary activity and at the cost of many missionaries' lives. The Chinese were strongly xenophobic, suspicious of imperialist ambitions and resentful of the 'unequal treaties'. This antipathy culminated in the Boxer Rebellion of 1900 when almost 200 missionaries and several thousand Chinese Christians were killed. A resurgence followed, with missionary numbers increasing rapidly. Yunnan province was a particularly fertile ground for conversions, since it had a large ethnic minority population who were not just looking for spiritual enlightenment but for anything that was anti-Han Chinese. Female missionaries were important as Chinese women were not allowed to interact with foreign men. They were expected to offer education and healthcare in addition to religious instruction and, indeed, the practice of foot-binding was brought to an end partly because of pressure from these female missionaries.

After his adventure on the road to Dali, Dad seems to have really enjoyed visiting the ancient town and its environs:

Tali is a pleasant walled city about one mile square. Much of the land within the walls is cultivated. It is almost completely untouched by modern 'progress'. Unlike so many Chinese cities which I have seen and which are built of stamped mud or wattle, Tali is built of stone. In consequence the streets are not inches deep in mud or dust but are comparatively clean. We ourselves lived in a courtyard of a most attractive Chinese house. The city is a great market centre for trucks coming from the north and Tibet. We saw in the streets a number of Tibetans in their peculiar leather boots and coats.

Tali lies in the centre of a plain about 2 miles in width between a range of mountains running up to 14,000ft and a lake about 30–40 miles long. The strip between the lake and a line parallel to the lake running through the city is cultivated, between this line and the foothills is one enormous graveyard. From a distance the countless stone tombs give an effect as of a vast grey cobweb woven over the countryside.

The day after our arrival we spent wandering around, calling on the local General and a French missionary bishop, to both of whom we had been given introductions by the Ambassador. That evening our hosts happened to be giving a large official dinner party and asked us to come along too. The food was wonderful (Cantonese cook), we drank local wine. The party became most convivial, so much so that one of our hosts seeing off some of the departing guests, lost himself and was returned to the house half an hour later by a troop of Boy Scouts.

Towards the end of our stay we (self, Standen and hosts) spent a day trying to climb up the mountain [Cang Shan, 4,122m]. Though it is 14,000ft high, Tali itself is over 7,000ft so it is a not impossible climb to do in one day. Unfortunately, two days before our attempt it snowed and though from down below it appeared to be only a powdering, by the time we had got to 11 or 12,000ft it was knee deep and quite impossible for us to reach the top.

The next day we started back for Kunming. We had an uneventful trip except for a broken rear spring which the mechanic patched up in about half an hour. The Chinese are really wonderful at improvisation.

The Burma Road is a magnificent engineering feat. It was built by the Chinese without foreign assistance. I believe they only started work on it in 1938. I shudder to think of the number of coolies whose lives must have gone into its construction. We passed over the highest section of the road where much of it is over 8,000ft above sea level and some of it over 9000. The surface by English standards is bad, but the alignment is wonderful. I think there is nowhere a gradient of more than 1 in 10.

The Ledo Road was completed in early 1945 and was soon renamed the Stilwell Road by Chiang Kai-shek. In July 1945, 6,000 tons of supplies were transported along the road, compared to 71,000 tons flown over the hump. Chiang's renaming of the road was possibly intended as an honour but, given the sour relations between the two men, it may well have been intended as a permanent rebuke for Stilwell's folly. After the war the Stilwell Road fell into disuse and has been steadily reclaimed by the jungle.

I left Kunming for India on the 13th January 1944 and had a most wonderful flight in brilliant sunshine over 'the hump'. The view was magnificent as we flew close by peaks of between 18 and 20,000ft. At the highest point we flew through a pass with mountains rising on either side of us. I had a very hectic time re-equipping myself in Delhi and arrived here [Quetta] on the 22nd. Cripes is it cold! Talk of brass monkeys! Fortunately the [Staff Officers Long War] course does not start for another week so I have time to look around and settle down.

How typical of Dad to take the bandits and wolves in his stride and to attempt a 4,000m peak in January! He was certainly single-minded in his passion for mountains, pushing on until actually knee-deep in snow. This 'pushing on' seems to be a heritable trait. It is useful when one is late for a train, say, and one keeps trying to get to the platform just in case the train is late. However, it can manifest as a tendency to overcommit and a refusal to stop and rest when faced with illness or injury.

I visited Dali in April 2015 and climbed the peak with no difficulty. The cable car probably helped. I noted that 'insane, intoxicated or hypertensive persons' were not allowed to use the cable car, but no one was actually checking. The old town is still intact, although it is now very touristy and cormorant fishermen ply the lake, posing for visitors and their inevitable phone or tablet cameras. Dali is where China starts to feel less Chinese and more Tibetan. The faces subtly change and the language is even harder to understand. The architecture begins to lose the characteristically Chinese pagoda-style roofs and gives way to tall, Tibetan, trapezoidal buildings.

In Quetta Dad took a 'long war' course until June 1944, covering operational planning, tactics and communications, and was then assigned to the recently formed 14th Army. This comprised a multinational force from a variety of Commonwealth countries, commanded by General William Slim. The 14th Army's mission was to repel the Japanese in Burma and thereby protect British interests in India and bring supplies overland to China. By the time Dad arrived in Burma in August 1944, the battles of Imphal and Kohima were over. These had resulted from the Japanese attempt to invade India but had ended disastrously for them, with over 50,000 Japanese dead (mostly from starvation and disease) and 100,000 casualties. They represented the worst setbacks for the Japanese so far in the war, and saw the beginning of their retreat. When Dad joined 28th Field Regiment, the Allies' task was to push back the Japanese and reoccupy Burma, code-named Operation Capital. According to the plans that had been discussed at the Washington Conference in May 1943, the recapture of Burma (code-named 'Anakim') was running about a year behind schedule.

Max Hastings comments on this moment in the Burma campaign, in his book *Nemesis* (2007):

> Slim's chief foes were now terrain, disease, weather, logistics. Mountbatten supported an important decision: to keep fighting through the monsoon, when in the past all significant operations were halted. Thereafter, Slim was called upon to move a modern Western army across hundreds of miles of the most inhospitable country in the world, devoid of road communications, to redeem the humiliations which Britain had suffered in 1941–42, and to keep alive a dream of empire which thoughtful men knew to be doomed. Churchill badly wanted to retrieve Burma and Malaya, but was determined, he told the chiefs of staff in September 1944, 'that the minimum effort should be employed in this disease-ridden country'. Here was a prospect rich in pathos, tragedy or absurdity according to viewpoint. As so often in wars, brave men were to do fine and hard things in pursuit of a national illusion.[1]

After a large-scale reorganisation of logistics for the overland attack, Operation Capital commenced in October. Dad was in command of 3rd Battery of the 28th Field Regiment, part of the 5th Indian Division of General Slim's 14th Army. During October and November 1944, they pushed steadily towards the Chindwin River in northern Burma. This laid the foundation for the subsequent recapture of Mandalay in central Burma. The fighting was heavy and sustained as the Japanese desperately defended their positions.

A magazine published after the event by the advertising agency J. Walter Thompson, called *Into Burma*, gives a flavour of the conditions:

> From Imphal the 5th Indian Division took up the chase down the 163 mile long Tiddim Road, known to all the footsloggers and tough transport drivers as 'the worst road

---

1. Max Hastings, *Nemesis*, Great Britain: HarperPress, 2007, 77

in Asia'. The feats on those days took on an epic quality. Tanks had to be winched up precipitous mud-clogged hillsides; in 65 miles the hard working sappers built 2,000ft of bridging. And before Tiddim could be entered the Division had to inch its way up the 'Chocolate Staircase', where the nightmare red earth road makes 40 hairpin bends in a climb of 3,000ft. These tough fighting men entered Tiddim on 14th October 1944. But there was no respite, only a month of gruelling mountain warfare on and up the slopes of 8,000ft cloud-capped Kennedy Peak and through the wild hill country around Fort White... [This] called for heroism, guile, improvisation, adaptability, patience and guts.

Incidentally, this is another example of my extraordinary luck. We were at a friend's house for supper and were talking about my book. Nick Ostler's father happened to have fought in Burma, and Nick – who has the most amazing library and a filing system that works – went to find his 'Dad's war file'. It included this magazine – I can find no reference to it online, though it may be in the JWT archive at Duke University – and it happened to be the edition about this moment in history, in Burma, covering the actions of the particular division to which my father was attached. The odds of that happening must be approximately one haystack to a needle against.

Once they had succeeded in meeting their objectives, the regiment were allowed to rest during December, when they were honoured by visits from Admiral Lord Mountbatten and General Slim.

Dad refused ever to mention Burma to anyone. I have to assume that those few months of jungle warfare were hellish for him and his troops, in the constant proximity of death and probably witnessing some appallingly gruesome sights. By 1944 the British had learned through bitter experience that jungle warfare did not follow the traditional rules of battle. In the jungle there was no such thing as a rear area, where administration and care of the wounded could take place in safety. Night did not bring a period of respite but rather an enhanced threat of guerrilla activity. Artillery was all but useless. Instead, close combat was necessary with grenades, tommy guns and accurate marksmanship from snipers. Visibility was poor and the portable radios often failed, making communication haphazard. The threat from the Japanese was only half the story – there was also the constant threat of disease and infection in the tropical heat. Two months in that nightmarish scene must have felt like an eternity. Even if Dad didn't suffer a nervous breakdown, I suspect his nerves felt rather frayed by the time the regiment reached its goal.

In February 1945, Dad finally left Asia and headed home. He stayed in the UK only briefly, being sent back to India in September 1945 to become an instructor of tactics at the School of Artillery in Deolali, not far from Mumbai [then Bombay]. In July 1946 he took a month's leave and headed up to Garhwal Himalaya to do some climbing with his old schoolmaster, Jack Gibson (1908–1994) and R.L. Holdsworth (1899–1976), both of whom were by then teachers at the Doon School in Dehradun, India, and experienced mountaineers. Also in the party were Lieutenant Nandu Jayal and schoolboy M.P. Chengappa, three Sherpas (Tenzing Norgay, Dawa Thundup and Dhian Singh) who would be their guides and technical support; and a group of porters to carry their equipment and supplies. They attempted to climb to the summit of Bandarpunch (6,315m), which had never been reached before. The monsoon was just starting, and they struggled to keep themselves and their kit dry in the rain and, higher up, in sleet and snow. Ordinarily, no one would choose to climb in the Himalayas in the monsoon season, but Gibson and Holdsworth were teachers and could only go climbing during the school holidays.

The five climbers and three Sherpas would make the summit attempt as a group, leaving the porters at a base camp. This kind of climbing is a logistical challenge, taking enough food, fuel and tentage to survive for a few days in freezing temperatures at high altitude, while minimising the amount that each person carries. The porters would carry everything up to a certain altitude, and could be sent down the mountain for resupplies, but they were not expert climbers and could not join the team in the summit attempt.

Dad was in his element and clearly loved every minute of it:

> I have had a most wonderful trip. We didn't reach the summit but despite this it was a huge success. The organiser of

the party was a man named Jack Gibson (Gibby) who was a very junior master when I was at school at Chillon and with whom I used to do quite a lot of climbing whilst I was there. He is a rather harum-scarum, methodless, untidy but very likeable chap. He has immense energy and great agility. He was captain of the Cambridge fencing team. He is now a housemaster at the Doon School, a scholastic experiment, a school run on the lines of an English public school entirely for Indians and as far as I can see very successful.

Gibby engaged three (sherpas) from Darjeeling, who had been on Everest expeditions, for the very high altitude work. Technically they are Indians but they are very Mongolian in appearance. They were immensely tough, always cheerful, very willing and most obliging and have my greatest admiration. At the end of the longest, wettest and most trying marches, carrying loads far heavier than us, they would bustle round, help us get our tents up, get up their own and produce a hot meal in an incredibly short space of time, all the while laughing, and joking and never a grumble amongst the three.

First we did a two-day march over a low pass about 6,000 feet up into the Yamuna Valley. From the pass we had our first views of our mountain as previously it had been hidden in cloud. Very impressive it looked. The second evening we camped on the banks of the Yamuna in an idyllic spot under some trees. However the place was infested with mushroom millipedes, like the centipedes we used to get in Hong Kong, only for every leg they had these must have had a dozen. They even got into some of our sleeping bags, fortunately I was undisturbed.

For the next three days we followed the pilgrim path up the valley of the Yamuna towards Yamunotri, its source, rising from about 3,000 to 8,000 feet. For Hindus Yamunotri is a very holy spot. We met many pilgrims mostly well to do old women and including the Ranee

John Monro, Tenzing Norgay and another Sherpa, 1946.

[princess] of Nepal who was a cheerful old trout. It must have been a terrific sweat for the old girls but I suppose it is really quite a good way of keeping their figures under control and better for their health than dieting.

The country was on a tremendous scale, even steeper than Switzerland. In places the river ran through gorges. At first the vegetation was tropical, then it gave place to pines, deodars, Himalayan oak and rhododendron trees. At the end of the third day we stopped at a little village about 5 miles short of Yamunotri, as our route here turned east and was along a ridge rather than a valley. We rested a day. The village was paved with large flagstones, which were also used to tile the roofs. The houses were made of wood, many of them were nicely carved. There was a large 'peel' tower and a funny wooden temple with the effigy of a goat suckling its kid on the roof. The village was surrounded by potato fields. The inhabitants wore a sort of brown woollen homespun trousers and smock which seemed to keep them warm even when they had been out in the rain for hours.

Most of them carried about with them a little basket of wool and a bobbin with which at every spare moment they span yarn.

The day after our rest we took a herd track up the side of a very steep ridge, through thick forest with occasional clearings. At about 11,000 feet we came out above the trees onto grass slopes covered with most lovely flowers. Yellow gems, dark wine red potentillas, acres and acres of forget-me-not and blue campanulas, blue poppies, a red flower called a polygonum which looks like a crimson grape hyacinth, and in places a very sweet-smelling primula with flowers like a primrose but arranged on a long stalk like a cowslip. Unfortunately we were too late for the rhododendron bloom.

Up till now we had had pretty good weather but when we got onto the ridge it began to rain. If it had been clear we would probably have had wonderful scenery but everything was in mist and cloud. I went on ahead to try and shoot a monal pheasant. I saw quite a number but they were all out of range. He is a very fine bird; dark metallic green in colour with a crest like a peacock, a white rump and, for a pheasant, a short chestnut tail. I managed to shoot one later. He was large enough for five hungry people to make a very good meal off the white meat alone. Unfortunately the porters followed me and I overshot our campsite by a couple of miles. When we discovered the mistake it came on to rain very heavily so we hurriedly pitched camp where we were. It rained hard all night and the next day so we stayed put, though the porters had a miserable time finding what shelter they could from one small tent and the surrounding rocks. Even though we were over 12,000 feet up our camp was near rather marshy ground.

The third day after leaving the village dawned rather less wet so we made a move. After several steep-ish ups and downs we crossed over a pass about 13,500ft and descended into a valley at the foot of our mountain where we established our base camp at 12,000 feet. We found some herdsmen and a few buffaloes in the valley and from them we got fresh butter and milk. We also bought a sheep which we ate. We rested here a day to dry out clothes and bedding. We discharged ten of the porters and housed the rest in a big cave. I was suffering from mountain sickness. A headache and a very bad go of the trots. After our day's rest we loaded up the porters with about a week's requirements and our minimum baggage and established what we called camp 1, at about 16,000ft. We had quite an exciting time getting there as in parts it was very steep and climbing up the rocks on the edge of the glacier we found many very loose, which the leading porters dislodged onto the rear porters. On a steep slope, slippery with ice, you can well imagine it was a tricky business avoiding falling rocks.

From now on we had to rely only on our own carrying abilities and that of the Sherpas. The following day when the clouds cleared a little we carried up a load of stoves, a steep and interesting snow and rock climb, and parked them on the top of the long ridge leading to the summit. The next day was very cloudy so we remained in our tents. My mountain sickness was better, but I found that I became very easily exhausted. The following day was much clearer so we humped the remainder of the camp up onto the ridge, up which we climbed for a further 600 feet and camped at 18,100ft on the ridge. It was very narrow – we had to knock the snow off the top to get a flat place on which to pitch the tents. It [the mountainside] just went down each side. I had quite a good night despite a headache.

In R.L. Holdsworth's account of the expedition in the *Alpine Journal* (May 1948),[2] he says about this night:

I have never before been cold at night sleeping at these

---

2. R.L. Holdsworth (1948) 'Bandar Punch Again', *Alpine Journal* Vol LVI, no. 276, 246–251

or at higher levels, but I have never before slept on snow without a mattress [they had cork mattresses but these were too heavy to carry for this part of the climb]. The weather was mild and even at this height there was only slight frost at night, but I was never really warm and slept little. I rather think the other members of the party felt the same, though perhaps not so acutely. Bad nights are bad for morale and it would, perhaps, have been better if we could have rested the next day and made our attempt the day after, but the impending end of Monro's leave made us all anxious to make an attempt without delay.

Dad continues the story:

> Next morning was fine and clear. We made our attempt on the summit. At first after leaving our camp the ridge was nearly level, then came a very steep patch of rocks for about 600 feet. 2/3 of the way up this Gibby and I found ourselves very exhausted. I had difficulty with my balance and found myself staggering badly. We decided that if we went on any farther we would probably not get back safely. I think the trouble was we rushed the mountain too fast. We didn't give ourselves time to acclimatise between 12,000 and 18,000 feet. This was my fault as I only had a month's leave. We made our attempt on 17th. It took us 14 days to get there and I had to be back on the 28th. So you see I hadn't much time. We did not have sufficient stores to remain longer in the top camp so we went down to camp 1.

Holdsworth continued up with Nandu, Tenzing and Dawa and they were soon confronted with an imposing tower of rock, snow and ice leading to the summit. They roped themselves together and began the steep ascent, with Tenzing cutting steps in the snow. They reached a point higher than any previous attempts on the mountain, but the weather was deteriorating. Climbing successfully is as much about getting down as it is about ascent, and Holdsworth sensibly called a halt, saying:

> If we were caught in an exhausted state in a violent wind coming down that long steep ridge ahead of us, I felt it would require more than a little favour from Lord Shiva to pull us through. So, reluctantly, and to everyone's great disappointment, I signalled retreat.

Dad, determined to summit a mountain, tried a neighbouring peak:

> Next day Gibby, I and Nandu had an interesting rock climb up one of the satellite peaks of about 17,800ft. Funnily enough the snow on the summit was black with fleas. There were little birds, pipits and alpine accentors, right up to 19,000 feet. We decided to try a different way home. We descended 1,000 feet and then found cliffs, so had to go right back to the top and down the way we came up. We went right back to our base camp and got in very tired about 4.30pm.

I have once visited India, in 1992, when I was contemplating a career change. I was attracted to the idea of a mountain retreat where I could clear my head and mull over what to do next. Having a guide and nothing to do but walk made for a blissfully simple daily rhythm, a roving version of meditating on the breath. I chose to go hiking in the Garhwal Himalaya, about 50 miles from Bandarpunch. Small world. I found the Himalayas thrilling, so steep that, as we walked up through the cloud forest, we could pick wild strawberries almost without bending over. We too met men spinning wool as they tended their flock, wearing the same outfit that Dad described from 50 years before. The highest point of our trek was at the Sikh shrine of Hemkund, 4,600m, the final approach to which was a lung-bursting 6km hike with a 1,000m climb. Devout Sikhs are then expected to dive into the lake (breaking the ice as they enter) to cleanse themselves before visiting the shrine. It was a stunning spot and it certainly did feel closer to heaven.

Dad returned to England in 1947, where he continued teaching artillery until being posted to command G Battery (Mercer's Troop) of the 5th Regiment Royal Horse Artillery in 1949. He was made second in command of the 5th Regiment, RHA in 1950. This fateful appointment took him to Larkhill in Wiltshire, where he met my mother. He had previously been engaged to two other women during the war, but they had eventually declined to marry him, perhaps fearing early widowhood. By now he was 36, the war was over and he perhaps felt that he really should be getting married.

My mother's father, Brigadier Howard Greene (who had also won a Military Cross, as well as a Distinguished Service Order and a CBE), was teaching artillery at Larkhill. Dad's opening gambit was to take Mum, Betty Greene, 13 years his junior and doubtless overawed by him anyway, to the opera at Glyndebourne to see Mozart's *Le Nozze di Figaro* for their first date. They were engaged within six weeks and would have been married very shortly after that, but for a delay caused by Mum developing appendicitis and having an appendectomy. My mother says that Dad was very conscious of the age gap between them, pointing out to her that she was likely to lose him long before her own death, and making sure that she made an informed decision in marrying him. That probably melted her heart even more, even though it sadly turned out to be an accurate prediction.

Babies Katharine and Robert followed soon after, along with Dad's promotion to Lieutenant Colonel in 1952. He was sent to Korea in 1955 to command 19th Field Regiment, RA, in a peacekeeping role after the Korean war. My parents had a couple of happy years based in Hong Kong in 1956 and '57 before Dad finally retired from the army in 1958, during the so-called Golden Bowler period, when the size of the army was being drastically reduced and officers were offered substantial redundancy payments to prevent the military structure from becoming top-heavy. Apparently, some people felt that Dad could have continued up the ranks to General if he had stayed in the army. If that is true, then why did he decide to retire at the age of 44?

He was a countryman at heart and there was a farm available to him that had been owned by his family for about a hundred years, but had until then been rented out. Perhaps it was simply a serendipitous combination of being a good time to exit the army and having an attractive opportunity to go to. At a deeper level, I can only speculate from my own experience. By the age of 30 I was consulting to some of the world's leading businesses and being very well paid for it. I was also bored, dissatisfied and fed up with long hours and lost weekends. I was fortunate enough to be made redundant and used my new-found freedom to contemplate my next step. I stumbled across osteopathy, and the more I looked into it, the more boxes it seemed to tick. Freedom was the thing for me – I didn't want to be attached to London, or a long working week, or a boss, or a repetitive job. Freedom was the thing for Dad too – he was a soldier and then a farmer, both professions in which duty, discipline and need hold one captive, yet both contain the purposes of freedom defended, and freedom lived.

I now live a life of my choosing in rural England, caring for a diverse range of human and animal patients, and I obtain deep satisfaction from seeing the direct results of my work. I wonder if Dad had had enough of army politics, or felt that the army was going in the wrong direction, or just wanted a new challenge and a more settled and peaceful life, with more control over his own destiny? We all have 'plusieurs cordes à l'arc' and we don't have to stick to one string just because we are good with it.

Dad attended Walford Agricultural College in Shropshire to learn his new career, and in 1960 the family moved to the farm, on the edge of the Shropshire Hills. He took full part in the local community and was one of the founders of the Riding for the Disabled Association. He recognised the essential similarity between being a captive of war and being a captive of your own body. Knowing the freedom of the saddle, he saw that riding could restore agency and freedom to anyone, regardless of their limitations, and so brought children from the School for the Blind in Condover, a couple of miles away, to ride our ponies at the farm. We would walk them down the lane, the children thrilled to be sitting above their carers, controlling their pony and experiencing a new perspective on life. The RDA has been going strong ever since, partnering the liberating power of the loyal horse with the needs of people oppressed by their own bodies.

My final destination in China was Shanghai, which I hoped would be a restful and cosmopolitan idyll after Chongqing. I had a day of travelling: getting to Chongqing airport took an hour, then the flight was delayed, it took two hours to fly to Shanghai, an age waiting for luggage and then an hour into the city centre through the sprawling suburbs, spreading like algae on the rich nutrients of the Chinese economy. The appalling smog would have made landing the aircraft tricky in pre-electronic times, and my nose gradually withdrew its services after I arrived. This wasn't what I'd had in mind for a relaxing couple of days back in civilisation.

My Shanghai guide hadn't read the briefing about my trip and its purpose. Instead, he asked me how long I had been in China. I told him it was about two weeks.

'Have you seen the Great Wall?'

'No.'

'Have you been to Beijing and the Forbidden City?'

'No.'

'You must have been to see the terracotta warriors in Xi'an!'

'No.'

'The panda sanctuary?'

'No.'

'Well, where have you been then?'

This had been my first visit to China and so I suppose I should have gone to see all the well-known highlights, but I felt grateful to have stuck to my own itinerary and had been duly amazed by the unexpected delights I had experienced. Still, I was in Shanghai now, and so some standard tourist sightseeing was on the agenda.

We visited the Jade Buddha Temple that was made into a highlight by the white jade statue of a sitting Buddha, about 1.9m tall. Carved from a single stone in Burma, this magnificent artwork had a glowing serenity to it, a sentience of its own. It was originally sent to Shanghai in 1882, but the temple housing it was destroyed in the unrest at the end of the Qing dynasty in 1912. Luckily the statue was saved and rehoused in the current temple in 1928. It is one of the most beautiful objects I have ever seen, and I held its calm image in my mind as we headed out into the real world of modern Shanghai.

I was taken to the Nanjing Road – Shanghai's Oxford Street. It is pedestrianised, but don't let that fool you. Just as zebra crossings in China serve only to lure the unwary, so the Nanjing Road is crossed by several trafficked roads, whose drivers seem to think that the pedestrians are there for sport. Eventually I was allowed to dive into the sanctuary of the Astor House Hotel, a Victorian building right by the river in the centre of the old part of town. Previous guests included Bertrand Russell, Albert Einstein and Charlie Chaplin.

The next day dawned cold and wet, but this contributed to the beauty of the Yu Garden, a classical garden built in the centre of Shanghai between 150 and 400 years ago. It was a delightful oasis, even in the pouring rain, mixing plants, rocks, water and buildings in the most aesthetically pleasing combinations. The pavilions serve to frame the view of successive 'scenes' in the garden, placing the visitor in the best positions to enjoy the garden as well as encouraging contemplation. The mountain peak was a symbol of virtue, stability and endurance, and this element is symbolised by the rockery. Water represents lightness and communication. It is also the complement to the mountain, the other central element of the garden, and represents dreams and the infinity of spaces. The golden koi carp in the water represent both fortune and the traditional yellow of the emperor's robes. The plants and flowers represent nature in its most vivid form, and contrast with the straight lines of the architecture and the permanence and immobility of the rocks.

Later we drove out to the 'Venice of the East', the ancient town of Zhujiajiao. It was fun to take a 'gondola' through the waterways and see all the traditional houses. We passed under the Fangsheng Bridge, or 'bridge of letting the captives free' – a large stone bridge built in 1571 and historically used by monks to set free their fish back into the river. On the last evening of my trip I went to an acrobatic show at a dedicated theatre in Shanghai. The troupe of acrobats showed what the human body is capable of if you know how to work it right. For kick-off we had a man balancing on four stacked trays, separated by tumbler glasses positioned at each corner, on top of a rolling cylinder. Then he kicked a rice bowl onto his head, then another, then two more, three more, etc., till he had the whole dinner service on his head.

I was very sorry to leave this fascinating land. The Chinese are charming, gentle, polite, friendly and helpful, and everything is scrupulously clean and well-organised. They also spit, sniff, slurp and belch for a pastime. In one local restaurant, a woman spat out the bones of her meal onto the floor. Perfectly acceptable, apparently. I was warned of smoky hotel rooms, but there seems to have been a major clampdown on smoking and now it is only allowed in limited places. I had nothing but fantastic experiences in China – the landscape was magnificent, the journeys were easy, the people endlessly kind. I felt safer there than at home.

It really is a land of yin and yang extremes. Ancient and modern rub shoulders but don't connect; everything is utterly foreign but comfortably familiar; the streets are swept clean but the air is almost unbreathable; the culture is laid-back but 'face' rules make being polite a minefield of unexploded intercultural bombs – you can't accept a compliment, for example, or accept food or drink too readily or you will appear greedy; they use poetic imagery and gentle ways of giving instructions, but bulldoze whole villages out of the way to make progress; they give some autonomy to the minority peoples while taking their world out from under their feet. They are indeed inscrutable.

In case you ever feel inspired to visit China, travel essentials include loo roll, hand sanitiser, a torch, a local adaptor (two vertical flat-sided prongs), VPN software for bypassing Big Brother on the internet, a China SIM card, a character-reading app (e.g. Pleco), your own alcohol/chocolate/treats of choice, nasal decongestant to counter poor air quality, digestive aids. Try not to be vegetarian. Always get a hotel card on check-in, with the name and address in characters, in case you need to get a taxi home. You will also need fully functioning knee joints – there are Western toilets only in posh hotels. Your gut will appreciate the squatting position, even if your knees don't. In the Second World War it was said that to visit China you needed a very strong constitution and a copy of *Alice's Adventures in Wonderland*[3] to cope with the utter paradox of the place and its people. Lewis Carroll's

---

3. Ride, *BAAG: Hong Kong Resistance 1942–45*, 104

book is filled with impossible and contradictory characters and situations, presented as though this were perfectly normal.

China still has a Wonderland sort of feel, but the strong constitution is no longer obligatory.

14

The Path into the Light

Dad and China are analogues, both undiscovered countries to me, both strangely familiar and impenetrably foreign. Each foray into their interiors raised more temptations to dig deeper, as clues flashed past the edges of my perception, as elusive and electric as kingfishers. After all my best efforts at exploring their character and spirit, they both retain their terrible secrets. I will never know what happened to Dad in Burma or how he felt when his youngest brother, Michael, died in his thirties. I know that Dad and his brother Robert, known to all as Bob, used to call each other Jing and Bing, respectively. They could have invented these names in childhood (was their brother Michael known as Ming?) but the nicknames seem rather Chinese to me. Jing means capital in Mandarin, as in Beijing, and it can also mean to bear or endure. Bingbing means military power. I looked at Dad's business card, which has his name in Chinese characters on the back, but sadly it only showed the translation of Monro – 'Meng luo', so no confirmation of this idea. 'Jing meng luo' is not really a phrase in Mandarin, but you could translate it as Dreamcatcher. Very funny, Dad.

His letters and diaries are more forthcoming than he ever was in person, but they alone could not bring this man to life. Having walked in his footsteps through China and in India, I have developed more of a sense of who he was. The research that I have done in writing this book has given me a deeper understanding. What he writes in his diaries and letters are the facts and events of his experiences. What I don't know is whether this is down to his personality or whether, at the time, it was simply impossible to say more, either due to security concerns or to protect his correspondents from anxiety. It has been the reports of others and the views of historians that have made me realise how incredibly courageous he was.

The Battle of Hong Kong, the perils of his escape, the destitution of Chongqing and the horrors of Burma are now documented and accessible, helping me to appreciate his courage in adversity. Even his jolly holiday in the Himalayas took some guts. Having recently read *Into the Silence: Mallory, the Great War and the Conquest of Everest* by Wade Davis, I am in a better position to understand the challenges of the early days of mountaineering in the Himalayas. Equipment was primitive: from poorly weatherproofed tents to needing to bring your own wood to fuel stoves. One of Dad's charms is that he seems to have had no idea of his own bravery. He simply regarded all the 'slings and arrows of outrageous fortune' as ordinary.

I share Dad's enjoyment of China and I felt a natural affinity with my Chinese guides. Dad's diaries about his work with BAAG in 1942 and '43 are full of his delight at the scenery and culture of China. He occasionally expresses frustration at the glacial rate of progress of his journeys, but he never complains about his accommodation (although there is sometimes a bedbug count!) and he clearly loved the food. He ranges from amused to resigned when he encounters Chinese idiosyncrasies – never condescension or disgust. He remarks on a Chinese dinner party that he attended in September 1942:

> I thoroughly enjoyed myself. Our hosts were all charming and educated people. There were to Western minds two incongruities to the general tone of the party. Mrs Liu [the hostess] did not eat any of the delicacies but contented herself with a little bread and butter. Someone remarked on this and she informed the table that for the past three months her diarrhoea had been very bad. The second was as we were saying goodbye. Everybody came down to the verandah to see me off. In the midst of handshakings a small girl aged about ten took down her knickers and piddled in the verandah gutter!

I think his escape from Hong Kong must have been one of the most exciting events of his life. He must have felt enormous satisfaction in succeeding, not only in getting out of the camp undetected but also in negotiating the many obstacles along the way. It was surely a boost to his confidence in his leadership abilities and taught him that even in an alien land, he could meet any challenge. That foundation must have stood him in good stead when he faced a relentless series of crises in the 1960s. In a letter to his friend Bren Trevor in May 1942, he says of his terrifying escape: 'It was really great fun. When peace comes I shall try and do the same trip again for the fun of it.'

I wonder to what extent he realised that there might have been reprisals against his fellow prisoners when his escape was discovered? Did his instinct to 'do his duty as an officer' simply outweigh any other considerations? Whitehead frets about the impact of his escape on the prisoners left behind but says that he later learned that the enormous morale boost of successful escapes made the resulting privations seem trivial. Dad's work with the BAAG was mainly concerned with helping prisoners and refugees, maintaining essential supplies and helping with escapes. He clearly had relevant experience for the role, but I think he was probably also delighted to have the opportunity to repay the generosity and kindness that had helped his own escape. I am curious that he didn't stay in touch with his fellow escapers – Baugh was killed in action in Burma in 1943, but Trevor (Captain I.B. Trevor, his escape companion, not his friend Arthur Trevor) survived the war and returned to his work on the railways in Hong Kong. Perhaps two months of each other had been enough. He did remain in touch with Norman Standen, the British Embassy man with whom he travelled to Kunming and the Burma Road in January 1944. Norman later became godfather to my brother Robert. My own godfather, Edmund Cowell, was a fellow Assistant Military Attaché and friend from Dad's time in Chongqing.

Dad took full advantage of his presence in China and went travelling when he had the chance. Even when he was in Chongqing, he would go for long hikes out into the surrounding countryside. He describes coming across an old temple, about three hours' walk from the city, perched on the top of a range of hills:

> Sunday, 11 April 1943: At first we thought that it was closed and disused but in the back quarters we [Edmund

Cowell, Major Day and Dad] found a young priest and two other men. We got permission to go in and passing through their living quarters, which were dark but clean, suddenly entered a lovely little courtyard of mellowed grey stone. In the centre was a pond with an ornamental bridge flanked on one side by a row of tea bushes and crimson and white peonies in tubs. It was a delightful experience suddenly to come upon such glorious colour. On a raised dais behind the peonies was an antique bronze brazier for burning incense or joss paper.

After admiring this courtyard we passed into one of the main rooms surrounded by little booths containing some most ferocious images. They were in quite a good state of repair though by no means in the first flush of youth. From this room we passed to the inmost sanctuary. Here there was one most lovely set of images which had only recently been made and painted. The gold leaf had not tarnished nor the red paint faded.

Finally we were taken out through the back of the temple through a small stone archway to a large flat rock on the very edge and summit of the cliff from where we had a magnificent view over the surrounding country. To add to the sense of unreality experienced standing there, a red rose in full bloom was growing in one of the fissures of the rock. We admired the view for about a quarter of an hour, chatting with the priest and his two companions about local conditions and wandered back through the temple admiring the drawings on the paper lanterns hanging before the altars.

This kind of wonderful experience and the lifelong friendships that he forged make it even more of a puzzle to me that Dad never mentioned China. I can only guess that by the time I was up to listening to the story he was in his sixties, much water had passed under the bridge, he was living a different life and perhaps it didn't seem relevant in rural Shropshire. Perhaps I just wasn't listening. Perhaps he couldn't bring himself to be positive towards what had become a Communist country. Perhaps he thought it was pointless enthusing us about a country we couldn't visit. China was completely closed to tourists between 1949 and 1974, and after that tourism was severely restricted. In 1978 there were only 230,000 foreign visitors to China, but by 2015 there were 56 million visitors.

Despite all the unanswered questions, I have learned much about my father. I can more easily detect his influence in my life and choices and those of my siblings. To my sister, Kathy, he was her opposite: he conservative, she a left-wing hippy; he sexist, she feminist; he patriotic, she preferring a different world view; he hierarchical and status-conscious due to his upbringing and military experiences, she egalitarian; he peacemaker, she confrontational. Yet she was his opposite only as one's mirror image is one's opposite. Of all of us, he had most right to be proud of her – fearless adventurer, clever, interesting, endlessly resourceful and compassionate, especially to those most disadvantaged. In the late 1970s when she happened to be home-based, Kathy learned that large numbers of Vietnamese refugees were being settled in Shropshire. She found that the Vietnamese men were learning English through their work, the children were learning English at school, but the women were becoming increasingly isolated at home with no support to learn the language of their adoptive home. She set up classes to teach them, being an experienced English language teacher, and made many friends as a result.

Kathy was always one to plough her own furrow, right to the end. Even after her diagnosis of terminal cancer, she doggedly completed her degree in Arabic and Islamic Studies at Durham University. That showed true grit, as she was feeling dreadful most of the time, but she had left school at sixteen and she wanted to test her academic abilities, even though she knew she would never return to the Arab world to make use of her degree. She is another member of the family who I regret not knowing better, and I feel I can only admire her from afar. She was twelve years older than me and left home when I was four. She returned home occasionally, but she was more like an exotic visitor than a sister and I never really connected with her. She had less of an affinity with the Chinese than she did with the Arabs. I'm not sure if that is simply a matter of personal preference or whether it was yet another way of opposing Dad.

My brothers have Dad's phlegmatic and long-suffering approach to life's trials and would have pleased him in their different careers. Interestingly, both of them have had complete changes of career – Robert went from zoology to the British Council, and James went from farming to become an independent financial adviser. James says that he would often dream of Dad, visualising the two of them sitting on the wall in the yard in front of the farmhouse, with James discussing his plans for the farm and seeking Dad's approval. It was very tough on James, taking on the responsibility for the farm and its employees, but he rose to the challenge and succeeded at a time when farm incomes were fluctuating wildly. Between 1990 and 1995, average farmer income rose rapidly to a peak of over £30,000, but by 2001 (when there was an outbreak of foot-and-mouth disease) average income had nosedived to just £7,500, according to DEFRA. James recently sold part of the farm to pay for a divorce settlement and, in any case, it is no longer a viable unit, but he is renovating the farm buildings for use as offices and holiday lets, determined to maintain Dad's legacy.

I now recognise Dad far more in me – from phrases I use to ways of thinking and being. Naturally, there were many influences on me, but his characteristics form a bedrock to my character that is unshakable. He'd admire my perseverance, I think – once I start something I complete it – but I'm not sure whether he'd recognise his influence in other aspects of my life. I think he would be puzzled and sceptical about my work as an osteopath (not a proper doctor) – and formerly as a marketing consultant (a job for people who grow up with no particular skills) and mystified by my lack of adventurousness (travel across China with *guides?*). He would probably have adopted the 'dignified silence' approach rather than actively criticising me, though. He was unsentimental and undemonstrative, a stoic who actively made his own luck. While he wouldn't have approved of my divorce, with his traditional values, I believe he would have taken the view that I was regaining control of my destiny. I'm sure he would have relished the opportunity to visit China with me, not least for the culinary experiences.

It is clear from his accounts that Dad admired and liked the Chinese. During the war the British were generally not at all respectful towards the Chinese and, in turn, the Chinese thought little of the British. I am heartened that Dad took them on their merits rather than adopting the majority view without question. Today, our view of China is largely based on whatever the media choose to serve up: economic growth, environmental desecration, human rights abuses, hostilities with Japan, natural disasters, exploitative investment activity in Africa and so on. But this is what is happening at state level – it is not the daily experience of people living in China, just as what makes the news about the UK or the USA does not reflect our daily experience.

China is an ever increasing force in our lives, but there are miniscule numbers of us with direct experience of the world's second-largest economy. The British Council calculates that Mandarin is the fourth most important foreign language to Britons (after Spanish, Arabic and French) but only 1 per cent of Brits can speak enough Mandarin to hold a conversation (and I bet that's an exaggeration of the term 'conversation'). There is increasing educational exchange, with Chinese universities opening campuses here, such as Peking University's new campus near Oxford, and more British students going to study in China. Similarly, the number of Chinese visiting the UK only increased by 36,000 between 2007 and 2012 (to 179,000), during which time total outbound tourism from China to the rest of the world increased by 42.5 million. By 2015, outbound trips from China had increased to 120 million, of which only 270,000 were to the UK. Expensive and unfriendly UK visa processes are largely thought to be to blame for the feeble increase in the number of trips to Britain. France receives three times as many Chinese visitors. Britain's universities, by contrast, have grasped the importance of the Chinese to their economic success, with over 90,000 Chinese students in higher education institutions in 2015/16.

Not that visiting the country makes it any easier to understand, with China's centuries-old inbuilt system of paradox. There is a beauty and a stillness held in the integration of opposites but sometimes it just seems baffling. Yet perhaps that is its purpose – to remind us that life is not reducible to simple, linear equations. We have to accept and embrace complexity and have the courage to keep trying when we are knocked back. I was really inspired by the story my guide told me about her childhood. There was no sense of bitterness about being unwanted by her parents and sent to poor relations in the back of beyond. She and her adoptive parents knew how to make the best of the situation and relentlessly weathered every storm until they succeeded. With a population like that, it is small wonder that after its 'century of humiliation' China has risen to become a world power. I'm no fan of the politics, but the people are amazing.

What impact did Chinese culture have on my father? I don't know what he was like before his wartime experiences, but he showed some signs of appreciating paradox and holism, both Chinese cultural themes, during my childhood. One day when I was learning to drive in our ancient Land Rover (the vehicle and I were both 17 years old), I put it in first gear and the gearstick came off in my hand. Dad was standing nearby and saw me anxiously waving the stick about, not knowing what to do next. I was frightened that he would be terribly cross. We looked at each other for a few moments and then he burst out laughing. I moved over and we drove round to the farm workshop where he welded the stick back into position. He had weighed up the danger of the situation and concluded that the farmyard was the best place for this to have happened; indeed, I think he was delighted.

'Wisdom, compassion, and courage are the three universally recognised moral qualities of men', said Confucius. And they are probably the three words I would use to summarise my father. He was also conservative to a Victorian degree, patriarchal and emotionally distant. A private man who liked parties. An adventurer who stayed home on the farm. A man who lived in the moment and planted trees that would not mature in his lifetime. An intellectual who worked with his hands. A pauciloquent speaker but an eloquent writer. Perhaps he's more Chinese than I'd realised.

Confucius also said: 'Choose a job you love, and you will never have to work a day in your life.' My father had two careers, in the army and then farming, both of which he loved. He worked very hard on the farm, the income was relatively low in the 1960s and '70s and he was often tired, but he never complained or thought of selling up and doing something less exhausting or more lucrative. He knew that farming was a way to be his own boss, to be close to the land, to allow time for his pursuit of country sports and to bring up his children in a healthy and wholesome environment. He wanted us to do well academically, but he also wanted us to be practical, self-reliant, adventurous and caring. My older brother and my sister rode, with their friend Jane, 80 miles across Wales on their ponies in their early teens. Dad helped them to plan their route and accommodation along the way and then let them take care of themselves. When I broke my kneecap out hunting (aged 17), I rode home, put the horse to bed and cleaned the tack before going in to tell my mother that I needed to go to hospital. It was just expected that you would do what was the necessary order of operations.

Was he a '20th-century Great', as our family friend described? It took me seven years but I did eventually call her and ask her what she meant. My siblings' friend Jane Cordingley said that Dad was a 'Great' in the sense that he represented a type. A leader, a man whose natural integrity, intelligence, fearlessness and determination generated the loyalty and support of his troops, who trusted his skill and experience to lead them to success in their endeavours. He was also trusted and deeply respected by the men who worked on the farm and who always referred to him as 'The Colonel'. He expected those under his command (including his children) to share his values, to know right from wrong and to act honourably and in the best interest of the greater good.

He was a type in the sense that there were probably thousands like him who contributed to the victory of the Allies in the Second World War. I recognised the words of Edwin Ride[1], describing his father Colonel Lindsey Ride, founder of BAAG: 'The academic physician and sportsman was to assume a role perhaps more suited to him than any other. As soldier, leader and administrator, he was to demonstrate great strength and determination. His selflessness, fairness and will-

---

1. Ride, *BAAG: Hong Kong Resistance 1942–45*, 49

ingness to disregard danger in pursuit of what he considered his duty was to inspire loyalty and confidence in those who worked with him.'

Another 20th-century Great. Perhaps not at the level of Gandhi or Churchill, but nevertheless one of a breed of men without whom the war would not have been won. We owe our comfortable lives to men like these, the very many unsung heroes who achieved feats during the war that made them shake their heads in disbelief after the event. Think of all the thousands of gallantry medals awarded in the Second World War – each one represents a 20th-century Great, leading (officer or rank) in a way that no corporate management team can hope to emulate, inspiring courage, giving meaning, generating hope. At the end of the 1978 film of Agatha Christie's *Death on the Nile*, Poirot quotes Molière: 'La grande ambition des femmes est d'inspirer l'amour' (The great ambition of women is to inspire love). Perhaps the great ambition of men is to inspire courage.

And who am I? Apart from being immensely proud of my father and even more upset than before that he's not here to talk to, I have an expanded sense of self. Since completing my journeys to China and writing this book, I have become more confident of my place in the world. I am doing more writing and teaching, speaking up. I have something to say and the confidence to say it. It seems that reliving my father's experiences has added a perceptible strength to my being. As though the flow of courage from parent to child was interrupted in its flight but has now landed. At last I understand and can internalise the Monro family motto – *alis et animo* – wings and courage, indeed.

So many of us share this experience – the loss of a parent or grandparent without knowing them as a person rather than just as a role. We often don't realise that their life contributes to ours in diverse and subtle ways; that if we had had the opportunity to really talk with them, they could have taught us so much about ourselves. The generation who saw the Second World War are steadily leaving us and they have a tendency to remain silent about their experiences. This reserve seems to me to be modest and protective, preserving their own sanity and hiding horror from us like a clutch of deadly eggs under a serene and soft-feathered facade.

The modern habit of sharing every thought and feeling is alien to them at the least, offensive at worst. But this is an enormous loss to us, even if we don't fully appreciate it. Those who were non-combatants have just as much to teach us about resilience in adversity and how to live well in difficult times. The two-minute silence on Remembrance Sunday helps to make many people pause and reflect, and maybe, now that research is so much easier to do, it will also encourage more people to enrich their lives by delving further into their family history. Bereavement is never easy, but it has been truly joyful getting to know Dad and feeling the full force of his personality. It's been like falling in love.

Structure of the Royal Artillery in the Second World War

Descriptor	Comprises	Leadership
Army	2 or more Corps	General (4 Star)
Corps	2–5 Divisions	General Officer Commanding (Lieutenant General (3 Star))
Division	12,000–18,000 men, usually 3 Brigades	Major General (2 Star)
Brigade	3 Regiments	Brigadier (1 Star)
Regiment (equivalent to Battalion in Infantry)	2–3 Batteries	Lieutenant Colonel
Battery	2–3 Troops	Captain or Major
Troop or Platoon	3 Sections	Lieutenant
Section	10 men	Corporal

Source: https://www.britishmilitaryhistory.co.uk/documents-units-formations-1930-1956/

Bibliography

Abram, David, *The Spell of the Sensuous*, New York: Vintage, 1996

Air Pollution in China, 2015. Accessed December 2015. http://www.theguardian.com/world/2015/aug/14/air-pollution-in-china-is-killing-4000-people-every-day-a-new-study-finds

Alison, John R, *'Interview'*, Private Papers of Merian Cooper, Hoover Institution Archives: Stanford, 1958

Alsop, Joseph W. and Platt, A, *I've Seen The Best Of It*, New York: Norton & Co., 1992

Bagby, W.M, *The Eagle-Dragon Alliance: America's Relations with China in WWII*, Newark: University of Delaware Press, 1992

Banham, Tony, n.d. Accessed 2015. http://www.hongkongwardiary.com/book1thebattle.html

Chen, M.J., *Transcending Paradox: The Chinese "Middle Way" Perspective*, Asia Pacific Journal of Management 19: 179-199: Kluwer Academic Publishers, 2002

n.d. 'China 1943.' President's Secretary's File, FDR Library. Vol. Series 3

Davis, Wade, *Into the Silence: Mallory, the Great War and the Conquest of Everest*, Croydon: Vintage, 2012

Douhet, Giulio, *The Command of the Air*, New York: Corward-McCann, 1942

Farndale, General Sir Martin. 2002. *History of the Royal Regiment of Artillery: The Far East Theatre 1941-46.* Revised Edition. London: Brassey's

Foot, M.R.D. and Langley, J.M. 2011. *MI9 Escape and Evasion 1939-45.* London: Biteback

Frayling, Christopher, *The Yellow Peril: Dr Fu Manchu & The Rise of Chinaphobia*, London: Thames & Hudson, 2014

n.d. 'Gen CL Chennault – Guide to Papers held at the Hoover Institution.' Accessed at the Imperial War Museum, London.

Grimsdale, Gordon, *'Private Papers'*, London: Imperial War Museum, 1950

Han, Suyin, *Destination Chungking*, London: Penguin, 1942

Hastings, Max, *Nemesis: The Battle for Japan, 1944-45*, London: William Collins, 2014

Havers, R.P.W, *Reassessing The Japanese Prisoner of War Experience: The Changi Prisoner of War Camp in Singapore 1942-45*, London: Routledge, 2003

Hessler, Peter. *Country Driving: A Chinese Road Trip,* Edinburgh: Canongate, 2011

Hewitt, Anthony, *Bridge with Three Men: Across China to the Western Heaven in 1942* London: Jonathan Cape, 1986

Hickman, Kennedy. n.d. 'Hong Kong Casualties.' http://militaryhistory.about.com/od/worldwarii/p/World-War-Ii-Battle-Of-Hong-Kong.htm

Holdsworth, R.L, 'Bandar Punch Again,' Edited by H.E.G. Tyndale. *Alpine Journal* LVI (276): 246–251, 1948

Jones, E, and Wessely, S, 'British Prisoners of War: From Resilience to Psychological Vulnerability: Reality or Perception?' *Twentieth Century British History* 21 (2): 163–183, 2010

Keay, John, *China: A History*, London: HarperPress, 2009

Lindsay, Oliver, *The Lasting Honour: The Fall of Hong Kong 1941*. London: Hamish Hamilton, 1978

Luard, Tim, *Escape from Hong Kong: Admiral Chan Chak's Christmas Day Dash,* Hong Kong: HKUP, 2012

Matloff, Maurice, *Strategic Planning for Coalition Warfare 1943–44,* Washington D.C.: US War Department, 1994

McLynn, Frank, *The Burma Campaign: Disaster into Triumph 1942–45,* New Haven: Yale University Press, 2011

Menon, Krishna, *Twilight in China*. In *The Chinese People at War: Human Suffering and Social Transformation, 1937–45,* by Diana Lary. Cambridge: Cambridge University Press, 2010

n.d. Mental Health Statistics. Accessed December 2015. http://www.youngminds.org.uk/training_services/policy/mental_health_statistics

1943. 'MI9 Reports WO208-3498.' War Office, London: The National Archives

Mitter, Rana, *China's War with Japan 1937-45, The Struggle For Survival*, London: Allen Lane, 2013

Moser, David, 'Why Chinese Is So Damn Hard.' *Sino-Platonic Papers* (University of Pennsylvania) 27: 59–69, 1991

n.d. *Pacific War Online Encyclopedia*. Accessed 2015. http://pwencycl.kgbudge.com/C/a/Casualties.htm

Post, Laurens Van der, *Yet Being Someone Other,* London: The Hogarth Press, 1982

n.d. 'Private Papers of Gen CL Chennault.' Vol. Box 8. Stanford, CA: Hoover Institution

Ride, Edwin, *BAAG: Hong Kong Resistance 1942-45*, Hong Kong: Oxford University Press, 1981

Spence, Jonathan D, *The Search for Modern China*. 3rd Edition, London: Norton, 2013

Tang, Yijie, *Confucianism, Buddhism, Daoism, Christianity and Chinese Culture*, Heidelberg: Springer, 2015

Tuchman, B.W, *Stilwell and the American Experience in China 1911-45*, New York: Bantam Books, 1971

n.d. 'War, Chennault Claire L.' President's Secretary's File, FDR Library. Vol. Series 4

Wheeler, Sara, *The Magnetic North: Travels in the Arctic*, London: Vintage, 2010

Whitehead, J.S, and Bennett, G.B., *Escape to Fight On: With 204 Military Mission in China*, London: Robert Hale, 1990

Acknowledgements

Lou Allison for drawing all the maps so beautifully and for being a supportive fellow Unbounder through the publishing process.

Tony Banham, archivist of the battle of Hong Kong and its aftermath, providing a great service to veterans and their families via http://www.hongkongwardiary.com/hkwdhome.html.

Julian Caldecott for endless support and encouragement, in this and in all matters.

Jenny and Joseph Cheung for maintaining the China connection.

Jane Cordingley for raising the question.

Jane Dunn for encouragement and advice on improving the book.

Jenny Fichmann for searches at The Hoover Institution, Stanford, CA.

Simon Fowler for relentless and efficient digging at The National Archives.

Martin Heyes of WalkHongKong for a fascinating tour of the battle site in Hong Kong.

Damien Lewis for encouragement and support.

Tim Luard for advice on retracing the journey.

Sadie Mayne and the rest of the editing team for insightful, eagle-eyed and comprehensive editing.

Betty Monro for keeping the documents and funding the trip.

James Monro and Robert Monro for sharing their memories of Dad.

Duncan Monro for filling in the gaps about uncle Michael.

My Odyssey Tours (www.myodysseytours.com) for excellent tour planning, guides and hotels.

Nick Ostler for the loan of relevant books from his extensive library, detailed feedback and correcting the sections about Mandarin and China.

Sim Smiley for searches at the American National Archive, Washington, D.C.

Rod Suddaby (IWM) for his enthusiasm and interest and great skill as a curator and archivist.

Patrons

Pauline Andrews
Ana Bertolossi
Sue Bishop
Joanna Durham-matthews
Hilary Franklin
Tracey Grigsby
Kate Groves
Jacqui Hughes
Terri King
David Longmuir
Alastair Macrae
Kate Nottage
Louise Owen
My Odyssey Tours
Susan Turner
Philippa Vick
Rachel Williams